A FACE
TO THE
WORLD

LAURA CUMMING

A FACE
TO THE
WORLD

ON SELF-PORTRAITS

HarperPress
An imprint of HarperCollinsPublishers
77–85 Fulham Palace Road
Hammersmith, London W6 8JB
www.harpercollins.co.uk

Visit our authors' blog: www.fifthestate.co.uk
Love this book? www.bookarmy.com

First published by HarperPress in 2009

9 8 7 6 5 4 3 2

A catalogue record for this book is available from the British Library

ISBN 978-0-00-711843-4

Typeset by 'OME DESIGN

Printed and bound in Italy by L.E.G.O Spa – Vicenza

In memory of my father James Cumming
And for Elizabeth, Dennis, Hilla and Thea with all my heart

Contents

Preface

'We were created to look at one another, weren't we?'

Edgar Degas

C harles Dickens once said that he lived in perpetual dread of any sudden new discovery about Shakespeare: the revelation of a letter, an image, a biographical fact, anything that might disturb his life's fine mystery. The little that was known was dismaying enough – that the Universal Genius had a hard head for business and thought nothing of pursuing the tiniest of debts through the courts; that the author of the Tragedies also found time to pester the government about the state of the roads around Stratford. At least nobody really knew what Shakespeare looked like. To Dickens's relief, there was no face to disillusion the faithful since not one of the portraits for which claims of authenticity were so often published in Victorian times was made by an artist known to have met him. The ruffed bust of the bard at Stratford, the Chandos dandy with his golden earring: these could be regarded as false idols for a credulous population. Dickens despised the public's need for a face and could not contain his scorn when asked to help fund a statue of Shakespeare, replying that he would not contribute a farthing for a likeness because the *work* must be the only lasting monument.[1]

The ideal Shakespeare for Dickens is the Shakespeare we have, a genius and an absolute blank. Immortal, invisible, unimaginably wise: something like God Almighty. This is exactly the comparison that occurs to Jorge Luis Borges in *Everything and Nothing*, his parable of Shakespeare's extraordinary elusiveness as an actual person. Borges imagines a conversation at the pearly gates between the two great creators in which Shakespeare, having been so many other people in his art, appeals to God to let him be just one man at last. But God offers not the slightest hope: 'I too have no self; I dreamed the world as you dreamed your work, my Shakespeare, and among the shapes of my dream are you, who, like me, are many men and no one.'[2] Shakespeare has no unified self, no single identity and certainly no fixed appearance. In fact, he is too great to have been visible at all; Borges describes him as a hallucination, a dream dreamt by nobody, a cloud of ethereal vapour.

For all those who would prefer Shakespeare to remain invisible many more long for a definitive face, perhaps hoping to find a trace of character in its expression, or to feel a direct line of communication opening before them, or just for the simple and irreducible fascination of knowing what Shakespeare looked like. This curiosity is not to be despised. You do not have to believe, like Schopenhauer, that the outer man is a picture of the inner, or that the face is a manifestation of the soul. From the infant's ability to read two dots and a dash as primitive features barely before its eyes can focus, to the instinctive imagining of the unseen correspondent or the speaker on the other end of the line, from our mass observation of passers-by in the street to the rage for Facebook, a compulsion to look at our fellow beings unites us. How can one not take an interest in faces, real or represented? It is almost a test of human solidarity.

Degas told Sickert he always took the omnibus across Paris because he could never see enough people from inside a closed carriage. 'We were created to look at one another, weren't we?'[3]

Yet the strain of antipathy towards portraiture that runs in and out of history, that once demoted it well below battle scenes or bathing nymphs, that derides it as face-painting and mistrusts its version of the truth, has something to do with faces and not just pictures. For faces do not always fit, people do not look as they should. Appearances may create a spurious sense of intimacy when they look right for the part – this is just how one imagined the famous person – or sudden and dismaying estrangement when they don't. Delacroix, passionate in painting, has a prim little toothbrush moustache. Stravinsky is a lugubrious bureaucrat. Rothko, his aim so spiritual, is a heavy lug in blue-tinted glasses. Almost everyone would prefer a better Shakespeare than the egghead of the First Folio engraving (which Ben Jonson, having known the original, worryingly endorsed on the opposite page) and nobody can stomach the portly dolt with his cushion and quill commemorated in the bust at Stratford. If Shakespeare made us most fully human to ourselves then surely he should look more like some other great soul; Shakespeare should look more like Rembrandt.

Or more like a Rembrandt self-portrait, to be precise; not Rembrandt as he might have looked to a fellow artist. Another painter could have settled a few pedantic questions about Rembrandt's actual appearance – the colour of his eyes and hair, the shape of his nose and so on – about which he is notoriously cavalier and inconsistent. But no matter how accurate such a portrait might have been, it could never give the sense of inner mutability, of a personality altered daily by experience, never fixed, ever-changing, that makes the Rembrandt of the self-portraits so human, so Shakespearean.

Of course it could be argued that self-portraits involve obvious conflicts of interest, that they may be less true to appearances than portraits. But they are not *just* portraits, for all that art history often treats them as a subset; and they often specialize in other kinds of truth. Artists have portrayed themselves, improbably, as wounded, starving or unconscious beneath a tree, as a baby being born or a severed head dripping blood, as younger or older or even of the opposite sex. We clearly do not consult self-portraits for documentary evidence. But no matter how fanciful, flattering or deceitful the image, it will always reveal something deep and incontrovertible (and distinct from a portrait) – namely this special class of truth, this pressure from within that determines what appears as art without, that leaves its trace in every self-portrait. In Rembrandt's case it might be the desire to appear head-in-air when most down and out, or the urge to portray oneself as laughing in the dark or all alone in the world. The pose could be an outright lie, for all we know, but the fiction always carries its own truth – the truth of how the artist hoped to be seen and known, how he wished to represent (and see) himself. Had Shakespeare been able to paint as he wrote, had Shakespeare left a self-portrait, not even Dickens could have denied its transcendent value.

    This book, like many, has its origins in childhood. Ill in bed, I was given what its owner called a portable museum: dozens of postcards of Old Masters in a shoebox. Among the many pictures of people were some that stood apart, having that intensity about the eyes that even a child recognizes as the sign of a self-portrait. Two stayed out of the box, probably never given back and as mysterious to me now as they were then; both appear in this book.

    Jacques-Louis David was a puzzling presence because he appeared puzzled himself; discomforting because he seemed in evident discomfort. I could not have said what was wrong with him or even what was odd about the picture, except that the artist seemed to be in some peculiar sense convalescent, which was exactly how I imagined my state. Or did I learn that from him? The painting drew me in so forcefully with its image of a man who seems strange even to himself that it gave me a sudden insight into how it might feel to be perplexed as an adult.

    The events leading up to this moment, what cinema calls the backstory, are exceptionally dramatic. (They are laid out in Chapter 11.) But they only explain the occasion, not the painting, and in re-entering my early response to it I have tried instead to get to the heart of that startling switch that self-portraits can effect, putting you on the spot – in the artist's position – through their involving intensity of look. You are as he was: contemplating himself; you see him through his own eyes. Growing up, I realized how this resonates with our own experience all the time, the way we consult the mirror to question our appearance, rearrange our looks.

The other self-portrait was not intimate at all: Dürer's painting of himself in 1500, the midpoint of the millennium, so eerie in its glacial charisma. It looked too modern to have been painted so long ago (a classic reaction to high illusion among children), too alive to be trapped behind ancient glazes and varnish. Although I was quite frightened by the picture, it made me aware for the first time that people in pictures could seem as exciting as people in real life. Much later, a German school friend sent me a postcard of the self-portrait, writing on the reverse that she had quite a crush on Dürer. My art teacher strongly disapproved when I showed it to him, probably suspecting my interest in the face, certainly doubting its status as an image. 'There's too much of the artist,' he declared, 'in the picture.' But both his words and hers strike at a defining aspect of self-portraiture – and of this self-portrait in particular – which is the fusion of person with picture. With all portraits, no matter how mediocre the image, how brief and faltering its illusion, there is always the sense of coming face to face with another person before that person reverts to an image. Self-portraits go further in claiming the two to be one and the same.

A person and a picture all in one, the artist as masterpiece: faced with the self-portraits of Dürer, Rembrandt, David, Dickens's opposition between man and work falls apart. And it is in the oscillation between the two that one perceives the mind at work, for whatever they show of the outer person, self-portraits speak of the inner self too in the character and choice of depiction. Sitters in portraits may assume their own pose, expression, clothes and so forth, although it is remarkable how often artists, especially portraitists like Sargent, control the whole show right down to wardrobe and hair. Self-portraitists do all this and more, true to their own desires about how to picture themselves from within and without, both in and *as* works of art.

I take these truths to be significant and am struck by the reticence of Poussin, fastidiously withdrawing into an enclosure of his own paintings, almost an abstract of his art; by the unstoppable ego of Courbet trying to thrust his way out of the space of the picture. By Rosa with his glowering mountain-man pose looming above a tablet engraved with the injunction to keep quiet if you've nothing better to say, the solemnity of both the words and the image half-mocked by the melodramatic pose.

Rosa speaks loudly, no matter that he is affecting to keep silent. Self-portraiture is rarely the 'singular, in-turned art' described by Julian Bell in his classic *500 Self-Portraits*, however introspective its reputation. Not even David is talking only to himself, as it seems to me. When Munch painted *Self-Portrait in*

Hell, in which he appears up to his waist in sulphurous paint, he wasn't simply describing the lonely anguish of being abandoned by a lover who had brought him so much grief the artist had turned a gun on himself (strategically missing everything but the tip of a finger). He was issuing a public accusation specifically for display in an Oslo gallery where anyone, including the press, could see it. Self-portraiture is an opportunity to put across one's side of the story and it has been exploited at times as a love letter, mission statement or suicide note by other means.

Its special look, so sharp, so expectant, shifts straight into the first person address, and self-portraiture has its counterparts in speech – soliloquies, monologues, laments – as well as the written word in the form of prologues, sonnets, memoirs (in addition to its sublime qualities as a painting, Velázquez's *Las Meninas*, with its maze of relationships, may also be the one great novel in art). But the directness and potential intimacy of speech come with peculiar dilemmas and anomalies. Should the self-portrayer show him or herself in the act of painting – true to the moment of creation – or doing something completely different that might appear more impressive but less plausible? And if painting, should the picture in view be this one or another? And if this one, what about the paradox of timing – I show myself in the middle of painting, but my picture is obviously finished. The supposedly direct relation between mirror and canvas is confusing and even compromised. Who is this in the mirror: myself or another, I or he? And when painted, has this self become someone independent of me? Some artists, for instance Sargent in an image so devoid of inner stresses it might as well be a portrait, or Titian in a magnificent self-portrait in which he is looking away and clearly impatient to be gone, justify their presence by appearing as far as possible in the alibi of the third person.

And why do artists choose to show themselves in the first place, exposing themselves and their art to the accusations of narcissism so often raised by critics who seem to confuse self-representation with self-regard? Historically, there has never been much money or glory in it; self-portraits, unlike portraits, are rarely commissioned or appraised as the high point of an artist's career, although well over a thousand have been painted specially for the Vasari self-portrait corridor of the Uffizi since the seventeenth century; an honour, incidentally, that appears to stifle creativity even among some highly original painters. But self-portraits are often called for in more intimate ways – a gift for a friend, a wedding present, the embodiment of reproachfulness, appreciation or love. Goya painted himself in the arms of the doctor who saved him from dying, in gratitude for his life. Murillo painted a self-portrait at his children's request that would live with them in all its touching benevolence (literally: the picture turns upon the tangible movement of his fingers) after the artist's death.

Self-portraits make artists present as the embodiment of their art; it sounds so neat and succinct. But they often do so only to ask who or what this person is who is looking back from the mirror, how dismaying it is to be alone, how hard it is to represent or even just to *be* oneself in the wide world of mankind. I only know for certain the exact circumstances in which one such self-portrait was made but my sense is that something in this artist's experience may speak to a universal truth.

She was my mother, Elizabeth Cumming, studying painting at Edinburgh College of Art not long after the Second World War and surrounded by men who fought that war, many of them still in uniform at the easel. Compared to these heroes who had seen — and changed — the world, she felt she knew about nothing more significant than herself. College days were spent painting the external world of which she had such a powerless grasp, but one night when everyone else had gone home she took a canvas into a studio and made a rapid self-portrait in secret. There was more conviction in that image, she said, than all the heaped apples and male nudes she ever painted. My mother had made herself real, momentarily, to herself.

She would be horrified to think that a painting kept hidden ever since should be mentioned in the same pages as Velázquez, but they have something in common. Self-portraits stand in the same relation to each other as human beings — possessed of a self, members of the same infinitely various race.

I don't say that this puts them beyond criticism, far from it. But if this book has the slightest hint of a unifying theory of self-portraiture (and it is by no means obvious that any theory which could be made to stretch all the way from *Las Meninas* to Andy Warhol in his fright wig would be of much ultimate value) it is that the behaviour of people in self-portraits has a strange tendency to reflect the behaviour of people in life. One might say this of portraits too, but it is not so easy to think of an example of a portrait in which the sitter tears at his face, pulls out his hair, looms up at a mirror in disbelief or recoils quite openly from it (still less where the sitter is masturbating or wallowing stark naked in cash). Nor do many portraits express what it is like to live deep inside the mind of the sitter. Rembrandt's depth of knowledge is not an illusion. Van Gogh's mind teems. Velázquez senses the brevity of our life's day in the sun as few other painters in art.

This is a book of inquiry as well as praise; it examines how and what self-portraits communicate and why they come to look as they do. And it considers something else that unites us — the representation of our selves — in terms of artists' self-portraits. We all have a self and a public existence, however limited, and it is the daily requirement that we put together some sort of face to the world. The thought of having to create a definitive face for all time, though, might make even an extrovert falter and there are chapters here on stage fright and the serial self-portraiture in which artists give themselves another mollifying chance. On the other hand the opportunity to put oneself across as completely as one cannot in life (*pace* those conflicts of interest, such as boasting and lying, also discussed here) as a rehearsed address instead of an off-the-cuff ramble has its obvious appeal. The most poignant self-portrait I know is the little picture by Carracci, reproduced at the end of this book, where the artist makes his address even while wondering whether any of his attempts to communicate will ever succeed.

Art historians do not concern themselves much with the power of art to move, disturb, inspire, indeed to affect the emotions of the viewer; yet it is hard to think of many artists even in the last century whose own concerns and ambitions are exclusively formal. Self-portraiture offers a perfect instance of this dichotomy. Historians sometimes treat it as the remote and insignificant twig of the far greater branch of portraiture, finding in self-portraits a profession's collective representation of itself, a way of signing works, signalling skill, exemplifying style; where there is no written evidence concerning a self-portrait, they prefer to avoid remarking on its human content. But I cannot believe that self-portrayers are never thinking of themselves and their lives, or that self-portraits have no subjective or personal significance, that they are not in some profound sense a fragment of someone's self. I cannot see Rembrandt's self-portraits solely in terms of the art market in seventeenth-century Holland any more than I can look at Dürer's 1500 self-portrait, even after historians have tried to put out its fire with theological explanations, and not be amazed. These self-portraits have ineluctable mystery as part of their content.

A history of self-portraiture may one day be written, though such a work would have to concede that there is no straight path in any case, that self-portraiture is a series of fits and starts, cul-de-sacs, detours and strange digressions. Still, these separate essays are approximately chronological and linked, one to the next, as a narrative with its own story. Most of the self-portraits discussed are paintings. No prejudice is intended towards video or sculpture, although sculpted self-portraits are comparatively rare; it is simply that paintings have fascinated me more.

Many of them fulfil Dickens's ideal of the lasting monument, are among the artist's greatest works, if not the greatest of all; others struggle with the multiple personalities that Borges imagines must have afflicted Shakespeare. Peculiarly testing in its demands upon the artist who has to hit upon some form of self to represent, peculiarly rich in the self-knowledge on which it can call, self-portraiture draws forth some of the most profound and advanced picture-making in art. It turns the subject inside out, and remakes him or her as an indivisible trinity: there is the work of art, the image of the maker and the truth of what he or she sensed, imagined or believed about themselves and how they chose, as we all must choose, to present themselves.

Chapter One

Secrets

'The world so conceived, though extremely various in the types of things and perspectives it contains, is still centerless. It contains us all, and none of us occupies a metaphysically privileged position. Yet each of us, reflecting on this centerless world, must admit that one very large fact seems to have been omitted from its description: the fact that a particular person in it is himself.'

Thomas Nagel, The View from Nowhere.

Portrait of a Man (Self Portrait?), 1433

Jan van Eyck (c. 1390–1441)

n a clear day, when the sunshine is bright, we cannot help glimpsing ourselves as spontaneous reflections, vividly present in polished metal and glass, more provisional in opaque surfaces. The pianist becomes aware of his fingers echoed in the sheen above the keyboard. The caller sees his face in the mobile phone. The writer becomes a shadow in the computer's screen when the glare gets too harsh, coming between her thoughts and her words as maddeningly as those vitreous flecks that drift across the optical field when staring at a white sky or during the prelude to a migraine; each is an involuntary manifestation of oneself.

At home we only have to draw a curtain to deaden our own image but the wider world is not so conveniently adjusted. We spot ourselves large as life in the windows of shops, tiny in wine glasses and spoons, in others' eyes and the lenses of their spectacles. Mainly we ignore these inklings of ourselves, except when the object that contains them is big enough to be exploited as a face-checking device, but the truth is that nobody actually needs a mirror to see how they look. The daylight world is a sphere of endless reflections in which we are caught and held, over and again, and even at night the curtainless window becomes a mirror when backed by outer darkness. Surrounded by these shining surfaces and the reflections they give back, there is no getting away from our selves.

Flemish painting loves this world of surfaces. It aims to do them to perfection, as if getting them exactly right was the guarantee of some higher truth than material reality. And this must have seemed the case nearly six hundred years ago when these painters very suddenly began creating images of God's universe so persuasive to the eye, all the way from the broad rays of the sun to the microcosmic fire inside a diamond, that contemporary viewers thought they could hardly have been made by human hand. A saint's golden cope and all the tinsel-bright threads running through it; a carpet and all its individual woollen staples, and then every thread in each: surely this must be some kind of God-given miracle, for such minutiae couldn't possibly be rendered by an ordinary mortal with a paintbrush. The old strain of incredulity rings true even today since one still marvels to see such immaculate illusions of life unfolding from the nearest dewdrop to the furthest range of mountains. And if Flemish art aspires to a visibility that amazes then the work of Jan Van Eyck goes even further, rising to a kind of godly omniscience — all you can see and more, as much of the world as can be gathered into the little compass of a painting, above, below and beyond. Van Eyck developed a way of expanding the field of vision by using reflections to show what was just out of sight as well as what was beyond the picture altogether: the entire skyline of a distant town reflected in the gleaming helmet of an archer, an offstage martyrdom in a heretic's breastplate. The armour will be super-real, so like the thing itself as to baffle belief; the reflections will make visible even more of the world.

When it comes to reality, Jan Van Eyck is the supreme master. His art is so lifelike it was once thought divine. But he does not simply set life before us as it is — an enduring objection to realism, that it is no more than mindless copying — he adjusts it little by little to inspire awe at the infinite variety of the world and our existence within it, the astonishing fact that it contains not just all this but each of our separate selves. What is more, Van Eyck makes this point in person, and not once but several times with a humility that amounts to a trait. Yet experts barely seem to notice the human aspects of these incidental appearances, or the startling solo portrait he left of himself, for arguing about whether they can be deemed self-portraits in the first place. This is one of the disadvantages of being a pioneer; Van Eyck is too early to assimilate. Because there is no flourishing tradition of self-portraiture in Europe yet, he is not allowed to be painting himself. Clearly there must have been great self-portraitists before him when one considers how much art of the period is lost (some estimate that only a quarter of Renaissance art survives) but even quite serious art historians seem to imagine that nobody could produce a sophisticated self-portrait without a sophisticated mirror, or that nobody had a self before its supposed invention later in the Renaissance and that Van Eyck is only fooling about with figments. But his art argues against such primitive and arrogant notions and does so with characteristic grace. Look at the way that Van Eyck finesses his own image into a great altarpiece such as *The Madonna and Child of Canon van der Paele* by way of drawing attention to the fact that anyone who looks at a bit of fiercely polished metal, no matter how grey the day, is pretty much bound to see himself.

The Madonna and Child are sitting in a space so cramped there is hardly room for their visitors: St Donatien on the left in a blue and gold cope, St George on the right in a cacophonous suit of bronze armour. George is a bumptious figure, disturbing the peace and treading clumsily on the vestments of the old cleric kneeling beside him, namely Canon van der Paele, who has commissioned the picture and is even now being introduced to the Virgin.

The point of the picture ought to be the relationship between these four large adults but there are so many other pressing attractions. The heavy eye-glasses in the Canon's hand, the circular ventricles of the windows, the individual design of every single chequerboard tile; above all the stupendous patterned carpet that begins beneath the Virgin, folds its way down the ceremonial steps and stretches right out of the picture as if to meet the viewer's own feet, a sensation fully underwritten by the staggering depiction of this woven stuff, too thick to make perfect right-angle bends down each step, its weave stiffening here, flattening there, casting the tiniest of shadows within in its own texture: infinitesimal.

Van Eyck seems to have started out as a miniaturist and part of his achievement is to sustain that technique on a larger scale without any loss of

effect so that his pictures never disintegrate into smaller catalogues of detail; you can be densely absorbed in that carpet without losing your sense of the circulation of air, the passage of light or the reflections that keep the space flutteringly alive. St George doffs a helmet ribbed like a conch, its volutes reflecting the mother and child over and again; and the entire scene, from the red granite column behind him to the cold Northern light of the window, is repeated in his breastplate and shield. But there is one reflection that has no identifiable source in the picture because the original stands outside it – a tiny figure in a red turban, one arm raised to apply a brushstroke.

To describe this self-portrait as modest would be an understatement; it is not even the size of a match. Only in a reproduction fully as large as the painting itself – approximately six feet by four – would anyone be able to see it in context. The hiding place is what gives it away, as well as the pose, for to be reflected in the saint's angled shield at this size the man in the turban would have to be standing back from the picture, near the centre, approximately where we stand to look. And what did the artist see when he stood there? Not the armour, of course, but the wet oil paint itself in which, working close, he must have been hazily reflected.

Madonna and Child with Canon Georg van der Paele, 1436

Jan van Eyck
(c. 1390–1441)

Detail of *Madonna and Child with Canon Georg van der Paele*, 1436

Jan van Eyck
(c. 1390–1441)

The conceit is that the armour he has painted is so sparklingly real Van Eyck can see himself in it, and perhaps there was an actual suit of armour in the workshop, a material object to summon in all its hard glory. But there were no saints and Canon van der Paele clearly never met Mary; the artist is making up his world. There is the fictional scene, the wily old canon sucking up to the mother of God, and there is the miraculous illusion of reality that abets it; between the two, slipped into the surface of the picture, is a reflection of the truth and reality outside it: the painter's side of the story.

Jan Van Eyck was probably born in 1390, possibly in Maastricht. He worked mainly in Bruges as court painter to Philip, Duke of Burgundy, who sent him on at least two ambassadorial missions by sea, voyages so weather-pitched the ships were forced to dock in England for safety. First he painted Isabella of Spain as a potential bride for the Duke and then he painted Isabella of Portugal; neither portrait survives, but the Portuguese Isabella won the contest.

Philip treasured Van Eyck's friendship as well as his art, giving him vast bonuses and expensive gifts, becoming godfather to his daughter and supporting his widow. That he prized their conversation is apparent from an outraged letter to some of the painter's clients who were withholding payments, an insult that the Duke takes personally, declaring he will 'never find a man equal to [Van Eyck's] liking, nor so outstanding in his art and science'.[1] Not just art but science as well, meaning knowledge of mathematics, optics, astronomy, geometry, all the learning that enriched Van Eyck's painting and no doubt his table-talk, but possibly something else too: the invention of oil paint itself.

According to Vasari, teller of tall tales, Van Eyck one day took a most painstaking piece of work out into the sunshine to dry. When he returned, the varnish had cracked and the wooden panel was splitting. Infuriated, but being a man who 'delighted in alchemy', Van Eyck experimented with numerous concoctions of egg and oil until he hit upon a secret formula of linseed and nut oil, mixed with ground pigment, that was not only heatproof but waterproof too and which brought a beautiful new lustre to his colours. Out of base substances, Van Eyck supposedly transmutes the precious stuff that 'all the painters of the world had so long desired'.

Oil painting existed before him, of course, but most artists were still working with tempera or gesso, mixing their pigments with egg white or damp plaster, and getting stuck with their quick-drying effects. Oil paint gives depth and luminosity and reflects light from within, layer by translucent layer. Fluid and lingeringly slow to dry, it allows for infinite variations of hue, tone and consistency and the subtlest of blends and transitions. Van Eyck exploited all these properties to the fullest degree as no other painter before him, inventing not so much a technique as an entire tradition of painting.

His own pictures look as if they have never quite dried, their surfaces shining with liquid light like the very substance of which they are made. Had he lived in the late twentieth century, Van Eyck might even have painted a stunning picture of oil paint itself: the texture and gleam of it on the palette, another wonder of the world. And working so intensively with the palette and so close up to the surface of each panel he must have glimpsed himself in the oil – not exactly a face, just an imprecise blur in whatever he was painting. As long as the sun shines, there is no getting away from ourselves.

Does this painted reflection amount to a self-portrait? It is too small to be much of a likeness, this indirect glimpse, and for some its size irresistibly reduces it to a joke. 'More playful than profound,'[2] comments one art historian, with a touch of patronizing indulgence, arguing that the artist does not show himself so much as his character. It is true that one could hardly extrapolate a recognizable likeness from the face and yet something more than character is surely represented in this little self-portrait.

Not at all, according to other experts, for this is not Van Eyck.[3] Lay people may want it to be a self-portrait but they only see what they want to see and there is no textual evidence to support the claim. Written evidence trumps visual evidence for art historians even more than for lawyers; without documentary support, such identifications are purely subjective.

Of course, the case could be argued in terms of custom and practice. Artists often appear at the back, in the margins or among the crowds in Renaissance paintings pointing at themselves – it was me, I painted this – and sometimes even gesturing at their painting hand – I made the whole thing with this. (One would have thought the tiny brush in Van Eyck's hand would have amounted to a form of positive ID too but his case proves more complex.) Some go even further, putting a name to the face. Benozzo Gozzoli included himself among the throng of Medici godfathers and hangers-on wending their way down a valley on horseback in his *Procession of the Magi* for the Medici chapel in Florence. He wears a scarlet hat with the words 'Opus Benotti' lettered in gold round the brim, a pun on his name – Ben Noti, well noted – which was also something of a self-fulfilling prophecy since his is practically the only name not now lost. The caption beneath Pietro Perugino's pretend 'portrait' of himself hanging from its *trompe l'oeil* chain among the frescos of the Collegio del Cambio in Perugia declares that if the art of painting had never existed then Perugino would have invented it, though since he lavished more care on himself than anyone else – the self-portrait could almost be Flemish – no one could be fooled by this third-person rhetoric. It is traditional to regard such self-portraits as elaborate signatures or advertisements, instances of attention-seeking painters asking to be elevated to some higher status than anonymous craftsmen, though even Gozzoli and Perugino show more conceptual wit than such narrow interpretations allow. But Van Eyck presents problems for experts. Unlike either of the Italians, he did not support this or any other self-portrait with written certification.

So there are supposedly no self-portraits by Jan Van Eyck because none can be substantiated; or there might be one; or they are all just stick-men in a running gag. If Van Eyck paints a reflection of himself in a pearl he is simply celebrating the shininess of the world, not alluding to his own place within it. If he paints a reflection of a man in a turban in *The Arnolfini Portrait*, it is just another way of signing the work. Right at the outset, the depth and complexity of self-portraiture are already being denied.

But it is not romantic to call these reflections self-portraits; it is a mark of respect. Van Eyck's art teaches the eye to see the world on an infinitesimally small scale, and it hardly belittles picture or painter to suggest that the miniature figure in the armour expresses self-consciousness in its maker: a figure in the visible world. What wit, moreover, to clinch this extraordinary illusion of reality with a reflection that introduces the here-and-now right into the picture, as if the real and painted worlds were continuous; while at the same time jamming that illusion with a reminder of the artifice involved in the picture's making personified in the image of its maker. Discount the possibility of a self-portrait and you deny Van Eyck all of these marvellous possibilities. Put simply, you refuse to allow that he could be such an intelligent painter.

———

Appearances are everything in Van Eyck's art, and his art is devoted to making them real. Most representational painters leave something to the viewer, requiring us to imagine or deduce some parts of the picture, but Van Eyck does the opposite: his paintings are stupendously complete. Not a hair out of place. Yet it is precisely this fullness of reality that Michelangelo dismissed in an early objection to the realism of the Flemish school: 'They paint stuffs and masonry, the green grass of the fields, the shadow of trees and rivers and bridges … And all this, though it pleases some persons, is done without reason or art.'

Without reason? Without art? Look at another painting by Van Eyck, in which the Madonna and Child are foolhardy enough to grant an audience to the Duke of Burgundy's intimidating chancellor. Rolin is a big man with a savage haircut and a look of brute cunning, much like the enforcer he was in real life. The Madonna appears to be drawing cautiously back, but the child on her knee is blessing the politician: exactly what Rolin had paid for.[4]

Behind the lavish chamber in which they sit a whole world unfolds through the windows: green fields, rivers, the shadows of trees and bridges, a sparkling city and beyond it brighter vistas yet. 'Even those landscapes which seem to extend over fifty miles retain the same degree of solidity and the same fullness of articulation as the very nearest objects,' wrote the art historian Erwin Panofsky in a famous passage of praise. 'Jan's eye operates as a microscope and a telescope at the same time.'[5] And all this reality – the palace garden and every leaf of it, the meadows and every blade of them to the furthermost glittering pinnacles – is paradise on earth, the landscape of the New Jerusalem.

Between this world and the next, near and far, two little figures are posted like watchers on a promontory. One is studying the view from the

Detail of *The Madonna of Chancellor Rolin*, c.1435

Jan van Eyck
(c. 1390–1441)

palace battlements, the other turns slightly, glancing back in our direction. He wears a red turban and carries the rod of a courtier. The crucial fact about this figure is once again its position, on the threshold between two worlds, present and future, and right at the epicentre of the painting. Draw the diagonals and they would meet on a point: the hand of the man in the turban.

The angel in the New Jerusalem, according to Revelation, has a rod to measure the glorious architecture of the city. The measurements of Van Eyck's New Jerusalem are exceptionally small – the whole picture is only about two feet wide – and his rod is thus sensationally tiny, a microscopic yardstick for a miniature vision. But even without the biblical aside, and Van Eyck's paintings are always theologically rich, the little man in his eye-catching turban has a modest humour all of his own: discreet enough to escape Rolin's self-centred attentions, you feel, but there for those who have eyes to see him.

Van Eyck places himself at the crosshairs of his own field of vision; painting the world, and all its contents, he numbers himself within it. This is not narcissism but modest logic: even without a mirror, or reflections, we are visible to ourselves somewhat. Shut one eye and the projecting nose becomes apparent; look up and see the overhanging brow. We have an outer as well as an inner sense of our own bodies that reflections confirm or confound; and catching sight of these reflections, we are made episodically conscious of our own bodily existence – atoms in time, maybe, but nonetheless the viewing centre of our world.

It has been argued that the only reason anyone ever imagines these little men in red turbans might be Van Eyck is because of another painting by him known as *Man in Red Turban*.[6] Or at least that was its title until very recently when visual evidence was finally allowed to outweigh academic caution just a fraction and scholars relabelled it *Portrait of a Man (Self-Portrait?)*.[7] In fact, there is a faint long-nosed resemblance between this man and the courtier with his rod that has nothing to do with turbans; and turbans are in any case off the point.

Van Eyck stares piercingly out of the picture, a tight-lipped man with fine silver stubble. His look is shrewd, imperturbable, serious. The eyes are a little watery, as if strained by too much close looking, and there is a palpable melancholy to the picture. Look closer, as Van Eyck's art irresistibly proposes, and you notice something else – that the eyes are not in equal focus. The left eye is painted in perfect register and so clearly that the Northern light from the window glints minutely in the wet of it – the world reflected; but the other is slightly blurred, you might say impressionistic. These eyes are trying to see themselves, have the *look* of trying to see themselves in some kind of mirror. 'Jan Van Eyck Made Me' is written below the image. Along the top runs the inscription 'Als ich kan' – 'As I can', and punningly 'As Eyck can'.

Van Eyck painted the 'Als ich kan' motto on the frames of other portraits too but it is far more emphatically displayed here to create the illusion that it has been carved into the gilded wood itself. It also appears where he normally names the sitter. But more than that, its play upon the first and third person epitomizes the I-He grammar of self-portraiture to perfection. Here I am, gravely scrutinizing my face in the mirror, and the picture; there he is, the man in the painting.

————

I am here. He was here. 'Jan Van Eyck fuit hic' is written in an exquisite chancery hand on the back wall of *The Arnolfini Portrait*. Ever since Kilroy was here and everywhere in the twentieth century the phrase has epitomized graffiti, which is, in its elegant way, exactly how Van Eyck uses it.

Everyone knows the Arnolfini – the rich couple with the dog, the oranges, the mirror and the shoes, touching hands in an expensively decorated bedroom. But nobody knows quite what they are doing there, in a bedroom of all places, an intimacy unheard of in Flemish portraiture. This joining of hands, is it the moment of betrothal, the marriage itself, the party afterwards, or nothing to do with a wedding? The bed awaits with its heavy scarlet drapes, the dog hovers, the texture of its fur exquisitely summoned all the way from coarse to whisper-soft. Perhaps he is an emblem of fidelity; perhaps this is a merger between two Italian families trading in luxury goods, as lately suggested, but all interpretations are necessarily reductive for none can fully account for the strange complexities of the painting. Even if one knew precisely why Giovanni Arnolfini was raising his right hand as if to testify he would still be a peculiarly disturbing presence, with his reptilian mask and lashless eyes, dwarfed beneath a cauldron of a hat. He touches, but does not look at the woman. She struggles to hold up the copious yardage of a dress that nobody could possibly walk in. Behind them is that writing on the wall that makes so much of the historic moment, and beneath that is the legendary mirror in which Van Eyck is reflected (in blue), entering into the scene.

Jan Van Eyck was here. It is not strictly accurate in terms of tense, of course, for Van Eyck has to be here right now as he paints his story on the wall. He sends a message to the future about the past, but it is written in the present moment; the paradox is its own little joke, as for every Kilroy. But the mirror also tinkers with the tense of the picture. Without it, you would simply be looking at an image of the past, a time-stopped world of wooden shoes, abundant robes and a sign-language too archaic to decode. But things are still happening in the mirror, a man is on the verge of entering, life continues on our side – the painter's side – of this room. For Van Eyck invented something else

Detail of *The Arnolfini Portrait*, 1434

Jan van Eyck
(c. 1390–1441)

too, not just a new way of painting but the whole idea of an open-ended picture that extends into our world and vice versa. Just as his reflection passes over the threshold to enter the room where the Arnolfini stand, so he creates the illusion that we may accompany him there as well. The tiny self-portrait is the key to the door. Art need not be closed.

The inscription in *The Arnolfini Portrait* announces the artist's role as witness and narrator – I was here, this was the occasion – though the self-portrait says something more about the reality depicted. The liquid highlights in the eyes, the pucker of orange peel, the flecked coat of the dog, the embrasure of clear light, reflected again in the brass-framed mirror: the whole powerfully real illusion was contrived by Jan Van Eyck, transforming what he saw into what you now see here. He is there in the picture connecting our world to theirs, a pioneer breaking down frontiers.

As usual, the painter makes no spectacle of himself. Van Eyck's self-portraits are conceivably the smallest in art, certainly the most discreet, yet their scale is in inverse ratio to their metaphysical range. The visible world appears to be outside us, viewed through the windows of the eyes, and yet it contains us all.

Chapter Two

Eyes

'There is a road from the eye to the heart that does not go through the intellect.'

G. K. Chesterton

Detail of *The Adoration of the Magi*, 1475

Sandro Botticelli (c. 1445–1510)

It would be hard to think of a more unnerving stare in Renaissance art than that of Sandro Botticelli, a painter better known for his dreamy visions of peace and love than for undertones of menace and coercion. Botticelli looks back at you, what is more, from a scene that ought to be all hushed and hallowed joy, the arrival of the wise men at Christ's nativity. But even without his presence there is a sense of threat, for the miraculous birth has taken place in a derelict outhouse of yawning rafters and broken masonry that looks on the brink of collapse.

Between the viewer and the Holy Family, hoisted high for maximum visibility, mills a large crowd showing very varying degrees of respect, all played by members and attendants of the Florentine Medici. Botticelli includes two of his current patrons, Lorenzo and Giuliano, but also Piero the Gouty and Cosimo the Elder, both of whom were already dead at the time of painting. At the far right of this hubbub, in which at least two of the posse seem more adoring of their bosses than the Christ child, stands the artist himself. Stock still, full length, perfectly self-contained, he is the only figure set apart from the scene, muffled in his mustard-yellow robes like an assassin in a crowd, a Banquo's ghost of a presence apparently visible only to us. The face is sullen, disdainful, unrelentingly forceful, the eyes trained upon you with a stare as cold as Malcolm McDowell's in the poster for Stanley Kubrick's *A Clockwork Orange*. A face, incidentally, that runs counter to the comfortable dog-and-owner theory of self-portraiture that artists tend to look right for their art —Van Gogh a fiery redhead with startling blue eyes, Rembrandt a rich ruin of a face — for it has no affinity with the sensuous rhythms of his work. The artist stands out not because he stands apart, but because of the look he gives the viewer. With a single glance, Botticelli turns the biblical scene into a confrontation.

Why is he here? What occasions his presence? Self-portraits often raise the question of their own existence. You might ask what could possibly justify the casting of the Medici as worshipful Magi, the rich miming the faithful, but this is obviously commemoration in the form of ostentatious prayer. Odd as it may seem to include a couple of deceased Medici, it was an expedient way of keeping their images alive before God and the congregation of Santa Maria Novella, just as Lorenzo and Giuliano would be eternalized in their turn; and if the patrons could appear in this elaborate fantasy, viewing and queuing and even occasionally stooping in awe, then why not the author of the painting itself?

Savonarola, apocalyptic preacher, burner of vanities and scourge of Florentine corruption who would later count Botticelli among his followers, railed against the shocking preponderance of secular portraits in religious frescos in those days. The churches were becoming a social almanac, a portrait gallery

The Adoration of the Magi,
1475

Sandro Botticelli
(c. 1445–1510)

for local mafias. There they would be, witnessing martyrdoms, watching miracles, gazing at the Crucifixion – anything to appear in the picture. At least Botticelli did not cast himself as a wise man, but he does not play the family retainer either. His presence, his *look*, has a far greater purpose: to intensify the whole meaning of the painting.

Eye-to-eye portraits were comparatively unusual in fifteenth-century Italy and congregations rarely saw a recognizable face looking directly back at them from a church fresco. Patrons generally appeared in worshipful profile. The sitters in independent portraits – paintings you could hang on the wall at home – were commonly presented in profile too, like a head on a medal, distanced and aloof, partly because they were often transcribed directly from frescos in the first place but also perhaps because profiles are so precise and economic, an enormous amount of information condensed and carried by a single authoritative line. The compiler of an inventory of paintings in Urbino in 1500 is surprised to come across a portrait 'with two eyes'.[1]

Until Flemish portraits by Van Eyck and others started to arrive in Italy, with the revelation of a three-quarters view, it was unusual for a portrait to show more than one eye. This shift towards the viewer, this turning to communicate, was beginning to happen when Botticelli painted the senior Medici as Magi, but they still have the idealized remoteness of dead legends, whereas a singular vitality radiates from his eyes. The eyes are the strongest intimation, of course, that this is a self-portrait.

But Botticelli is not just putting in a proprietorial appearance, the painter painted. In *The Adoration of the Magi*, the self-portrait activates both the scene and its meaning. Just by turning and looking so challengingly at you, he shifts the tense so that the nativity no longer seems like ancient history but an incident of the moment, its significance forever urgent. There is fixation in that look, not just born of strained relations with the mirror, but perhaps of the kind that made Botticelli labour for twenty years over his never-finished illustrations to Dante's *Divine Comedy*, or that would eventually drive him to destroy his own paintings in Savonarola's notorious bonfire of the vanities. At any rate, the stare is a deliberate pressure, almost a demand or accusation. You who look so complacently upon this scene that I have envisaged for you – how deep is *your* adoration, *your* love?

––––––––

Self-portraits catch your eye. They seem to be doing it deliberately. Walk into any art gallery and they look back at you from the crowded walls as if they had been waiting to see you. The eyes in a million portraits gaze at you too, following you around the room, as the saying goes, but rarely with the same heightened expectation. Come across a self-portrait and there is a frisson of recognition, something like chancing upon your own reflection.

This is self-portraiture's special look of *looking*, a trait so fundamental as to be almost its distinguishing feature. Even quite small children can tell self-portraits from portraits because of those eyes. The look is intent, actively seeking you out of the crowd; the nearest analogy may be with life itself: paintings behaving like people.

Eye-to-eye contact with others – a glance, a stare – is the purest form of reciprocity. Until it ends, until one of us looks away, it is the simplest and most direct connection we can ever have. I look at you, you look at me: it is our first prelude, an introduction to whatever comes next; if we smile, shake hands, converse, get married, it will always be preceded by that first glance. We talk of eyes meeting across a crowded room, of recognizing each other immediately even though we had never met; we speak of love at first sight. Conversely we could not stand the sight of each other. Just one look was enough.

Since painted faces cannot hold your interest by changing expression, much depends on the character of that look. It is the first place we go, as in life, and if it is too tentative or blank or disaffected it might also be the last; the overture rebuffed. Some artists are disadvantaged from the start because they cannot get a fix on their eyes in the mirror, an aspect of excruciating strain that shows up in the picture exposing the pretence that they were ever looking at anyone but themselves. Others have to deal with spectacles or

Self-Portrait,
c. 1546–1548

Jacopo Comin
Tintoretto
(1518–1594)

myopia or some insurmountable affliction, although the Italian painter
Guercino movingly transformed the brutal squint he suffered from birth
(Guercino means squinter) into a sign of unimpaired imagination by painting
his eyes so deeply shadowed that one understands that this man's vision turns
inwards. His self-portrait shows, by concealment, what it might be like to
have partial sight; *mutatis mutandis*, one sees what he sees. This is in the gift of
self-portraits with perfect sight too of course. Whenever the look that
originates in the mirror stays live and direct in the final image then the viewer
should have a vicarious experience of being the artist – standing in the same
relation he or she stood to the mirror, and the picture.

    This sharpening of vision is very marked in a self-portrait Jacopo
Tintoretto made in his late twenties. The Venetian turns to look our way and
there is inquiry in his dark-eyed stare, a hook so strong you cannot immediately

pull away for the sense of being held in his sights. The look is charged, the intensity meant, and abetted by other aspects of the image: the turning to stare over one shoulder, the gathering frown, appearing to cast a cold eye upon oneself in the encroaching darkness – no illusions, no fears – not to mention Tintoretto's burning good looks.

It is an obvious and much-remarked fiction of self-portraiture that the viewer, rather than the artist, is the focus of all this intense interest. Tintoretto perfects the illusion. He has not gone right through the looking glass the way some artists do, their eyes worn blank by staring; he is not lost in self-contemplation, not caught in some infinite regression of looking at himself looking at himself, and so on. He is all attention.

The eyes are unusually large as if they dominated the other senses. Light catches the upper lid of the left and the lower rim of the right so that one has an uncommon sense of their spherical form within the socket. Perhaps these are the red rims of a man who painted with insomniac drive right through the night, creator of the tumultuous murals that cover wall after wall of the Scuola di San Rocco in Venice. At any rate, the eyes have their own special force of character and they have the reciprocal effect of making the viewer stare hard in return. It is no stretch of the imagination to feel you are both equally intent upon the other, but that you have also slipped into his position, seeing what he saw, entering into his self-knowledge. Centuries before anyone discovered how the eye actually works, Tintoretto has hit upon a true metaphor, for the eye is indeed an extruded part of the brain, drawing whatever it can of the outer world in through the retina to be transformed into neural images. Nowadays some specialists consider the eye a part of the mind itself, its freight of information modified by individual cognition, and even in Darwin's day its curious status was enough understood for him to have written that 'the thought of the eye makes me cold all over'.[2] But Tintoretto, without any knowledge of the mechanics of seeing, senses the connection between mind and eye: to see is to know.

———

Look at me when I am talking to you, we say in pain or exasperation to those who have turned away – putting us out of sight and by implication out of mind. The simplest way for anyone to thwart our attentions, to block our access, is to look away. The barman who does not want to take an order will not meet the customer's eye. The pedestrian who has stepped out in front of the car looks into the middle distance to avoid the motorist's glare. An especially chilling way to deny another person is to stare straight through them as if they were just not there.

This is precisely the look of many portraits where the sitter is supposedly a cut above – the royal portrait, say, or the duke on horseback – but most portraiture aims for some kind of connection. The Italian artist Giulio Paolini made the point in the 1960s by showing just how disconcerting it feels if this communion is deliberately thwarted. Paolini displayed a black and white reproduction of a Renaissance painting, Lorenzo Lotto's *Portrait of a Young Man*, which shows a beautiful youth staring very candidly, and captivatingly, back at the viewer; or so it seems. But Paolini killed that illusion at a stroke simply by calling his version *Young Man Looking at Lorenzo Lotto*.

Common sense says this can only be true, that the sitter's eyes were always on Lotto while he worked; but common sense is exactly what we naturally suppress when looking at the eye-to-eye portrait. It is our willing suspension of disbelief, our contribution to the occasion, and if the young man is no longer looking at us, if his eyes are refocused on someone else, then the party is over. The painting withdraws, becomes the record of two dead people looking at each other in some previous century, an effect of deflation and exclusion. It is the end of the rapport most portraitists want and exactly the opposite of self-portraiture's aspiring eye-to-eye transmission of a first person encounter.

But an inept self-portrait will prove Paolini's point quite unintentionally just by botching the eyes. The artist gets into a loop of looking at himself in the glass and reproducing that look that meets nothing but itself.

The Swiss-born painter Anton Graff is doing his best to see what he looks like, visor in position, brows pinched with effort. He poses as if turning aside from his latest commission, a portrait of some portly and presumably once-famous patron, but the pretence is not plausible for a moment. The Graff in the picture who wants to show himself doing what he does best – he was a very successful portraitist whose sitters included Schiller, Gluck and Frederick the Great – cannot really be working on that portrait, since he must be working on this self-portrait instead. And sure enough, he is trying so hard to paint both eyes in focus that you know he is really painting his own face. Graff's gaze swithers; he cannot see us for the struggle to see himself.

A few decades earlier, Jean-Baptiste-Simeon Chardin looks over the top of his pince-nez, one eyebrow raised with perceptible interest in an attitude of scrutiny that could not appear more sociable by comparison. The pose is almost humorous – who is not familiar with the rhetoric of lowering one's spectacles as if pretending to consider someone else more pointedly – and the artist is at home in his jaunty bandanna, neck cloth loosely knotted against the cold, a note of domestic intimacy that runs through his work. But Chardin, now in his seventies, is both watchful and grave.

His eyesight failing and the smell of the oil paint he had used for half a century now making him ill, Chardin was forced to give up oil for pastel instead. The light focusing through the lens, the steel frames, the eyes with their glint of curiosity: all are achieved with this tricky medium, so easily blended and yet so fragile and fugitive.

Chardin is one of those artists whose self-portrait comes as a surprise – not because the face is so intelligent, for he has to be at least this clever to be the greatest still-life painter in art, but because it exists in the first place. Born in Paris in 1699, he never left the city except for a trip to Versailles. He has nothing to say about the wars, politics or public misery of his times, still less the private excesses of the aristocracy, although he must have seen it all for he had a city-centre flat in the Louvre. Chardin stayed at home, secretive, industrious, painting his apricots, strawberries and teacups, hymning the softness of a dead hare, the molten glow of a cherry. His power of touch runs all the way from the silvery condensation on a glass of water to the reflected glory inside a copper pan and the downy cheek of the housemaid dreaming over her dishes. Diderot, his earliest champion, called him 'The Great Magician', trying to fathom the mysteries of his art, of those muffled rooms where everything is misty and slightly distanced and warm air circulates like breath. But nobody ever saw him paint and scarcely a single anecdote attaches to Chardin's life. That he should have left anything as personal as a self-portrait goes against the person of his art.

That it is outwardly turned and makes such vivid eye contact is even less to be expected. For the look is distinctly interpersonal, making a quizzical

connection with the viewer from the centre of the image, the perceptual heart of the picture. Chardin turns the same unhurried, penetrating gaze upon himself normally used to gauge the weight of a plum, the quiddity of an egg. You feel what it is to be one of his subjects, and what it is to be Chardin, eyes testing the truth of life directly.

––––––––

Rembrandt is acting with his eyes. He hooks you by reeling back and showing the whites. The etching has been given the title *Self-Portrait, Wide-Eyed* but it might as well be called 'Shocked to See You'. It is as if you personally have caused this effect: you come before him and *he* reacts, that is the one-two action of the image. The meeting of eyes amounts to an incident. And it is the same with almost all of Rembrandt's self-portraits: he paints the eyes as pinpricks in shadow, or black holes, or dark discs you have to search for in the gloaming, trying to make the man out. He squints and he leers and he creases up to get a better look at you, a better sense of who you might be, identity always at issue.

One of Rembrandt's contemporaries, the Florentine poet and painter Lorenzo Lippi, goes even further with this line of inquiry, this idea that artists' eyes do not just follow but actively seek you out, questioning who you are, with comic trepidation in his case. Lippi turns timidly towards us from the safety of

Self-Portrait, c. 1655

Lorenzo Lippi
(1606–65)

the shadows, one eye out of sight as if hiding round the corner, the other
swivelling fearfully in its socket. Who is there? The picture puts everyone on the
spot.

Lippi's ambition, he said, was to write poetry as he spoke and to paint as
he saw[3] and this likeness is quick and colloquial. But it is also a neat parody of
the eyeballing business of self-portraiture: here is an artist bold enough to
paint a portrait of himself yet who seems almost too scared to look. He has
one eye on the viewer's amusement.

Lippi seems to have been better known for his humour than his portraits in any case, spending much of his life at the court of Innsbruck painting respectful likenesses of the aristocrats while at the same time writing a serial mock epic satirizing their behaviour and mores to the mirth of devoted readers back home.[4] His jesting image is now in the Uffizi self-portrait collection, still amusing the people of Florence. Unlike most of the many hundreds of paintings in that collection, it was not made especially for the occasion yet seems to have its current neighbours in mind, a mouse that hardly dares squeak among the great lions all around it whose pomp it quietly mocks. With his one-eyed peep Lippi achieves in a blink, what is more, what other artists can only hope for: an intimacy of connection, a kind of wink, in his case, that immediately brings the self-portrait to life.

Where to look? Anywhere but the mirror is an answer for the rare artist who rejects the rhetoric of intimacy. One of the few self-portraits to avoid eye contact altogether is also one of the greatest, painted by Titian in his mid-seventies. By now, the artist's patrons have long since included popes, dukes, doges and most of the crowned heads of Europe and he shows himself as splendidly dressed as any of them, wearing the gold chains given him by the Holy Roman Emperor Charles V who is supposed to have bowed his own knee to retrieve one of Titian's dropped brushes (a folk-tale so gratifying to later artists that more than one painted the royal genuflection).

Titian sits at a table, this painter of kings and king of painters, one hand tensed against it, the other braced upon his thigh with the fingers powerfully outspread. A fellow artist who had been admitted to his studio in Venice reported that in these later years Titian often painted directly with his fingers, and one might imagine that the artist painted these magnificent hands with his own fingers, his supreme sense of touch evident in their very tips. But Titian is not painting in this self-portrait, of course – he is waiting, and this is the central tension of the picture. The body faces front, massively present, but the eyes turn away towards some invisible point beyond the picture. That you should still be here, that *he* should be here at all: these are the burdensome but inevitable conditions of self-portraiture, of appearing and being seen. But Titian manages to command your attention by diverting it, his eyes glancing free of yours.

Where to look when submitting oneself to scrutiny? It is a question that presents itself to the public-minded self-portraitist every time. In reality, we usually have some sense of who might be looking at us, especially if the circumstances are familiar. But artists can only see one person looking back from the mirror and have to imagine all the rest – anyone and everyone who might one day see their image – to compose a representative face. The politician filmed

in some satellite studio unable to see his interrogator may be analogous, having no rival eyes on which to latch and forced to frame an expression without any guiding response. Under these circumstances, interviewees frequently look up, down or wanderingly off-centre, flustered by the voice in their ear, infuriated by the questions, or just withdrawn into tense concentration.

The eyes of self-portraits can expose an artist in just this way as dazed or perplexed, lost in thought or self-consciousness, or just defeated by the harsh technicalities. But few have retreated so far into self-consciousness as to have forgotten the world altogether. No matter how intimate the exchange between self and self-image, not many self-portraitists address only themselves, muttering alone in the studio. Self-portraiture is rarely an act of total introspection; attention is what it generally seeks. Some artists aim straight for the public address; others do so while making a pretence of seemly privacy – lowering the eyes, looking away off into the distance. Still others simply want to *appear* intimate, without giving much away. Joshua Reynolds manages to combine all three just by playing upon vision as a conceit.

Reynolds painted a great number of self-portraits with the public squarely in mind and many of them are unbearably self-serving. But in the best and most original, painted in his mid-twenties when he was just up to London from a Devonshire village and about to set off for the glories of Rome, his sights are set on the future and the road is open before him.

The dynamic young hero stares straight ahead, shielding his eyes against the light with one hand. Literally, he is looking at himself in the mirror but the gesture implies far wider horizons. With the maulstick held across the body like a sword, he also looks ready for the cut and thrust. He is on guard: the artist as saluting swordsman.

It is a variation on the studio self-portrait – the palette, the stick for steadying the hand at the canvas, even a hint of that canvas – but such an advance on the usual scenario. Reynolds makes a character of himself in a drama that is all about seeing and being seen and trying to get a better look at the

'A beautiful eye makes silence eloquent, a kind eye makes contradiction an assent, an enraged eye makes beauty deformed. This little member gives life to every other part about us; that is to say, every other part would be mutilated were not its force represented more by the eye than even by itself.'

Joseph Addison

world. The world, and himself, and his audience, and his painting – the gesture is pointedly specific yet all-encompassing; and then comes a further twist. His eyes are so deep in shadow, like those of Rembrandt, Reynolds's hero, that it is impossible to tell whether they are truly fixed upon the viewer; and the implication of that shielding hand, what is more, is that it is in any case too bright to make out what lies ahead, that the artist can hardly see. Artist and viewer are ships in the night. Yet the hand against the light tells of a sighting!

Reynolds painted himself in Rembrandt beret, in the doctoral robes of Oxford University, contemplating a bust of Homer in the manner of Aristotle in Rembrandt's etching. His sense of achievement was highly developed and his self-portraits are ceremonial – the one painted when he got the freedom of his home town, the one for the king when he took over the Royal Academy – and made for public display within a month or two, usually at the Royal Academy.

But he sometimes produced less grandstanding works in which he comes more modestly downstage. In a late painting, now deaf, he cups a hand to his ear the better to hear us in a poignant reprise of this early gesture (his vision would eventually fade as well). Both pictures have a theatrical intimacy – Garrick on stage – that seems to single you out, to signal to you and you alone. They crave, and declare, an audience with these focusing gestures. But although Reynolds salutes the viewer, he has eyes not just for you but the whole wide world.

————

The eyes of most self-portraits are outwardly directed, seeking to be seen, but they may signify inner vision just as keenly. A head in close up, eyes like dark stars, was rare when Tintoretto painted himself in the sixteenth century but it became very common with Romanticism. The self is concentrated in the mind, the mind in the eyes, twin wells of feeling and thought. *Cogito ergo sum* translates as *video ergo sum*, and what I am may be manifest in my powers of vision. Self-portraiture's special look goes well with this idea of the artist as seer, possessing gifted powers of insight. It is a look popular among the young – Samuel Palmer, at twenty-one, appears charismatically far-sighted, although it is partly the effect of not being able to draw both eyes in focus – and mocked by Picasso in old age. At ninety-one, eyes like mismatched marbles in a primitive mask, one dim and myopic, the other stuck open for ever like some dreadful twist of fate, he is halfway between animal and crazed old totem.

There is a little self-portrait drawing by Paul Klee where the eyes are tight shut, so that one deduces that it cannot have been made by looking in a

mirror but must effectively be a self-portrait from within, and quite possibly with sex in mind, for there is orgasmic concentration in the features. But what it enchantingly expresses is this idea that inspiration, vision, imagination, soul, everything that really matters in art, come in the end from within. And an extra quirk is that humorous Klee can never be accused of self-regard (an old accusation against self-portrayers) for he was not even looking at himself. What these eyes must have seen, what thoughts, what dreams: Klee's self-portrait draws one intensely into his mind without following the usual invitation through the open eyes, a sweet retort to the old line about souls and windows. And one remembers that he did not make any distinction between the inner and outer worlds in his work. 'Art does not render the visible,' Klee said, 'it renders visible.' He was speaking mystically and what is rendered visible in his art is surely at the very least his own spirit – lightsome, benign, visionary, intimate and as comical as this little self-portrait.

What the eyes have seen, literally and metaphorically: this is the concern of all art. In this sense the eyes are the artist's truest emblem and attribute. How perfect that they should also become the crux of an artist's self-portrait, the focal point, the first line of communication between artist and viewer.

Yet no self-portraitist actually needs to meet our gaze directly to exert continuous pressure or keep our eyes upon his. This is nowhere more apparent than in an etching by Francisco Goya that speaks as powerfully with the eyes as Botticelli even though it does not even have the advantage of two and never fixes fast, or unequivocally, upon the viewer.

Goya turns slightly out of formal profile, throwing a sidelong glance out of the picture. The look is withering, as pungently directed outward as inward. It is an opening shot; it is the etching with which he prefaced *Los Caprichos*.

This volume of prints, unsurpassed in their terrifying visions of human violence and folly, avarice and cruelty, their riddling captions like the overheard speech of mysterious offstage commentators, goes so far beyond explanation into nightmare that it is often perceived as purely a figment of the artist's tormented imagination, no matter that the voice of the captions declares 'I saw this' or 'I was here'. Goya originally opened the volume with that deathless image of a man slumped over his desk, the air thronged with bats and evil critters that might indeed be issuing from his nightmares; and 'The Sleep of Reason' has been taken as an allegorical self-portrait depicting the source (and modus operandi) of all that follows. But Goya replaced it, significantly, with this likeness of himself as a top-hatted man of the world casting a cold eye upon the viewer.

It is an acerbic pastiche of the conventional famous-author portrait that has prefaced so many books, then and since. The profile puts the self-portrait straight into the third person: there is the author, Señor Goya, his name written below, corresponding precisely with Goya's verbal description of himself

throughout as *el autor*, or *el pintor*. And yet he breaks out of that profile, as if coming alarmingly alive. Facing left, he appears to turn his back upon what follows as if in disavowal; but then again, isn't he rather like the kind of figures who occasionally turn up in the book? Goya may be the maker, or the narrator, but he is not above the vileness depicted herein.

We always say that in his images of sexual corruption, torture, war crimes, bullfights, Goya is the master of modern documentary, that whatever he had to say about the Spanish Inquisition or the horrors of the Napoleonic invasions of the early nineteenth century applies to Afghanistan or Abu Ghraib. The priest lusts, the paedophile rapes: the artist has seen it all and brought it back to us in its absolute horror. But it is very hard to read the tone of Goya's art, to know who is speaking, who saw what, whether the talk is ever straight.

Look at that telling eye: it seems to swivel between there and here, then and now, between immediacy and distance. Pose and eye, taken together, make Goya both an observer and a man observed, the creator but also the subject. Yet the look is insinuating, and deviously incorporates the viewer. That left eye, half obscured by the heavy eyelid and nearly disappearing out of view, has you snared in its sights, for you and I are part of this too.

Dürer

'You make us to thyself and our hearts are restless until we find rest in thee.'

St Augustine

1500

Albertus Durerus Noricus
ipsum me proprijs sic effin
gebam coloribus ætatis
anno XXVIII.

Self-Portrait, 1500

Albrecht Dürer (1471–1528)

ne winter's day in 1905, a museum guard was meandering through the galleries of the Alte Pinakotech in Munich when he noticed that one of the paintings had changed since the last time he looked. The eyes of Albrecht Dürer's self-portrait, the most famous eyes in the museum – the most famous eyes in German art – had somehow lost their piercing charisma. The right eye appeared dim and the liveliness of the left severely diminished, as if they could no longer see, and when the painting was taken down, ferocious little rips were discovered in the irises and pupils that had most likely been made, it was agreed, with the tip of a hatpin. The man – or woman – who assaulted the painting may well have used such a weapon, swift, efficient and very conveniently produced and concealed, for it appears that nobody noticed the attack. Somebody unseen, somebody who was never caught, had tried to put out Dürer's eyes.

Dürer's eyes – this is how we put it, not bothering to distinguish between the painter and his self-portrait; and we do the same with portraits too. Mona Lisa is what we call both the picture and the young lady from Milan who sat for Leonardo da Vinci. But it feels more natural with self-portraits since artist and sitter are one and the same, being in some profound sense related, image to person. And in the case of Dürer's 1500 self-portrait, as never before in the history of art, the one would become the counterpart of the other in unique and mysterious ways.

The impact of this painting cannot be overstated: so immediate and yet so remote. At a distance it seems to transmit an unearthly glow that draws viewers across the gallery, and the power intensifies the nearer one gets, not least because the picture is such an unqualified close-up. Dürer presents himself front on, waist up, formidably fixed, immediate and erect. One of his hands is just out of view, as if under the counter, the other fingers the tufts of his fur lapel in a curious gesture that draws attention to both the garment and the wearer, so present and correct, this man who is representing himself. His long moustache is waxed in two scimitar curves that echo the fine arcs of his eyebrows. The hair streams down over his shoulders, a triangle of metal-bright locks, not a single tendril out of place. The face is closed and eerily symmetric. Above all, the eyes transfix.

Even if you knew nothing about German society in 1500, or this period in art, you could assume that Dürer's contemporaries were amazed by this self-portrait because it still astonishes today. No gold is used in the paint, apart from the inscription, and yet the picture has this peculiar golden radiance. The face appears exceptionally precise and distinctive – strong nose, more of a limb than a feature; slight cast in the eyes; blemish on the left cheek – yet the evidence, for all its heightened clarity, is bizarrely impersonal. What colour are those pale eyes? How old is this person? What is the expression in his look, so pertinacious and yet so withheld? The picture seems both immeasurably more than — and yet strangely unlike — other self-portraits.

It is a double take so improbable one hardly believes it at first. The long hair, centre-parted, the beard and moustache, the gesture of the fingers, the symmetry and stillness and remoteness of countenance, out of time and out of this world: the resemblance startles, incredulity immediately sets in and yet the thought builds like a quake. Is it just chance, a coincidence of fate, or could this man actually have meant to make himself look like Jesus?

———

People attack portraits when they no longer see, or want to see, them as pictures so much as surrogates or even real people. This is especially true of statues, which are abused exactly as if they were alive, their noses broken, their genitals mutilated, heads and hands brutally severed. Painted people ought to be less vulnerable, safe indoors and protected by guards, but they are victimized too and the connection between people and pictures is held to be so much closer that unlike statues — sightless objects, things apart — we commonly class them together. Nobody would dream of correcting a child who points to a baby in a book, and calls it a baby instead of a picture, and the same is true of our portraits. Even grown-ups plant kisses on images, carry them like champions through the streets, worship them, savage them out of spite or fury, become excited by them as we are excited by people in reality. What is so singular about Dürer's image, in this respect as in so many others, is not that it has been adored or loathed but that it has excited both extremes of passion and to a greater degree than any other portrait.

This old painting of a man with prodigious hair and alarming eyes has been kissed and excoriated, worshipped and attacked, carried through the streets and mounted on an altar like an icon. It has been accused of self-love and sacrilege and shocking froideur, in spite of which, or perhaps because of which, women have loved it like a man. The German writer Bettina von Arnim became so infatuated with it — or him — that she had a copy made, one she would send to Goethe, for whom she also felt unrequited love, on the curious grounds that it was so precious to her that she might as well be sending herself.[1] But was von Arnim in love with the portrait, or the man, or the idea of an artist who could create such an image? The idea that image, man and artist might somehow be one and the same, a trinity, may well be the most potent claim of self-portraiture.

In any case indifference is not what Dürer's painting invites or inspires, and this sense of agency is crucial to its power; for all its preternatural stillness, the self-portrait feels almost oppressively vital. Just as things seen in a dream may seem clearer than those in the waking world, so one imagines that this self-portrait might have appeared more vivid than the real man himself, and perhaps the attacker felt this vitality was focused in the eyes. The damage to the self-portrait was clinically specific: just the irises and pupils, not the whites or any other part of the face, as if whoever tried to blind him could not stand the drilling fixity of Dürer's gaze.

Mercifully the rips did not penetrate the Renaissance varnish and the painting was successfully repaired, except for a minuscule spot of dullness in one of the eyes that is invisible to our own but was fastidiously noted in the museum records. It is here that the details of the crime have been buried for almost a century. Museums do not often acknowledge — are perhaps even embarrassed by — the power of art to entrance, frighten or enrage and any viewer affected to the point of violence is inevitably described as insane. So it was with the unknown assailant at the Alte Pinakotech, who is described as categorically mad in the records. This may have been the case; the paranoid and delusional often believe that paintings are staring at them. But among the dry reports of each minute abrasion, the experts cannot help wondering whether the painting itself supplied motive. Why was the painting attacked? Because of the way it looked at its attacker, of course, a person presumed to have 'taken exception to Dürer's penetrating stare'.[2] It is not beyond belief, even among those who make strong professional distinctions between art and life, that someone — anyone — might experience the eyes as a personal affront. But it is also possible that the attacker may have taken exception to more than the artist's stare.

———

All self-portraits are prefaces of a sort. Just as our faces in some sense introduce us, so these painted faces are perceived — and treated — as the prefaces to artistic utterance. They are reproduced on the covers of autobiographies, monographs and fictional lives. They are displayed at the beginning of the museum retrospective like the host at the party, and sometimes at the end in farewell (in which respect, they are once again being construed as surrogates).

In any case indifference is not what Dürer's painting invites or inspires, and this sense of agency is crucial to its power; for all its preternatural stillness, the self-portrait feels almost oppressively vital.

The self-portrait is cast as a frontispiece, a prologue before we get down to the *real* work, no matter that it may be among the artist's greatest achievements, and this Dürer both courts and defies. He puts his self-portrait forward very consciously as a frontispiece but also as an unprecedented work of art. You are not to think that this is just any old painting of him so much as the *defining* image of Dürer the man and artist.

That he looks like Christ, that the painting resembles a frontispiece: this much is apparent all at once, but neither observation can quite explain the surpassing strangeness of the image. Strangeness is its first and last note. While there are other masterpieces of which this could be said very few of them are portraits, and still less self-portraits, which commonly have as part of their content the artist's manifest desire to be the very opposite of strange: in fact, to be quite clearly understood.

The figure occupies a peculiar middle ground somewhere between two and three dimensions. There is no backdrop, but no foreground either and no obvious source of light. In fact, the tawny glow that illuminates the scene, beginning at the crown and rippling down through the hair, appears to emanate from Dürer's own body. This hair, with its unnatural sheen, spreads in triangular curtains from the top of the head to the exact edge of the frame, perfectly contained as if made to measure; and the inscriptions on either side make an opposing triangle, its base the pointing finger below. These inscriptions – Dürer's famous AD logo and the date 1500 on the left; the details of name and place on the right – are not written on any depicted surface but that of the picture itself, as part of its symmetrical composition; pendant as the scales of justice, they weigh Dürer's face in the balance. Nothing is allowed to detract from this sense of order, geometry and design, of very close and insistent frontality. All is congruent. The artist is perfectly fused with his picture.

Dürer does not turn, he does not move, he is not looking out at you from any given time or place. He is simply and starkly himself – self-portraiture at its least equivocal – and yet he is also somebody else.

It is not quite accurate to say that Dürer looks like Jesus so much as an icon of Jesus, since nobody knows what the most famous man in history actually looked like. This is an obvious advantage for anyone who wants to slip his own features into the picture, but what kind of artist would do such a thing? It scarcely seems possible that Dürer could propose anything so flagrant and one cannot help thinking, faced with what appears to be an act of astounding hubris, that there are no other self-portraits like it. No other artist of the period represented himself in the image of Christ, and it has not exactly become a convention in the meanwhile. Egon Schiele's self-portraits, naked, agonized and arms out-flung, could be construed as metaphorical crucifixions lacking only the wooden cross. Paul Gauguin's comparisons of himself with

Jesus — two martyrs united in suffering — are not so much messianic as ironic in their abundant self-pity. Surely the comparison of oneself with Christ would have been considered sacrilegious in its day (if not now) or at the very least maniacally boastful? So the lay viewer might think. But there is no evidence that the painting shocked Dürer's contemporaries, despite the fact that they were late medieval Christians.

This fact, however, has troubled modern scholars. Ever since German art historians began to devote decades of their lives to Dürer in the late nineteenth century, the question of what he meant and how he was understood in his day has dogged our interpretation of the painting. If there is no evidence of outrage, then the iconography of the self-portrait must have been seen as (or must now be made to seem) completely unexceptional.

Dürer was not a Protestant; it would be another seventeen years before Martin Luther nailed his ninety-five theses to the church door in Wittenberg. Nor, despite his famously bantering correspondence with the humanist Willibald Pirckheimer, his close friend in Nuremberg, can anyone say for certain whether the artist was even a humanist. Historians have gone to great lengths to work up theological justifications for Dürer's conceit, each opposed to the next. Dürer represents himself as Christ because he is trying to live up to Christ in life as well as art (*Imitatio Christi*). Dürer takes literally the idea that man is made in God's image. Dürer sees the human form as an expression of the divine (consider the perfect proportions of the self-portrait) and therefore as a different kind of *Imago Dei*. It is possible that the painting represents all these possibilities and more, but what is striking about these interpretations, each a counterblast to the last, is the way they *neutralize* the actual painting. By the time it has been exhaustively theorized, Dürer's self-portrait has been made to seem not only simple but really quite orthodox and straightforward — precisely what it is not.

Nobody knows whether Dürer's contemporaries were vexed by the picture. We do not know why he made it, how many people saw it or where it was hung during his lifetime. No such thing as art criticism existed. As Dürer's great exponent, Joseph Leo Koerner, has written, 'the entire body of literature about any specific painting of the 16th century in Northern Europe as written at the time can be fitted on one sheet of paper'.[3]

We do know that Dürer exchanged works of art with Raphael and that his gift to the Italian was no simple depiction but an extraordinary mock-up of the Veil of Veronica. Dürer had painted Christ's face in gouache on transparent cambric so that it looked the same from both sides and appeared to float in thin air when held up to the light. Christ's features were those of Dürer.

Since this fabled item disappeared long ago there is no way of gauging how shocking it might have seemed. But it clearly played on the idea of the *vera icon* as a sort of supernatural self-portrait, Christ's image mysteriously transmitted without human hand on to Veronica's veil as he wiped his brow. No human hand; the brushstrokes in the 1500 self-portrait are almost indiscernible.

The painting, with its power of looking, its hieratic solemnity and remoteness, so alien in its lack of intimacy or ingratiation, was evidently made to look like an icon – and yet it is emphatically one man's portrait. The figure may aspire to imitate Christ, or to resemble icons of Christ, but the inscription pulls hard in a secular direction. 'I Albrecht Dürer of Nuremberg painted myself with everlasting colours in my twenty-eighth year.' Nobody is to be in any doubt about which mortal painted the picture, or that it is a self-portrait – as against an icon – resolutely made to last for ever. The more one contemplates this painting, the first proleptic leap in self-portraiture, so cunningly conceived as a double identity, the more it seems to be poised in perfect tension between icon and portrait.

————

Albrecht Dürer was first in so many ways. Born in Nuremberg in 1471, he was the first great sightseer in European painting, making the hazardous crossing of the Alps more than once, living in Venice, travelling back through Germany, the Netherlands and Belgium. He once voyaged for six days on a small boat in the middle of winter in search of a whale that had washed up on a beach in Zeeland. Like his contemporaries he was fascinated by marvels and his journals are full of astonishing sights – a great bed in Brussels sleeping fifty men; soaring comets; Siamese twins; the bones of an 18-foot giant. And whatever Dürer saw, he drew: a ferocious walrus, a dragonfly landing awkwardly on the ground, even what appeared to him in dreams; the face of Christ as it came to him one feverish night, a hellish deluge flooding a plain. Dürer was the first to paint a landscape purely for its own sake and to make the sights he saw available to the world in the form of mass-produced prints, a medium in which he is the true pioneer and the first genuinely international artist.

It may be anachronistic to say that Dürer was the first to use his own image as a brand – others did this for him, issuing his self-portraits in the form of prints and medals even while he was alive – but he does seem to have felt as no artist before him the value of putting a face to one's name. How easily reputations could be forgotten must have been clear to him in his native city where he was surrounded by the masterworks of artists whose names were unknown, their histories forgotten, in the city's cathedral and churches.

In Italy, in 1494, Dürer complains in a letter home of the bitter contrast

between Nuremberg and Venice where painters like Titian and Giovanni Bellini are spoken of as heroes. 'Here I am a gentleman, at home no more than a parasite.'⁴ In Venice he also signs his works with new flourish. 'Albrecht Dürer the German brought this forth [*exegit*] in five months' is the exultant inscription on one altarpiece, alluding to the poet Horace's boast of bringing forth (*exegit*) a monument. That Dürer was alive to the originality of his own work is apparent from his campaigns against the pirating of his prints, and the AD logo, with which he signed every painting and drawing, was central to the celebrated lawsuit (a precedent, needless to say) in which he defended his intellectual copyright. Dürer's first drawing is also his first self-portrait, made at the age of thirteen – the first example of such precocity in art.

It is a marvel in itself, this queer little drawing in silverpoint. Even so young, even starting out, Dürer does not do anything conventional. He does not draw in pencil or chalk, he does not draw something or someone easier. He does not even portray himself from the front but in three-quarter view, looking and pointing to the right, a set-up so challenging it probably involved more than one mirror. The medium is as tricky as possible since silverpoint, which involves drawing with a fine stylus on specially prepared paper, cannot be erased or corrected. Dürer's father, a goldsmith, had already made a silverpoint self-portrait, in the same pose and holding one of the delicate tools of his trade; his son does nothing so humble. The right hand is not drawing, as it might have appeared in the mirror, nor holding anything so rudimentary as a stylus. In place of the tool is the boy's gesturing finger, pointing to a world beyond that of the picture. And sure enough the future is all there in this little sheet of paper: virtuosity, incisiveness, the intense scrutiny and detachment, the fascination with everything from the individual strands of hair to the crumple and fold of fabric, stiff as carved wood. Even the elongated finger, elegant as his friends attest, is seen again in the 1500 self-portrait where pointing becomes even more significant.

Dürer's art is always pointing things out, defining their likeness, making them visible and more of them than ever before. The tusks of a walrus, a greyhound's quiver, the muzzle of a bull: superbly drawn and zoologically exact. Isolated on a page out of context, they look newly strange and wondrous; and things that are genuinely wondrous because imaginary – a merman, a horned devil, the Four Horsemen of the Apocalypse – seem actual because they are visualized out of observable truth.

The thirteen-year-old Dürer is a strange creature, too young to be producing such a work, and yet preternaturally wizened and aged: the child as father to the artist. Decades later, Dürer annotated the page with something like paternal pride: 'This portrait of myself I made from a mirror in the year 1484 whilst I was still a child.' Just noted for the record, as it seems, but to whom are these words addressed? Not to his descendants, for Dürer had no children, but to everlasting posterity.

'I made this in five days.' 'This I made in awe when I was ill.' 'I saw this in Antwerp.' Everything is annotated. There is more writing in Dürer's art (and upon it, in the form of postscripts) than practically any other of that era and had he been an author there would surely have been meticulous volumes of autobiography. Time past can never be regained, or so it is said, but Dürer labours continually against this miserable dogma. He preserves everything, records everything, nothing must be lost to dust and oblivion. There are notebooks, travelogues and a long family chronicle; he wants to record in word and image everything he experiences, from the quotidian to the momentous. On the flyleaf of his copy of the new edition of Euclid he writes, 'I bought this book at Venice for one ducat in 1507. Albrecht Dürer.' On the tragic drawing of his mother in later life (which also records the strong family resemblance) he puts down the date, of course, and then 'This is Albrecht Dürer's mother when she was 63' so that we would always know who she was and how she looked. Perhaps Dürer feared that she was mortally ill (he made portraits of both of his parents on the eve of his first trip to Italy, presumably in case he never saw them again). Not many days later, he adds the last words: 'She passed away in the year 1514 on Tuesday before Cross Week two hours before nightfall.' The portrait that begins as her living likeness becomes her epitaph.

Some years later Dürer draws himself half naked in the dire illness that probably overcame him during his search for the whale. One hand behind his back like a gallant about to bow, he points with the other to a circle inscribed around a point on his side and painted a delicate yellow. 'There, where the yellow spot is located, and where I point my finger, there it hurts.' The drawing was intended for his doctor and must be the most elaborate diagnostic aid in all art for it is a fully realized self-portrait in which the artist cannot suppress his mania for observation despite the suffering.

Self-Portrait in the Nude,
c. 1503

Albrecht Dürer
(1471–1528)

There are other drawings that probe — struggling to keep his face still in the mirror, head in hand, cheek awkwardly squashed; getting older; growing emaciated. But starkest of all is a full-frontal nude in which Dürer leans towards the glass to get a better look at himself, light striking his bony kneecaps and cheeks, the veins of his legs visibly standing, the long locks in a hairnet. Perhaps this is a man in his prime (he was approximately thirty-three) and certainly the torso is lean and strong, but it is an unstinting anatomy of nakedness, the dangling scrotum insidiously echoing the protuberant eyeballs, the cast in the left eye now more explicitly noted. Dürer is a peculiar sight even to himself, an alien creature in the world. The sense of an objectivity approaching estrangement is acute; Dürer, examining himself, sees something as strange as the wonders on his travels.

———

Dürer painted two self-portraits before the climax of 1500 and they have both been deplored as appallingly narcissistic. At twenty-two he looks pretty and girlish, clean-shaven in his raked cap with its scarlet cockade, fair hair artfully disarrayed. Other men in portraits of the period wear these ruched white shirts but never as low-cut as this. Between his fingers he holds an eryngium, an allusion to Christ's suffering but also supposedly an aphrodisiac and guard against impotence. Whatever it meant to Dürer's contemporaries in the arcane symbolism of the times it is displayed here, and depicted, as if it were some kind of outlandish scientific specimen, an object to be handled and examined. Some say this is a betrothal picture, painted on parchment so that it could be conveniently dispatched to his future wife. If so, and very unusually for Dürer there is no written evidence, then the inscription reads oddly. Next to the date, he makes the ambiguous announcement, 'My affairs run as ordained from on high', or in another translation, 'as written in the stars'. Perhaps it is a declaration of piety, but if pious then not quite humble; and if a reference to the wedding then not quite enthusiastic, as if Dürer was having to resign himself to what was indeed an arranged marriage. It remains

Dürer was teased for his long hair in an age of collar-length cuts and took real pride in his outlandish coiffure, including the moustache — 'sharpened and tuned' as an acquaintance quipped — calling himself 'the hairy bearded painter' in a surviving fragment of doggerel.

extremely hard to match the words to the image in any clinching sense, partly because it is impossible to read the tone and expression of the face. One commentator claimed to find nothing but vanity there; arguing that if the 'painting breathes love at all, it is love of self'.[5] Love of clothes, maybe; love of symbolism or botanical forms: this much is evident from the picture. But as for Dürer's sense of himself, the face – expressionless, uninflected, exacting as a study of cowslips – gives nothing away.

Goethe, who owned a complete edition of Dürer's prints, praised his supreme vigour and 'wood-carved manliness'. That is there in the prints, of course, but there is nothing manly about the way Dürer looks either at twenty-two or four years later in the Prado portrait. The costume is a deliberate

challenge, part troubadour, part op-art couture, from the black and white stripes to the doeskin gloves (a Nuremberg speciality). Not only does the artist not portray himself painting, he defies the very notion of manual labour by presenting himself prophylactically gloved.

Dürer is dressed as lavishly as the patrons he portrayed, striking the same pose and raised up to their social level. By now he was celebrated in Venice, had published the *Apocalypse*, his best-selling folio of prints, been praised to his face by Bellini. His clothes are a reward and a proof of success, along with the Italian landscape (a compositional first) framed through the window. The point of this picture is the whole combination: experience, money, cosmopolitan style, the picturing of oneself as a work of art, as a third-person portrait. For the painting says portrait – Nobleman with View – even though the inscription says self-portrait: 'I made this from my own appearance when I was twenty-six.' The face, all stillness and social standing, declares nothing except the strain of representing binocular vision. Far from the 'pharisaical self-admiration' that so appalled the English art historian John Pope-Hennessy, the narrow eyes do not speak of pleasure. There is no disclosure of self, no hint of the interior life. If you believe that clothes maketh the man you might conclude that this one is a peacock but the discrepancy between the showy clothes and the show-nothing face is sharply pronounced, almost a disconnect between outer and inner beings. Dürer may be his own protagonist here but subjectivity is by no means his subject. It is as if he has slipped himself into a portrait, adjusted the pictorial conventions so he can speak of himself in the third person as a man of mode and culture, a well-travelled man, a man who wears gloves when posing for a portrait. Dürer is thinking – as always – about pictures and picture-making and how he can exploit and reinvent them, just as in 1500 he would produce the most completely *pictorialized* of all self-portraits.

———

Painted at the midpoint of the millennium and exactly halfway through Dürer's life, though he could not know it, this picture is cherished by German commentators as the epochal image of the German Renaissance, the triumphant face of German painting. Surely a man so conscious of his reputation must have envisaged such an outcome for his self-portrait, it is implied, and it is true that the image seems explicitly *ordained*. Scholars have been able to show that Dürer was looking at an actual frontispiece, in a new book by the German humanist Conrad Celtis,[6] from which he may have extrapolated the configuration of lettering and image. At any rate, the Roman lettering, the insistently frontal depiction, the figure symmetrically cropped and contained by the frame: this is certainly the authorized face, Dürer as he intended to be seen and known. It was obviously never meant to stay quietly at home with the family for ever, like so many self-portraits, and indeed it must have had at least one ceremonial viewing within months of completion. Celtis, who was also Germany's poet laureate, published a poem in its praise before the year was out.

How far did Dürer have to go to transform his own person into an icon? The earlier self-portraits, from the age of thirteen, add up to a time-lapse sequence in which the face is more or less recognizably that of one man, and he does not look very much like this. It is true that German mirrors were still quite primitive when Dürer was young – pieces of tin backed with lead, very often spherical – whereas the Venetian glass-blown mirrors he could later afford were comparatively sophisticated. But still the 1500 face is smoother, the cast in the eye less apparent, the hair a different colour; and to see what lengths Dürer would go to in the interests of advanced art you only have to consider those locks.

Straggly but generalized at twenty-two, they could still pass as approximately the same hair at twenty-six, softly brushed and realistic. But by 1500, there is nothing natural about them. They look more like the curling tendrils of a Wallachian ram than human hair, and in fact more like some sort of metal twine. Dürer was teased for his long hair in an age of collar-length cuts and took real pride in his outlandish coiffure, including the moustache – 'sharpened and tuned' as an acquaintance quipped – calling himself 'the hairy bearded painter' in a surviving fragment of doggerel. Even in crowded religious scenes his passing self-portrait will always be identifiable by the hank of hippy hair, but it is never as long as in the 1500 self-portrait and never so preternaturally curled and intertwined. This is fantastical hair and sticklers for forensic evidence can even consult the real lock taken from Dürer's head two days after his death and cultishly preserved in a silver reliquary, now in Vienna, to see that the former looks unreal by comparison.

Dürer chose to represent his extraordinary hair and its weird reflective sheen with a precision so spectacular his contemporaries could scarcely believe it was done without magic, or at least without a magic brush. Bellini, according to Dürer practically the only painter in Venice who could view his works without envy, was so dazzled by the strand-by-strand depiction he imagined Dürer must possess a special brush that could be used to paint several hairs at one stroke; Dürer apparently responded with a private demonstration of his extra-special steadiness of hand. But against these exceptional powers of realization – the numbering of every hair, every twist – is an extreme and opposing artificiality that goes several ways. The hair is a triangle that points to the picture's dimensions and the proportions of the figure. Or you might say it is arranged like a ceremonial headdress, or draped like a veil, or that its metallic sheen suggests something more numinous, like an aura or halo.

Certainly it alludes to the hair of Christ in icons, and specifically an icon by Van Eyck that Dürer is known to have admired. Anyone who saw the painting in Dürer's day may even have been not so much struck as deceived by the resemblance. Koerner points out that the artist's contemporaries would have seen so many icons, and so few portraits, especially with such distinctive compositions, that to them it probably looked more like an icon than a portrait.[7] Dürer actually became the face of Christ for future German artists. His self-portrait appears in many prints and images as the face on Veronica's

Veil and a century after his death, Georg Vischer even cast Dürer without offence in *Christ and the Woman Taken in Adultery*. There he is, right at the centre of the picture, radiating celestial light, his self-portrait by now a sacred relic; Dürer as the Holy Redeemer of German painting.

Vischer's very queer picture, almost a collage with its cut-out figure and mismatching styles, makes one significant alteration to the original. His Dürer is making a straightforward gesture of blessing, whereas the hand in the 1500 self-portrait only teases at a benediction and it is not entirely clear what the fingers are actually doing.

This equivocation goes to the strangeness of the picture, the gesture being as hard to divine as the remote expression in the face. It also breaches the presentation of the portrait as an icon. It might seem that Dürer is just signalling his own identity according to a fairly conventional formula – here I am, here is the hand that made me – but he is not just, or not precisely, pointing to himself. He appears to be fumbling the fur of the lapel between his fingers, perhaps drawing attention to its texture as well as his own virtuosity in depicting such luxurious softness. But this fiddling is a taunt because it is so ostentatiously private. Whatever he feels, whatever he senses in his fingers, ought to connect straight up to the face, but when you get there all explanations are frustrated.

If the hand is a sign – pointing upwards, pointing to Dürer, pointing out his virtuosity – it is also a geometric crux that sends you back to picture-making. The principles of its own construction are so much part of the picture's content that the little A of the logo chiming with the big A of the head is no accident and repeats the ingenious point in miniature: A is the artist, the artist is the image, a sign literally embodying the person, and incomparable art, of Albrecht Dürer.

––––––––––

Dürer died in Holy Week, 1528, a significant time for those inclined to worship the artist. 'Whatever was mortal of Dürer,' sighs the epitaph over the saint's grave, 'is covered by this tomb.' Two days after his death the cherished lock of hair was cut and given to his assistant, the artist Hans Baldung. Three days after his burial, adoring students exhumed the body in order to make a death mask. By a most resonant coincidence, when the grave was again reopened in the nineteenth century by fanatics hoping to measure the divine proportions of Dürer's head the body was gone and they found instead the corpse of a recently departed printmaker.

If Dürer had never painted the 1500 self-portrait then the unprecedented plethora of festivals held in his honour right up to the present day would all have lacked a figurehead. There would have been no face to carry like a monument through the streets of Nuremberg when he died. There would have been no altarpiece at which to worship for the nineteenth-century Nazarenes, those German artists also known as the Albrecht-Düreristen for their long hair, who gathered every year to celebrate the anniversary of his birth. There would have been no model for the bronze figure erected by mad King Ludwig of Bavaria in Nuremberg in 1840 – the first public statue ever to commemorate an artist – or for the miniature replicas of that statue, like little Eiffel Towers, that immediately went on sale as souvenirs of Nuremberg and its celebrated son.

Other works could have come to represent Dürer's genius: the famous watercolour of the quivering hare, *Knight, Death and the Devil*, with its man of steel in a German helmet assailed by forces of evil, the mysterious *Melancholia* with its morose angel, face like thunder, sitting in her junkyard of allegorical symbols. But what else could represent the cult of Dürer, man and artist, better than the 1500 self-portrait in which he sets himself forth as an icon?

An icon ought to be awesome and so this one is with its coldly glowing charisma. Dürer comes before you, but he is as remote as a deity ought to be and fully as unreadable. In the very act of showing his face, Dürer put an unbreachable façade between himself and his viewers. You can see what he might have looked like, what marvels he could make of himself and his art, feel unnerved or entranced, but whatever your feelings before this self-portrait you are on your own. The artist remains a closed question. And although he supposedly establishes the whole tradition of self-portraiture, Dürer also shows that it has no straightforward course, for the example he set in 1500 was the first and last of its kind. Nobody could repeat this idea, this act of creation. It is the alpha and omega of self-portraits.

Chapter Four

Motive, Means and Opportunity

'I write not my exploits, but myself and my essence.'

Michel de Montaigne

Detail of *The Last Judgement*, c. 1538–41

Michelangelo Buonarroti (1475–1564)

At the dead centre of *The Last Judgement*, within touching distance of Jesus Christ, Michelangelo makes an appearance. He is not on the ceiling of the Sistine Chapel, where you would have to crane your neck to spot him in the soaring multitude, but right there in plain view above the altar. The artist who has painted the dawn of creation, from the moment God imparts the spark of life to Adam, now appears at the last trump to face God; but all he shows of himself is a ragged epidermis, limp as chamois leather, dangling from the hand of a saint. There and not there, Michelangelo is no more than his own outer casing, displayed as the flayed skin of Bartholomew who was martyred for his faith. And while this Bartholomew is a magnificent creature, muscle-bound, heroic, turning his classical head towards Jesus — exactly as one might imagine Michelangelo, a figure powerful enough to wrestle whole worlds into being — the artist is just an empty overcoat hitched to a rubber mask. Yet Michelangelo was immediately recognizable to his contemporaries, as he is now, even in this exiguous state.

Detail of *The Last Judgement*, c. 1538–41

Michelangelo Buonarroti (1475–1564)

He is known to have scorned portraiture, especially the scrupulously accurate Northern European variety James Boswell hoped to emulate when depicting Dr Johnson in his biography in 'the style of the Flemish … exact in every hair, or even every spot on his countenance'. To the Florentine this was just tedious imitation, aspiring to nothing more than the banality of fact. A child of the Italian Renaissance, a student of the classical fragments in the gardens of the Medici villa, Michelangelo believed in the poetry of perfection, the ideal figure, the transcendence of the spirit over the mortal clay. Vasari, who knew him well, even claims that Michelangelo refused to make portraits because 'he hated drawing any living subject unless it were of exceptional beauty' and when commissioned to sculpt Lorenzo and Giuliano

Medici the artist himself confessed to giving them a grandeur they certainly were not born with. In fact, these effigies in the Medici chapel scarcely look like human beings at all, and when critics descried them as implausible, Michelangelo famously retorted that in a thousand years nobody would know or care what the Medici looked like.

The same is not true of the artist himself, a man who presents such an image of total creative power – the immense scale of his imagination, the sheer force of his labour, from the gigantic block of marble to the sleepless nights and days on the Sistine scaffold, always striving to achieve ever greater figures – that admiration for his art shades into admiration for the imagined man. Long before Charlton Heston bared his biceps in *The Agony and the Ecstasy*, Michelangelo was already in danger of becoming art's superman, a cartoon Vasari inspired with his praise of the artist's prodigious muscle-power. But Michelangelo does not collude with this legend in the Sistine self-portrait, quite the opposite; he presents himself as a man entirely *without* power.

In his self-portraits, Michelangelo is always more concerned with the inner soul than the outer man. As the model for Nicodemus, helping to bear the body of Christ in a marble Pietà, he sculpts himself with head reverentially bowed and hooded, prayer embodied; as the flayed skin in *The Last Judgement*, he is not so much portrayed as disembodied. Yet each self-portrait has its distinguishing characteristic that alone might represent him; as Van Gogh has his wounded ear, as Dalí has his moustache, Michelangelo has his broken nose.

It was smashed in a fight with a fellow artist, Pietro Torrigiano, who finally lost his temper, it is said, after years of sharp-tongued provocation. Michelangelo often spoke of his ruined nose – though not the incident – and he alludes to its ugliness more than once in the long sequence of sonnets begun in later life. Of course, it seems to suit his physique, wiry and with a boxer's build even into old age; but it also fits his temperament, this titan of *terribilita* who said he took in chisels and hammers with his nurse's milk. Michelangelo's nose is his emblem, and it is all he needs to stretch a self-portrait out of the nearly formless Sistine mask.

Michelangelo was in his late sixties when he finished *The Last Judgement* and much preoccupied by thoughts of dying, death and the resurrection of the body, the end of time and the punishment, or forgiveness, of sins. He often wrote about shrugging off the mortal coil, escaping his ugly and sinful body in hope of spiritual redemption, and in Sonnet 302, appealing to God's grace, he recalls the sacrifice of Christ on the cross:

> *You peel of flesh the same souls you apparelled*
> *In flesh; your blood absolves and leaves them clean*
> *Of sin, of human urges, all that is mean.*[1]

The self-portrait epitomizes this longing for absolution, the peeling away of the flesh in order to be reborn. It imagines the exact nature of this out-of-body experience and makes it visible to all. Here is Michelangelo as he once was, a remnant of his former self, spirit flown; and here is how he might be in the full-scale bodily resurrection, more like Bartholomew with his nose intact. For the point about the saint is that he is an ideal figure, a higher being compared to this discarded rag.

How one is to achieve this transfiguration was the great anxiety of Nicodemus, the elderly Pharisee who repented his sins the minute he heard Christ speak. In St John's Gospel, Nicodemus asks Christ directly 'how a man can be born again when he is old', to which Christ gives no answer except that he *has to be* reborn. Michelangelo asked the same question in a late sonnet: 'How might I find salvation, with death so near and God so far away?' Like Nicodemus, uncertain of salvation, he must neither presume nor despair since both are sins against hope. And hope is all; hope and prayer.

The alleged relics of Saint Bartholomew lie beneath the altar of a church only a few miles from the Sistine Chapel, a shrivelled parcel brought to Rome in the tenth century. One imagines them folded like garments. Yet Michelangelo, who had dissected corpses and peeled back the skin to study the anatomy within, would have known that the membrane does not come away like a coat. The flayed skin in *The Last Judgement* is not remotely realistic, any more than the impossible pose of Adam reaching out that tentative forefinger to God; Michelangelo's profound understanding of anatomy is not put to the service of knowledge, as with Leonardo, so much as passionate faith. As for the likeness, no Flemish artist would have called it a portrait. Yet this coat has a face, and this face has vestigial animation, the head turning dolefully sideways. It needs to look like Michelangelo, even in this unimaginably debased state, to be part of this vision of bodily resurrection, to personify the artist's prayer. Michelangelo offers himself up to God not as Dürer has – in His divine image, perfectly beautiful – but as the shucked skin of a repentant sinner.

————

Nobody seeing this image in the Sistine Chapel could imagine that mere self-depiction was the artist's object. Michelangelo is there at the last judgement, suspended between heaven and hell, appealing to God for redemption. One might add that the difference between saint and skin is also the opposition between Michelangelo the idealized artist and Michelangelo the broken-nosed mortal, a warhorse who wore the same dog-skin leggings for months on end until his skin came away when he peeled them off, an old man who had no use for his body other than to keep on working for the greater glory of God.

Nor would one imagine that anybody could construe this as simply a *signature*, and yet that is the received tradition of art history. Self-portraiture starts in the margins as a way of signalling authorship – painters should be seen as painters, not just anonymous craftsmen – and develops as a way of promoting one's art in person. It becomes more prevalent with better mirrors, better paints, a bigger clientele, more competition and thus a greater need to promote oneself. Before self-portraits eventually break free of the crowd, becoming the image of I, myself and me alone, artists are generally there as witnesses – the self-portrait in *assistenza* – which is really a cover for signing the painting with one's image. Histories of self-portraiture tell this originating myth over and again, beginning with Masaccio in the Brancacci Chapel in 1425, his eyes on Christ (a giveaway), and ending a century or so later with Raphael chatting to Ptolemy and Zoroaster (another giveaway) in the School of Athens, as if these artists had no larger concerns than self-promotion. In between, of course, there is the troublesome precedent of Albrecht Dürer; but he is just freakishly early.

Whether Dürer was the first artist to paint an autonomous self-portrait can hardly be said for sure since so few works of art from this period survive. The tenacious idea that people never painted themselves alone before the Renaissance, or with any degree of self-consciousness, is in any case rather like the idea that people had no selves to paint, that a sense of self was something that had yet to be invented. This idea was promoted early on by the founding father of art history, Jacob Burckhardt. But Burckhardt's vision of the Renaissance as the moment when the fully rounded modern self finally steps free of medieval mass-uniformity is challenged even by paintings themselves: lost masterpieces such as the legendary self-portrait of Apelles, famed as the greatest artist of Ancient Greece, or Van Eyck's grave self-portrait in which he seems to be contemplating both himself and death. Conversely, the artist's face among the crowd never really disappears; all self-portrait traditions come round again in perpetuity. Frans Hals is there among the Amsterdam burghers in the seventeenth century. Velázquez appears in *The Victory of Breda*. Edouard Manet listens pensively among the milling figures in *Music in the Tuileries*. The British sculptor Marc Quinn's rubber cast of his own skin, still bearing his features, hangs upside down from a hook, flapping open like a skinned banana but completely empty as if Houdini had flown (its title is *No Visible Means of Escape*). Quinn is always trying to free the spirit in his self-portraits, like Michelangelo half a millennium earlier.

Even where conventions develop – the artist as witness, as religious adherent, as professional painter – self-portraits often have far more complex origins and motives. They are made as love letters, appeals for clemency, campaigns against specific people or the art world in general. They are made in revolt against one's patron or to exorcize one's demons, like Franz Xaver

Detail of *St Benedict's First Miracle*, 1502

Giovanni Bazzi
('Il Sodoma')
(1477–1549)

Messerschmidt with his stricken, gasping, grimacing bronze heads made to see off the Spirit of Symmetry. Sometimes they are made out of madness or fury.

When the monks of Monte Oliveto hired Sodoma to paint a fresco of the first miracle of Benedict, their patron saint, he arrived with a menagerie of horses, dogs, guinea pigs, badgers, swans and a raven he had taught to shout amusing insults when people knocked at the door. Sodoma insisted they all be stabled, and then demanded numerous items of clothing for himself and his assistants – Florentine stockings, new shoes, even the ostentatious yellow cloak of a Milanese nobleman who had come to take orders. The monks kept a written account of the visit in which they refer to the artist as 'Il Mattaccio', the buffoon. He did not leave for three years.

Sodoma was supposed to be painting the boy Benedict successfully praying that his nurse's broken tray will be mended by divine intervention, and sure enough you see the tray and Benedict praying on the left, and then receiving congratulations on the right. But bang in the centre, far larger than anyone else, dressed in the Milanese cloak and the Florentine hose, is the artist. Around him flock the badgers, swans and raven, as if he were St Francis of

Assisi. Way in the distance hangs the mended tray, to which Sodoma gestures — here, take a look at this! — as if he had performed the miracle himself.

It is impossible to view the painting without being completely distracted by Sodoma. He is not there because he believes, like Botticelli. He is not there as a witness so much as the main protagonist. This is simply an insane folly that the monks never managed to prevent, if they ever tried, worn down by his obstreperous presence.

One assumes piety in Renaissance artists because the alternative seems too heretical for the times, just as one assumes that any artist of any era appearing in a Bible scene must be on the side of right. But Caravaggio, in his early self-portraits, is among the dramatis personae of some very violent biblical incidents in which he is no simple onlooker, nor even on the side of virtue; never entirely innocent, he is always in some measure complicit.

Caravaggio is there, for instance, in *The Taking of Christ* in which Jesus is being arrested with appalling force in the garden of Gethsemane the night before Good Friday. The sense of motion, of figures gesturing and twisting in the darkness, is vividly proleptic, as if they might burst right out of the canvas. Christ is the only still figure, hands calmly clasped in the brutal onslaught, withstanding the terrible right to left motion as Judas and a rush of soldiers in jet black steel close in as if for the kill. Violent, crowded and tight, the event is caught in a flash-bulb glare — and at the far right is Caravaggio himself, holding up a lantern to illuminate both scene and picture.

Caravaggio has made it visible, brought this vision of Christ's courage and suffering into the light. But the lamp is not some trite symbol, any more than the self-portrait is a signature.

The Taking of Christ is not just a revelation, it has the *character* of a revelation, of darkness suddenly vanquished by light. Caravaggio shows us the scene and his face in profile, craning to see over the heads of the soldiers, bearing the same expression of open-mouthed awe we all might wear before this violent kidnap. He is on the very outskirts of the picture, struggling to see

'Pinching himself from time to time, Messerschmidt would cut a terrifying grimace, scrutinise his face in the mirror, sculpt and after an interval of about half a minute repeat his grimace… He seemed afraid of these heads and admitted that they represented the Spirit of Proportion. The spirit had pinched him and he had pinched back… at last, the defeated spirit had left him.'[2]

and make the gospel story visible, this artist evangelist. But his light also aids the soldiers he appears to accompany. Is he not in some sense their accomplice?

Some people have seen mutiny in this self-portrait, a sort of take-me-as-I-am retort to a patron who may have been trying to control the contents of the image. Certainly, almost half of Caravaggio's paintings were regarded as too independent for the Church. But even if it started this way, which seems a limited motivation — my vision as I have conceived and shown it — this self-portrait is profoundly uninterested in drawing attention to Caravaggio. It is a work of spiritual empathy; Caravaggio enters into the scene in every way.

Why do artists paint self-portraits? It is not a question prompted by portraits. One does not stand before images of monarchs, philosophers, aristocrats or popes trying to guess why they were immortalized in paint. The ruffed courtier, the periwigged anatomist, the uniformed soldier: their place in history, complete with

The Taking of Christ,
c. 1602

Michelangelo Merisi da
Caravaggio
(1574–1610)

details of occupation and status, and a discreet essay on personality, is pictorially assured. Even if the entire lives of anonymous sitters are lost, one thing is known about them: that somebody wanted their portrait; somebody paid an artist, or perhaps the artist himself wanted to record their image. But even this last possibility does not necessarily hold true in the case of self-portraiture, for many artists have dragged forth a likeness only under duress; at least one was painfully extracted in the mistaken assumption that it was required (see Chapter 12) and many more have been created, then rejected, in a state of heightened disgust.

Some are made with nobody in mind, others for anyone or everyone. A select group was commissioned (and continues to be commissioned) for a very particular audience, namely visitors to the Uffizi self-portrait collection in Florence. This began as the private gallery of Cardinal Leopoldo Medici, who had become obsessed with images that embodied both artist and style. He started with Guercino in 1664 and amassed a hundred more, past and present, before his death. Now there are over a thousand including works by Titian, Rembrandt and (questionably) Velázquez, and the Uffizi has had to ban unsolicited donations from those ambitious to join the club.

Anyone managing to get an appointment to visit the Vasari corridor where a portion of the collection is displayed will see that Leopoldo did not always get much return on his interest in style. An early etching of the collection, hung three deep floor to ceiling, shows what is still apparent today: that it contains some of the dullest self-portraits ever made. Head and shoulders, facing the same direction, many are not much more than variations on a passport photograph. Formal to a fault, but rigorously avoiding anything personal, they end up in opposition to everything that makes self-portraiture interesting: no sense of self, or negotiation between the self and the world, no implied milieu, no distinctive stance, gesture, expression, intellectual or conceptual ideas, just a conformity to type. Of course, there are tremendous exceptions, many discussed here, and the sense of collegiality is strong and affecting. But the official honour appears to have crushed the independent spirit.

Self-portraits do have other coarse and uncomplicated functions. Sir David Wilkie, in a rush to complete his enormous tavern scene *The Blind Fiddler*, inserted his own face in the wig and mobcap of a tipsy woman as if it were no more than a handy set of asexual features. Francis Bacon said he painted himself only because 'everyone else was dying off like flies',[3] although the idea that artists make images of themselves *faute de mieux*, being so compelled to paint a face that even their own will do, strikes a false note when one considers that the struggle to describe oneself is hardly a casual experience. Even Picasso, superfluent draughtsman, complained that he could never catch the look of himself on paper and would have to cut a hole in a canvas and put a mirror behind it in any case just to glimpse what he really looked like.

When an artist wants to join the great art club of tradition, the ambition can be outrageously flagrant. Sir Anthony Van Dyck reprised Raphael's double portrait with friend; Rembrandt painted himself in the distinctive poses of Peter Paul Rubens and Titian; Otto Dix went right back to the purity of Hans Holbein, drumming home his claim to German cultural inheritance. James Whistler tried to paint himself in the pose of Velázquez's *Pablo de Valladolid* and spent the last three years of his life intermittently trying to raise some trace of the Spaniard's spirit in this ghostly failure of a seance. Even the smallest anthology of artists showing off royal gold chains would include Titian, never seen without Emperor Charles V's special gift, Rembrandt, who probably had to buy his own, and above all Van Dyck's *Self-Portrait with Sunflower*. Made when he was court painter to Charles I of England, this startling image is nothing less than an awards ceremony: Van Dyck, in scarlet satin, turns his head our way while lifting his important chain with one hand and pointing at the outsize flower with the other. The triangulation of hands, eyes and flower joins the dots – I got this royal gold for that painted gold – though the symbolism of the sunflower was enigmatic even in the seventeenth century. Did it imply art or nature or the sunshine of the king's favour, this dark oval crowned with golden petals turning its face upon the artist?

The picture is a glowing self-appraisal, but like so many of Van Dyck's portraits that smooth away the flaws and bestow ineffable glamour on the English court, the artist cannot seem to stop himself from undermining the perfection with contradictory details. What tells against all this glory is the tendril of damp hair clinging to Van Dyck's slightly clammy brow; the artist would be dead at forty-two, it was said, of overwork.

Self-Portrait with Sunflower is a public performance, a star turn. It implies and requires an audience. The triangulation within it projects directly outwards too: Van Dyck looks at us, we look at the sun-king, who in turn gazes upon his favoured painter. It is a picture that calls for applause.

But it is not congenial; it is not, so to speak, on our side. Even the most out-turned of self-portraits, those that invite a two-way encounter, or where the artist is explicitly appearing by popular demand, are not necessarily sociable. Some artists want to appear in public, and tell you so in their self-portraits, others have been forced to do it and show it in defensive recoil.

Compare two paintings made a few years apart. We know precisely why Nicolas Poussin portrayed himself for his motives are laid out in an irritable letter; about the origins of Judith Leyster's self-portrait we know nothing except what the painting reveals. In fact, so little is known about Leyster that for centuries her paintings were attributed to Frans Hals, whose fame obscured her reputation quite literally in the case of a picture that was found to have her monogram (JL entwined with a star, punning on her surname, which means

Self-Portrait with Sunflower, c.1633

Sir Anthony van Dyck
(1599–1641)

lodestar) hidden beneath his forged signature. Leyster's existence might eventually have been forgotten but for this buoyant picture.

Intimacy is its trick: she was just working in her studio when you walked in, whereupon she pulled up a seat for you too. Cropped like an informal photo, just below the waist and so tight that one elbow and part of the collar do not make it into the frame, she leans casually back with a conversational smile, off duty for a sociable moment.

Leyster smiles, the work-in-progress implies, because she is the kind of artist who paints merry fiddlers, and perhaps because she is fond a joke. She is not trying to downplay her art, in which she takes evident pride, so much as play up its levity. The neat positioning of the two heads, inclined in different directions but both looking at you, embraces you in the mutual warmth of the circle. Like Walt Disney side by side with his animated Mickey, Leyster gestures lightly at the fiddler with the tip of her brush inviting you too to smile at the antics of the little fellow sawing away with his bow. You could not have a warmer welcome.

Poussin, by contrast, distances himself from the task. He sits back from the picture plane, enclosed by his own paintings – the three behind him, the

Self-Portrait, c. 1630

Judith Leyster
(1609–60)

one before him – in an attitude of fastidious withdrawal. He has only agreed to paint a likeness of himself because nobody else in Rome is up to the task, and only to satisfy a friend. 'I should not have undertaken anything like this for any other living man,' he informed his old friend Paul Chantelou, who hardly needed to be told since he had years of difficulty persuading him to paint the picture in the first place.

Poussin is sequestered in gloom, black hair, black cloth draped over his shoulder like funeral weeds swathing a coffin, black diamond glittering in his ring. His shadow falls ominously across the Latin inscription on the canvas behind him: an effigy of Nicolas Poussin from Les Andelys at the age of 56 in the year of the Roman Jubilee in 1650. It reads like an epitaph, proclaiming his affiliation with classical Rome in an austere third person as if someone else was speaking. The painting is resonant with solemn music.

Yet it is not the mood, or even the strange composition of the picture with its quadratic forms and its mysterious air of deliberation and finality, that strikes some commentators so much as the trail of visual 'clues' waiting to be deciphered. His toga: a Masonic robe? The four-sided pyramid of his diamond: an emblem of Freemasonry, or a symbol of Stoicism (constant as a rock)? The eye on the diadem worn by the woman in the canvas behind him: the Eye of All-Seeing Vigilance that represents the Supreme Being to Freemasons? Why, the picture was practically painted for Dan Brown to decode.

That this woman represents friendship or art, as prescribed in iconographic dictionaries of the period, seems a good deal more feasible and makes sense given that the picture was a gift for a friend. But the character of the picture would hardly be altered even if she turned out to be All-Seeing Vigilance; it is her positioning in the composition – as much deliberated as every other

Self-Portrait, c. 1650

Nicolas Poussin
(1594–1665)

EFFIGIES NICOLA... ...SINI AND... E...
YENSIS PICTOR.S ...ANNO...TATIS...
ROMA ANNO IVBILEI
1650.

element – that matters. She looks the other way from Poussin, her animation balanced by his absolute composure, just as his hand rests motionless upon the book while the golden frames of the paintings shoot back and forth like trains rushing in different directions behind the stationed gravity of his head.

For Poussin these paintings, whatever they show, are his life. By the time he finished this self-portrait in his mid-fifties he had a reputation across Europe as one of the most intellectual and disciplined of masters. He had left France more than twenty years before, despising French painters as *strapazzoni*, glib hacks who 'make a sport of turning out a picture in 24 hours'. Truth could only be distilled from intense and protracted cogitation. Compositions had to be tested over and again in advance, rehearsed with wax forms in a toy theatre. Even the most violent action in his work is marked by stasis and meditation. His paintings require you to stop and think, learn, mark and inwardly digest their mysterious dramas, and so it is with this self-portrait – a summation of his art as well as himself, neither offering instant disclosure.

These paintings spread like a hand of cards behind him – an allegory, a blank canvas, the back of a canvas – are all easel pictures. Being an artist in Rome at that time still meant producing frescos, panel-paintings and altarpieces to order, their subject matter generally dictated by the patron. But for Poussin it meant only one thing, easel paintings on landscape-shaped canvases, stretched, framed and painted exactly like the ones in this picture. His landscape-narratives, moreover, and his great religious paintings were never some compromise with a patron. Poussin, considered to have had a stern and melancholy temperament, prone to irritation and loathing constraint, avoided all the usual professional conventions to the point of bypassing the market altogether. He worked only for patrons who had become friends. That he sits in a booth of his own paintings feels majestically apt for an artist whose sense of freedom depended on making art for himself. He would not have painted himself 'for any other living man' and he never painted any other living person.

The public reputation encloses the painter, and the painter's passionate sense of vocation dominates the picture, a passion that has its ultimate testimony in his face. Poussin appears worn out, hypertense, his eyes red-rimmed with the effort of achieving such a high degree of probity. And yet the expression pulls in another direction too, from this fierce look of honour and discipline to something that looks surprisingly like sorrow. It is often said that Poussin was two different artists, that the younger Poussin was a proto-romantic whose pictures were charged with all sorts of conflicting and dangerous emotions, a man who could draw himself tousled and scowling in the early years in Rome, the kind of man who could be arrested during a street brawl like Caravaggio. This artist cools and contracts into the later Poussin, strict classicist and mythologizer whose paintings are above easy pleasures. Perhaps Poussin has moved from intensity to profundity, but something of the younger man's strength of emotion is alive in the older man's face.

Deep-seated within the picture, Poussin avoids social contact. He makes an appearance, as all self-portraitists must, with a marked sense of withdrawal. But this refusal to draw close, to be on our side, is elevated to the level of pictorial principle.

———

Self-portraits raise the question of their own existence but also of our common mortality. Michelangelo appears as the skin of a corpse, alluding to his disappearance from this world (a self-portrait that might alert one to the pathos and humility of his work instead of the usual narrative of power). Goya painted the doctor who saved him from death raising a cup to his lips, supporting his body as in a pietà. The artist's gratitude is repeated in words beneath; without Dr Arrieta, extinction. Murillo also explained the purpose of his self-portrait with an inscription that is unusually prominent, scrolling out of the bottom of the picture like a document from a fax and transmitting its message just as effectively: 'Bartolomé Murillo portraying himself to fulfil the wishes and prayers of his children.'

Murillo was the leading Sevillian artist of the seventeenth century, more successful even than Velázquez; after his death, the government had to enforce an export ban simply to stop the last remaining Murillos flooding out of the country. Although he was Spain's foremost religious painter, he was even more celebrated abroad for his images of street urchins. Children were his subject and his passion; orphaned at the age of eleven and brought up by one of his sisters, he had twelve children of his own. When his wife died, he remained a widower, raising the entire family by himself. Cholera and typhus orphaned many of the models depicted in his pictures and he lost several children during the worst of the epidemics. The words beneath his self-portrait are not empty but a tender expression of paternal love for his surviving offspring, tinged with deep knowledge of mortality.

Murillo is specially dressed to appear after his death in a fine lace collar and black silk tunic (he was, by all accounts, generally more threadbare). Although the highest paid artist in Seville, he gave most of his money to charity and regularly worked for the church without pay; the strain of labour registers in his face. He appears in an oval frame propped on a shelf; perhaps it is a mirror – there is that silvery play of light across the face – or perhaps it is a painting. Either way, it is modelled on contemporary frontispieces representing pictures within paintings.

Bart. Murillo seipsum depin
gens pro filiorum votis acprei
bus explendis

Self-Portrait, c. 1670–73

Bartolomé Esteban
Murillo (c. 1617–82)

But the illusion is broken, literally and metaphorically, by the artist's own hand which reaches out to rest casually upon the frame, signalling subtly towards the palette and brushes on the right, balanced on the left by a drawing – what else? – of a child. Between the tools he used to make art, and the art that supported Murillo's family, are the words he wrote for his children; the chain of creation is complete. The inscription is poignant but so is the gesture, for in that breach of illusion where Murillo's hand moves between the two pictures there is a brief sense of freedom, a quickening, as if he were still living.

Murillo's self-portrait makes nonsense of the claim 'that self-portraiture merely renders explicit the wider claim to authorship that takes place whenever an image is stated to be by somebody'. It is signed in writing, as an aside, but an aside that alludes to the preciousness of all portraits in an age before cameras; and of this self-portrait in particular that can speak so directly – in person, in prose, in style – to one's children. The loved one no longer leaves them in dying.

Murillo would not have painted himself for anyone else. He left no other images of himself. A self-portrait is not, after all, just any kind of work; it is in some deep sense a manifestation of oneself and since most artists have no idea what will become of their self-portraits in the end, especially when made for no particular person or destination, the impulse to keep them private may be strong and increased by a fear of exposure. Sometimes the risks are beyond ordinary courage.

Felix Nussbaum's *Self-Portrait with a Jewish Identity Card* is an urgent message smuggled out of hiding to the people of the future. It was made in 1943 and shows the artist with his collar drawn tight around him holding up the card stamped 'Juif-Jood' and displaying the yellow star the Nazis forced Jews to wear. The scene appears premonitory – the storm clouds literally gathering, the wall behind Nussbaum beginning to crack, the trees bare, birds hovering only in the distance; one remembers that no birds sang over Auschwitz. Nussbaum's fearfulness does not need to be exaggerated: here is the star that could damn him. He painted the picture after escaping from a detention camp in France and while hiding with his wife in a series of attics and cellars in Brussels. The Nussbaums were still alive one month before the liberation of Belgium, but they were betrayed, sold to the Wehrmacht. The Gestapo herded them on one of the last trains transporting Jews to Auschwitz.

It has taken many years to find even a fraction of the pictures Nussbaum produced between his flight from Germany in 1933 and his murder in the gas

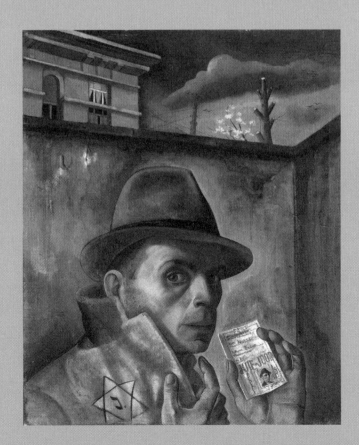

Self-Portrait with Jewish Identity Card, 1943

Felix Nussbaum (1904–44)

chambers. He evidently made many more drawings of the atrocious conditions in the French camps, for instance, but some still survive showing the effects of hunger and raging dysentery. 'If I go under, do not let my paintings die,' he begged one of his protectors in Brussels as the war closed in. Nussbaum's work is partly a testament, but he is not just a witness to history. What strikes about this self-portrait, lead-grey and lonely, with the great world visible only at the top of a wall, and the artist on the wrong side of it, is precisely that nothing in it is symbolic. The birds, the trees, the wall beside which the artist huddles, his eyes alert like those of a hunted man: everything is absolutely true to the life he was living – with one exception. Nussbaum never wore a star and never owned such a card precisely because he was trying to survive underground. They are the only symbols in the picture, a display of solidarity with the Jewish victims of the Nazis.

––––––––

What are the hazards of letting a self-portrait out of the studio to make its way in the world? Not the least among them is that it may be interpreted as a coded message, read as a text, or treated like a mirror, all its subtleties reduced to facts; that it may be classed merely as a professional advertisement or some sort of self-serving signature. In short, that it may not be regarded, still less appreciated, as an actual work of art that has passed through the imagination and intellect. Sometimes it seems surprising that so many artists are willing to take the risk.

A century and more after his death, Georges Seurat remains nearly as mysterious as he appears to have hoped. He wrote few letters, had no intimate friends and barely let anyone into his studio. Although he attended meetings of the Independent Group in Paris, he seems to have been an enigma to all the other members. Pissarro, who loved and learned from his work, found him cold and dispassionately rational; Degas called him 'The Notary'. One friend wrote that Seurat became immediately 'suspicious and reserved if one probed the interior self he cultivated in secret'. The two-page document in which he set forth his 'scientific' theories of art – mostly quite conventional – tended to fix attention on his methods, those little pointillist dots and dashes of colour, so carefully measured and graded, rather than on the paintings themselves. Seurat was regarded as a white-coat, his art abstruse, his paintings available for a song. His death went almost unreported.

Seurat fell ill on a Thursday, was taken to his parents' home the following day and died at six in the morning on Sunday. He was thirty-one. The cause of death was probably raging diphtheria, which killed his baby son a few days later.

Nobody knew Seurat had a son. Nobody knew he had a lover. His parents met mother and baby for the first, and last, time when they appeared at the door that Friday. His friends were amazed to hear that he had had a mistress at all, although he seems to have been living with her for more than two years. If they had bothered to ask the identity of the eponymous *Young Woman Powdering Herself*, a recently exhibited portrait, they would have learned that her name was Madeleine Knoblock. Perhaps they took her for a model, or one of his performers sitting in her corset backstage; perhaps they could not see it as a portrait. But an indifference to the sitter's identity had already had a destructive effect on the painting.

Seurat's pictures, it is true, do not tend to occasion such questions. Nobody looks at the great motionless dream of *A Sunday Afternoon at La Grande Jatte* and wonders exactly who these people are on the riverbank outside Paris: the couple walking the monkey, the woman daintily fishing, the show-off practising his trombone. Faceless, featureless cut-outs, these are not flesh-and-blood personalities but elements in a modern arcadia, along with the geometric trees, the clockwork butterflies and the sweep of abstracted green lawn. You notice the rhyming shapes of bustles and umbrellas, furled parasols and fans, the loop of the monkey's tail, the Euclidean geometry. You notice the dots.

But there is one painting in which the dots have a perfect relevance to the subject, are in lyrical accord, and this is *La Poudreuse* in which Madeleine Knoblock sits at a tiny ornamental table before a mirror, powder in one hand, downy puff in the other, poised between looking and dabbing.

All of Seurat's touches seem to imitate the dabs of this puff, as if he too was gently brushing the plump curves of her breast, neck and cheek. The particles of paint radiate out from puff and body like fine scented dust. Even the light is powdery and soft, stroking her shoulders and forearms, dimpling chin and full breasts. It glimmers from the little mirror and from another hanging on the wall in which a vase of flowers is reflected. Seurat has surrounded his lover with blossoms, real ones, reflected ones and a wallpaper pattern that seems to shimmer freely in the air.

Much about the picture seems strange – the size of the table compared to the woman, her elongated arms, the brioche of her hair – although only if one had never seen a painting by Seurat. But nothing is as odd as the mirror, with its bamboo frame and open doors like a cheap votive icon. Why is it so high on the wall? Surely the vase would have to be standing on a particularly tall piece of furniture to be visible at such a height, and the flowers themselves are uncharacteristically crude and cursory. The image in the mirror looks like an afterthought – which is exactly what it was, for it seems that Seurat originally painted himself in the mirror.

One of the few visitors ever admitted to his studio happened to see this painting in progress one day. He recognized Seurat, but not the woman or the nature of their relationship. Imagining that she must be a prostitute, he

remarked that Seurat's face, rising behind this half-naked woman, might provoke vile innuendo among the gallery-going public. Seurat took up a brush and painted himself out.[4]

In 1958 under X-ray a ghostly image was found beneath the flowers: the

La Poudreuse, c. 1888–90

Georges Pierre Seurat
(1859–91)

head and shoulders of the painter. But thirty years later, after another X-ray, the results were deemed too illegible to be conclusively Seurat. Everyone agrees that there is a man's face there, and the difficulty of reading all the dots beneath the dots may easily be imagined, yet science aside, who else could it possibly be but the painter? Why would Seurat even think of painting some other man's face in his lover's mirror?

Now consider how much more intimate the scene would have been, the two of them together in that little room: a couple of lovers, a couple of parents; Knoblock had already given birth to their first child and would soon be pregnant with their second. Although they were never married, a double-portrait would have marked their union, just as Rubens's self-portraits with Isabella Brandt and Hélène Fourment celebrated both of his marriages. What a delicate touch too, for Seurat to squeeze himself into the small space of that chamber as a cameo in the mirror, reflecting the compass of their private world.

Perhaps he painted himself painting, the tip of a brush just visible in the mirror, or even the edge of an easel. That would deepen the relationships in the picture: between artist and model, lover and mistress, two kinds of painter, both looking at themselves in a mirror.

Or perhaps he was gazing at her. A complicated task, involving some technical business with mirrors to get a view of himself looking in her direction and not his own, but worth it if Seurat wanted to imply beguilement, confirming the pervasive tenderness of the picture. It would also have directed out attention towards her, making us look even more closely at this bounteous young woman.

If, on the contrary, he was looking at himself then the whole picture alters again. His eyes would lock with ours, establishing a you–me relationship, getting up a conversation between us. It might be a kind of dramatic soliloquy, communicating something about himself, or her, or the state of play between them. Maybe he wanted to appear watchful but protective, appearing indirectly as a reflection in the glass instead of imposing himself right there in the room. There is no variation that does not immeasurably deepen the significance, and poetry, of the painting.

Naysayers, who refuse to believe that there was ever a self-portrait, complain that the account left by the visitor has made it impossible for people to see the picture for what it really is – a satirical and unkind image of a prostitute.[5] Seurat's motives are impugned and all the gentle parallels the picture proposes between the artist painting the woman who is painting herself, quite possibly for him, are overlooked. Hard as it is to credit the blindness of such critics to the tenderness, the palpable affection of the artist for his sitter, there are those who think this is an exercise in mockery. Had Seurat appeared, it would have given them eyes to see these two souls in one work. Without the self-portrait, both remain traduced by disgraceful innuendo.

Chapter Five

Rembrandt

'I give my soul now one face, now another, according to which direction I turn it. If I speak of myself in different ways, that is because I look at myself in different ways. All contradictions may be found in me.'

Michel de Montaigne

Self-Portrait, c. 1663

Rembrandt van Rijn (1606–69)

R embrandt is the soul of self-portraiture, its leading light. He personifies artists and art at their most profound, and if we sometimes speak of him in terms of Shakespeare or late Beethoven it is because the depth of his humanity, especially in the late self-portraits, seems to have no equal in painting.

Think of an artist depicting himself, alone with the easel, and you must surely think of Rembrandt. He is the solitary spirit, the lone genius, the hero in a brown study, bearing the marks of life's sufferings with inspirational courage. He is what we should all be when coming to terms with ourselves, when facing our end – the exemplary being, the exemplary artist. For think of Old Masters and Rembrandt comes first, looking out from the tawny shadows of the past, so familiar from the scores of self-portraits that he can be summoned to mind in an instant. Rembrandt looks as he should, as Old Masters look; his art is one with his face. We would know him anywhere, recognize him in any street. But what did Rembrandt actually look like?

His long-dead face looks out of more than eighty paintings, drawings and prints beginning with the smooth-faced student and running all the way to the hard-up old veteran close to death and burial in an unmarked grave almost forty years later. It is the longest lifespan of self-portraits ever painted, a record of change and decay unparalleled in the history of art. The Dutch film-maker Bert Haanstra, commissioned to commemorate the 350th anniversary of Rembrandt's death, took this to its logical conclusion by merging one self-portrait into the next in chronological order on screen so that one saw the face starting to sag, the eyes gradually shrinking beneath the creases and the hair eventually turning wispy and silver. But what colour was the hair in the first place? Red, auburn, tawny brown? What shape were the forehead and jowls? Haanstra's film is as inconclusive as it has to be because Rembrandt's appearance is so extraordinarily hard to pin down in the first place; the eyes are hardly ever the same from one picture to the next, wider apart in one decade than another, the famous nose waxing and waning by the year.

In the earliest solo image, Rembrandt downplays this nose for a sidelong squint at his own dark-eyed defiance. A few months later, etching himself again, he gives the nose colossal breadth, wide as the mouth itself. Above it the eyes are two startled black discs, faintly dismayed by what they see in the glass. At twenty-one, Rembrandt is already expressing far more than the facts.

The nose expands into a leonine muzzle, impossibly large, contracts into a narrow and almost elegant nib. The eyes don't just crease with laughter, bulge with tension or cloud over with care, they actually appear to change colour. Rembrandt paints them as dusky ovals, black pools, amber lenses washed with golden light. They are buttons, sultanas, fish-holes in snow; they are as abstract as Mickey Mouse's rectangular peepers. Sometimes Rembrandt avoids mentioning them at all except as punctuation marks in a fleshy expanse that seems to melt into different forms from one self-portrait to another.

Perhaps there is a measure of ordinary truth in Rembrandt's mutability, perhaps this is how we all look to ourselves, week by week, year after year, never the same from one day to the next. Look at the reams of photographs of Marilyn Monroe through the decades and she comes and goes, getting closer or further from Andy Warhol's clinching silk-screen icon as she loses weight, gains weight, acquires artificial lashes, grows more strained or puffy around the eyes, appears more but then less like herself; and even though she is the most famous actress of the twentieth century who can remember what *her* nose looked like? Everyone appreciates the old adage that at forty you get the face you deserve, with its presumption of plasticity finally hardening into place after many years of flux, just as everyone knows the bittersweet fascination of seeing oneself alter in a lifetime of photographs, anthologies of one's dead and irrecoverable selves. To see yourself as you were at twenty is to recognize the rudiments of your present face without being able to re-enter the past, or take advantage of hindsight. We live life forwards, as Kierkegaard laments, but are condemned to understand it backwards.

Rembrandt is so young in the first self-portraits, so unformed, that he hardly seems related to the old chieftain at the end; yet everyone feels that they recognize him every time. The connection is deep and immediate, the sense of intimacy Rembrandt's perpetual gift and crucial to this perceived familiarity. He may be a boastful boy from Leiden posing in a flashy steel collar, or a shrunken old Lear in a threadbare cap, and still you would know this was Rembrandt. Every self-portrait convinces you that *this* is the truth about him, the faithful expression of the man as he was. How remarkable that he can make you feel this not once but time after time, that if you saw his self-portraits all together (as was possible with an unprecedented show in 1999) you would feel that all the changes were somehow true to his nature as well as his physiognomy, that for Rembrandt an immense variety of character goes with a whole range of life-altered looks, that having multiple personalities is the human condition; in which sense, Haanstra's attempt to unify Rembrandt's face by locking the eyes of each self-portrait in the same position on screen is a travesty of everything these images have come to represent. That we change and lose our past faces is both agonizing and the commonest thing in the world. It is beyond belief that this great priest of humanity never had this in mind as he painted himself in sad and gradual decline, for if we feel this then how could he not, Rembrandt our Shakespeare – our contemporary.

———

Except that Rembrandt has no sense of self. Self-awareness has not yet been invented. This at least has been the steady assertion of some very eminent scholars over the years who insist, pretty much against the entire body of self-portraiture from Jan Van Eyck onwards, that artists before the nineteenth century cannot possibly be conscious of – still less actively contemplating – their inner selves.

This was the curatorial principle of Rembrandt by Himself, that once-in-a-lifetime show: that while some might fancifully believe in Rembrandt's self-portraits as a form of self-scrutiny, a search for identity, the artist coming to terms with himself, the paintings were, in fact, stimulated by the market and commerce. That the term 'self-portrait' did not exist in Rembrandt's day is submitted as proof, as if concepts cannot exist without the framework of language. Before the nineteenth century such images were described as pictures or likenesses of artists by their own hand, then all of a sudden the new term self-portrait appears 'because from the end of the eighteenth century the experience of one's own individuality was very different to that current in Rembrandt's century'.[1] Rembrandt is not the only one who couldn't possibly have had any sense of his own personality; even Montaigne's marvellous essays on his inner self, mind and mores 'should not likewise be confused with a romantic, individualistic desire for self-knowledge'.[2] In the interests of demythologizing self-portraiture it has even been asserted that artists in Rembrandt's day 'did not step to the mirror with questions and doubts, but with a carefully planned *programme*'.[3] Anyone tempted to believe this assertion might start by consulting Annibale Carracci's profoundly doubting self-portrait from the same period.

Scholars often reflect the society of their own times, despite being otherwise so leery of anachronism, so perhaps it is no coincidence that the Rembrandt of the late twentieth century turned out to be a model of advanced capitalism. He has to develop new products, evolve new forms of portraiture to meet the demands of the new middle classes of the nascent Dutch republic, has to thrive in a highly competitive market where every town has its local painter and every profession from banker to orthopaedic surgeon wants to be depicted. Needs must, even when it comes to portraying oneself.

Of course Rembrandt had to survive, and his interest in getting and spending has long been attested, from the letters requesting ever higher prices for his pictures to the purchase of a prodigiously expensive house in Amsterdam that brought him to financial ruin. It is also true, and unarguably important, that Rembrandt's self-portraits were sold during the artist's lifetime. Documents show that three were in famous collections, one of them belonging to Charles I of England, before the artist was out of his twenties and his self-portrait prints were in high demand as patrons vied to complete their set of Rembrandt etchings. When the artist went under in 1656 and all his possessions from clothes to studio props and even little sketches by his son Titus were inventoried by rapacious brokers, not a single self-portrait appeared on the list as still in the studio unsold.

But if Rembrandt's self-portraits were so successful one might have expected him to repeat them, as he so often did with other kinds of picture, instead of resolutely avoiding the temptation. Those who regard his self-portraits as product, albeit superior product, aren't inclined to notice their evolving originality, or to concede that they might be enriched by insight or exceptional depth of personality. Faced with such incomparable paintings, these experts retreat into issues of quantity, asking why he painted so many self-portraits rather than how, and the answers given are ruthlessly impersonal – as a way of practising facial expressions for subsequent pictures; as a standard type of self-advertisement; as a model for painting figures from Bible and myth, as well as speciality 'characters' of the artist's own invention; even just for the humdrum reason of adding to the popular stock of images of famous men that etchers would turn out in printed anthologies and which by now included not just philosophers and kings but artists all the way from Raphael to Rubens. When Rembrandt stepped to the mirror, it seems he saw money.

There may be some truth in these claims, though we do not know of a single Rembrandt self-portrait that was painted for the market, and it does not follow that because a painting was sold it must have been made expressly for sale. Nor does the discovery that these images were passing from one collector to another quite early in his career, and not piling up in the studio as once thought, mean that they had no private or personal meaning for him. The economic and professional functions of pictures are not the only motivations painters have for making them and others arise, beyond doubt, in the process.

Rembrandt left no documents about his self-portraits and there is no record of him saying anything about them. Although this puts him in the company of practically every self-portraitist who has ever lived for some scholars it is proof positive that they cannot have meant much to their maker. Yet for all that has been written about Rembrandt, very little is known about his views on art of any kind. We know he bought Dürer's prints, admired Leonardo and Titian and Raphael's *Portrait of Baldassare Castiglione*, which he copied when it was up for sale in Amsterdam and then emulated in a self-portrait etched not many weeks later. But he did not theorize, or if he did, his ideas have been lost except for a meagre six words whose meaning is still in dispute. What he aimed for in his work, Rembrandt wrote to a patron, was to produce '*die meeste ende die natureelste beweechlickheijt*' – 'the greatest and most natural movement'.

But whether he meant the movement of bodies and faces or souls is unclear; perhaps he was aiming to move *our* emotions? The last word has also been translated as emotion and Rembrandt's gift for conveying feeling was famous in his own lifetime. His patron, the poet and composer Constantijn Huygens, declares in his memoirs that Rembrandt's uncommon ability to portray emotions is already widely extolled.

Huygens's autobiography, moreover, contains a passage that goes right against the line that nobody had any awareness of their inner being in the seventeenth century. Huygens had commissioned Jan Lievens, Rembrandt's professional partner in Leiden, to paint his portrait but reports that everyone criticised the finished picture for being too sombre, 'a contemplative rendering that detracts from the vivacity of [my] mind'. Yet the gloom in his face was true, and something the poet had hoped in vain to suppress. 'During this period I was involved in a serious family affair of some importance and, as is only to be expected, the cares which I endeavoured to keep to myself were clearly reflected in the expression of my face and eyes.' Huygens admired the perspicacity of Lievens almost as much as Rembrandt.

If no sources exist – other than the paintings themselves – from which to deduce Rembrandt's sense of self, there is plenty of documentary evidence of him as a man who drove hard against society and its standards. It is well known that more than half of the members of the militia who paid to see respectable likenesses of their faces in *The Night Watch* were appalled to find themselves summarily reduced to profile or crepuscular sideline, at least one powerful patron rejected his portrait altogether and Rembrandt was habitually late, wayward and defiant. From the 1640s, as tastes changed to the smoother Flemish style and the classicism of Poussin, Rembrandt began to lose prestige but still did not alter his approach to suit the changing market. One of his earliest biographers, Filippo Baldinucci, drawing on the testimony of Rembrandt's pupils, says that 'after it had become commonly known that whoever wanted to be portrayed by him had to sit for him for some two or three months, there were few who came forward'. Van Dyck, by contrast, could paint a client in a morning. Another biographer, Arnold Houbraken, tells of Rembrandt's irrepressible individualism. The artist had been labouring for ages on a family portrait and was nearly finished when his pet monkey died. To the family's horror, he chose to commemorate the beloved creature by introducing its corpse into the painting: 'an effect that so impressed him that rather than remove it to satisfy his clients he left the work unfinished'. Art before money; monkeys before clients.

We expect a certain consistency of behaviour and thought among our higher beings that we do not require of ourselves. That the artist capable of bringing forth *The Jewish Bride* or *Belshazzar's Feast* or *The Anatomy Lesson of Doctor Nicolaes Tulp* would not easily submit to convention feels apt; our ideal, in fact, of the proto-Romantic artist. One wants to believe that Rembrandt knew his own worth, that his eventual poverty was as proudly borne as his late self-portraits are brave, and it is gratifying to learn that he sometimes behaved as though he was the country's only great painter. The early self-portraits may declare their own originality for strategic purposes, quite possibly for money; but the late self-portraits go way beyond those functions.

———

The standard account of Rembrandt's self-portraits is that they amount to an autobiography in paint. You see him as a truculent youth in Leiden posing in the soldier's collar he has no real right to wear, or trying to outdo Caravaggio in spectacular lighting; as a young star newly translated to Amsterdam as the money starts to come in, wearing a gold chain or with ostentatious feathers in his cap. You see him as a well-fed husband dandling his wife on his knee, messing about with the fancy-dress trunk for portraits and self-portraits alike; as a successful businessman in furs and even once or twice as a prosperous

Dutch burgher. Then widowed, weary and even perhaps a little shame-faced, as some claim, after having one mistress locked up in a house of correction while taking up with another, much younger lover.

After a mysterious gap of nearly a decade, he returns as the bankrupted old sage, overextended, out of favour, increasingly isolated as he outlives not just his father, mother and wife but both of his mistresses and his only child Titus. In the late self-portraits, in his lonely and beleaguered sixties when there are no more students to teach and no more collectors at the studio door, he drops the make-believe of the youthful self-portraits for the honest scrutiny and celebrated depth.

It would be inhuman not to perceive some sort of life story in these pictures, not least because they so evidently follow, to a certain degree, the trajectory of our own lives: the arc from aspiration to achievement and then to retirement, from intensity to profundity, the seven ages of man minus the mewling infant and the schoolboy. If Rembrandt sometimes dresses up as an actor in costume – a Turkish potentate in gleaming tassels and turban, Saint Paul in prison holding one of his letters to the Ephesians, the painter-king in golden robes with sceptre – it is because his life, our lives, are surely experienced as a drama, performance its perfect metaphor. When Rembrandt appears in theatrical darkness it is not to invite an exchange with the viewer; his is strictly an actor's monologue from the other side of the limelight. At thirty-three, he leans on a wall, beret rakishly angled, magnificently dressed, but in no sense conversing over the fence. Ten years later, squaring up with defiance, full frontal with hands on hips, making a comeback after the longest absence, he defies you to say anything about it. Even at the very end, he does not stoop to discourse.

These late paintings are monuments of silence. Dark and knotted images that close in on the face, with all those sad stories of the deaths of kings in the eyes, they make you feel you are seeing the old man himself, in person as well as in painting. They are all candour and truth and from them we learn what it feels to be old, if we do not already know it; and in Rembrandt's case, what it is to be prematurely aged by grief and disappointment, to grow puffy and weak, to have to squint because your vision is losing power and your eyes are sinking into their sockets. Rembrandt in the dying yellow light, the last life in his eyes, makes himself felt in the brushwork, distressed, gnarled and haphazard, perfunctory, thickening in veiny skeins or wearing paper thin, as if the paintings themselves were on the way out.

We are so used to thinking of these images as unimpeachably honest, their intensity the very measure of that candour, that we tend to see them as straight and unstaged compared to the earlier self-portraits. But Rembrandt, young and old, is always in performance.

Take two early show-stoppers, the self-portraits in Amsterdam and
Munich where Rembrandt is a lone soul in the forests of the night, his eyes
blacker than the darkness around him. He has drawn back from the single shaft
of light, deftly positioning himself at the exact boundary between brightness
and darkness where the light catches his smooth cheek and the flash of white
lace, showing off his already superb ability to make flesh and fabric tangible,
but obscuring his features, allowing his true face – his true self – to remain
unreachable. It cannot have been easy to make himself out in the mirror from
such deep shadow, let alone paint in such lighting conditions, if indeed he did,
rather than making some of it up. The dazzle is in the staging, yet the staging
is all concealment. You have to search for the artist in the picture, and when
you find him there's the shock that he already had you in sight.

These two paintings were made within months of each other and at the
same time as a sequence of etchings where Rembrandt pulls faces, turns
suddenly, looks shocked, goes into a peculiar fugue state where his eyes shrink
to sightless dots. He is young and cocky, he is old and past it; in no time at all
he inexplicably ages. Pulling his cloak about himself he shoves forward a mug
so blank it is almost aggressively vacuous. Rembrandt is never sociable,
appearing only once in company with his wife Saskia, and he makes
considerable play of his solitude, coming forward a fraction but then looking
away; or retreating into tantalizing shadow. There is no attempt to ingratiate.

The paint at every stage rises to the level of performance. People came
from across Europe to see his alchemy, the way he could turn paint into gold
with a few irregular nubs of impasto that picked up the light, the way he could
make an incisive contour with a casual swipe. He applied paint so thickly you

could pick his portraits up by the nose, it was said, and so complex were the effects, so persuasive the illusion, some contemporaries saw his paintings as sorcery. In fact, his brushwork is everywhere revealed, particularly in the self-portraits where he makes the paint mimic precisely the grain and stubble and soft hang of flesh. The paint folds and creases beneath the eyes, the nose is a pile-up of marks mounding into a pocked tip, tear ducts are divots in impasto. He uses the brush handle to etch tendrils of hair into still-wet paint, smears the pigment with his fingers, scumbles and smudges it to get the tangible surface of life. He fashions this face, this human clay, and he shows himself making it up.

And making himself up too as he goes along, in a sustained act of improvisation. He adopts the pose of Rubens's self-portrait, then Titian's *Man with a Sleeve*. He transforms himself into a snarling beggar. He dresses up as an Oriental, even orientalizing his own features while still recognizably Rembrandt. The face, or at least the painted face, is so plastic from one self-portrait to the next that all you could say for certain is that Rembrandt looks Dutch.

But where the performance was once signalled with props, costumes and poses, in the later self-portraits it is more apparent in the violent contrasts. When you compare the Edinburgh self-portrait with the *Self-Portrait as Zeuxis* roughly two years later there is so little relationship between them, you feel they

can hardly be the same man. In the first he is deeply pensive, a look of wintry self-scrutiny in the eyes. In the second, where he is apparently coming on as the legendary Greek painter Zeuxis who died of mirth, his face is a frightening rictus of empty laughter.[4] Compared to switching roles between beggar and Turk, the psychological distance between these late self-portraits feels so much greater. Nothing settles, nothing resolves. The sufferings of a lifetime don't lead to peace and a united front to the world.

Rembrandt seems to be the oldest of Old Masters. It is strange to think that Caravaggio was already dead before he was born, and that Velázquez is his senior. Yet though he appears as old as time, he is every generation's soulmate.

This timelessness is not an illusion. Rembrandt deliberately painted himself out of time, set himself free of the moment. Compare any of his self-portraits with a portrait by his contemporary, Frans Hals, and you will see two different ways of picturing time. Hals catches the moment with the flashing dabs and spots so admired by the Impressionists; his sitters are in the here and now, leaning out of the picture, turning and laughing, equally struck to see you. Rembrandt avoids spontaneity. His self-portraits are manifestly premeditated.

They don't catch time so much as stop it altogether; he endures through the centuries.

Rembrandt consciously removes himself from the present. The look of the self-portraits is partly drawn from an era before his own, from the portraits of Titian, Raphael and Dürer. And the clothes from the studio trunk aren't contemporary either; some were made in the previous century. When Rembrandt dresses in furs, feathers and velvets he is in generic costume for the performance. On the rare occasion when he appears in contemporary dress – black and white with ruff – the focus narrows and shifts and he more resembles an unusually glum sitter in Hals's studio.

Our sense of Rembrandt as Everyman or the great actor-painter is inflected, somewhat, by these antique clothes but also by the genres peculiar to seventeenth-century Holland in which he makes his appearance. The *tronies*, for instance, were character studies that appealed to collectors as types or classifications of humanity, though presumably as entertainment as well. The scholars most likely to sneer at anyone sensing self-awareness in Rembrandt are also those who contend that the self-portrait etchings would have been considered as nothing but *tronies*. Yet Rembrandt became recognizable through his self-portraits comparatively early and paintings that were both of and by him were evidently treasured. To be recognized for oneself, to be a famous face in an age before cameras is at the very least to be something bigger than a *tronie* and considerably more than a type.

Rembrandt's clothes also fit another pictorial fashion of the time, the popular *portrait historie*, in which contemporary sitters posed as historical figures; a young couple might be represented as Venus and Paris, for example, or Ulysses and Penelope. Rembrandt depicted his wife as Flora and himself as Saint Paul. The sitters were meant to look like themselves, of course, real people but in historical costumes; the point was to be depicted in fanciful scene or metaphor, not buried beneath a disguise.

Rembrandt went much further with this than any other artist in Golden Age Holland, infusing the portraits with such mystery that it isn't always possible to tell the actor from the role. Who, for example, are the two people in *The Jewish Bride*, so tenderly adoring of one another, standing in undelineated space? Are they models for a Bible story, do they represent the virtues of marriage or the gift of conception, are they characters from a popular Dutch play concerning King Cyrus and a beautiful shepherdess named Aspasia, as has also been advanced?[5] Or are they patrons sitting for a *portrait historie*? One sees and remembers them as distinct individuals, and profoundly observed, but that gesture of love – his hand gently placed on her breast, hers tenderly covering it – seems to exceed portraiture so that the picture becomes a kind of secular altarpiece, an inspiration to patience, humility and love. We do not know if Rembrandt knew these people; whether they were just models enacting the visions in his mind. It is, in turn, very hard to say at what point a Rembrandt self-portrait in costume turns from a role performed to an individual portrayed. Always one knows this is Rembrandt, the actor beneath the clothes, but the effect of these pictorial elisions remains elusive.

———————

John Berger once advanced the theory that Rembrandt painted himself without a mirror, or that he began with one and then covered it up, relying entirely upon his own self-knowledge. For Berger, this helped to explain both the depth and the extreme variations in the face, as Rembrandt turns inwards to paint the *sense* of himself in all its innumerable nuances, profound and unique. Sure enough, if there is a constant in Rembrandt's self-portraits it is the impression of a soul-penetrating individuality that could never be reproduced.

And yet it was, over and again during his lifetime and often at Rembrandt's own behest. In the studio he maintained for over twenty years, students frequently copied his self-portraits (and quite possibly forged them) as well as mimicking their style. Self-portraits exist by Govert Flinck and Ferdinand Bol, for instance, that have been painted to look precisely like the master. Until quite recently, the Flinck was even though to *be* a Rembrandt self-portrait, and the resemblance was deliberate. Flinck found it hard to make a name for himself when he left Rembrandt's studio and Houbraken says that it was more profitable for him to imitate 'the handling of paint and manner of painting of Rembrandt since every aspect of Rembrandt's touch was praised at that time, everything had to be cast in that mould if it was to please the world'.

Uniqueness is what one might reasonably expect from self-portraits, uniqueness and authenticity. They should be deep and true (Rembrandt sets the standard) and irreproducible. These versions of Rembrandt that have convinced us for so long, and are painted with so much more than mere skill – something more like insight, in fact – perhaps deserve to be called Rembrandt self-portraits as well. He licensed their production, after all, had his assistants copy his signature, invented and propagated a self-portrait type into which other artists could fit themselves. Isn't this some kind of cheat? Certainly, if one thinks of one's self as entirely out of bounds, an island, impenetrable, beyond the comprehension of other people; and of the self-portrait as therefore having the unique status of DNA or fingerprints. But paintings are fictions, and self-portraits too; there is not a novelist alive who does not believe it possible to enter the mind and voice of someone else, real or imaginary, and the same is true of painters.

There is a mid-period self-portrait of Rembrandt, for instance, by one
of his pupils that has every aspect of the look right, even down to the
disappointment and self-reliance. The execution is very nearly indistinguishable
from a Rembrandt, but far more striking is the empathy. The artist understands
– or has learned from studying his art – what it is like to be Rembrandt.

If there is a Rembrandt self-portrait *type* then that is its commanding
characteristic, this sense of an inner imagination, a gift for seeing from within
as well as without. You might say this is true of all of his portraits, and in that

Portrait of Jacop Trip,
c. 1661

Rembrandt van Rijn
(1606–69)

sense the self-portraits are a variation within a strand. But compare one with the other and there is still something else, something more – the very thing that distinguishes portraits from self-portraits.

Rembrandt painted Jacob Trip in 1661, the year of his death. Trip was the richest of all Rembrandt's clients, an arms dealer and merchant; the portrait shows a wizened but hawkish potentate enthroned with something like a sceptre in one hand. The light is benign, the paint fluently laid and Trip, whatever he has done in his life, receives the greatest respect. Although his face is sunken and shrewd, and the skin of the hands so knotted with veins they appear as thick as gloves, he is not a spent force, not a shadow of his former self but a figure of terrific authority, an authority partly endowed by the pose and clothing – the robes that give him stature – but also by the rich massing of Rembrandt's paint.

A prince among men, possibly a king: this is to some extent a very grand instance of the *portrait historie*. Which is exactly how you might also describe the magnificent self-portrait that hangs in the Frick Collection in New York: Rembrandt with the same clothes and pose, the same sceptre and authority that would be bestowed on Trip some three years later.

Here he is, presiding over the great hall of the Frick among the Persian carpets and marble urns and in one of the most extravagant frames ever made: Rembrandt finally at home, king of art. Here the great chief is kept in the style to which he was accustomed during the golden years in Amsterdam before bankruptcy, lawsuits and social opprobrium brought him down. With those great hammer hands, golden tunic and sash and the copious furs that take him out of time, this is surely the most regal, magisterial, dazzlingly self-possessed of all self-portraits. Until you look into the deep shadow beneath the velvet hat and see those penetrating eyes, watchful, wary, impatient, perhaps even defensively sceptical, keeping up appearances against all kinds of turmoil and doubt. The face is fallen, the man prematurely old and scarred but bearing up. It is not the kingly attire that gives dignity and power to this self-portrait but Rembrandt's sacrifice of himself to his own merciless scrutiny. And this distance between performance and performer is the source of the painting's tragic aura.

Jacob Trip is powerfully intelligent, you feel, but single-minded and self-protecting. There is no reciprocal inquiry in his face (perhaps because this portrait is based on an earlier version) and the same is true of nearly all of Rembrandt's sitters; whereas the artist, looking at himself, is driven to search and explore. The depth of his self-portraits is not an illusion or an anachronism invented by the Romantics and reinforced ever since, it is real and a function of that pressing look of exploration quite apart from anything else. Unlike Rubens, his contemporary, whose solo self-portraits turn a supremely steady face to the world , the same face every time, Rembrandt sees nothing so simple or fixed before him.

There are Rembrandt self-portraits, for instance, that are very hard to love, and not just the porky adenoidal youth or the cackling prodigal in the tavern, but some of the late self-portraits where he leans unpleasantly close to self-pity, sweating and absurd in his hats, making an old curmudgeon of himself. Such paintings put one in mind of the affecting afterword in Gary Schwartz's monumental biography: 'It would hurt me if the reader thought I was painting too black a picture of Rembrandt's character by leaving out evidence of his humanity. Believe me, this is not so.'[6] Having published every available contemporary document, which intermittently show Rembrandt to be litigious, careless, vain, abusive, conniving and even underhand, Schwartz has struggled to find just one proof that he was anyone's loyal friend, anyone's godparent, anyone's beneficiary in a will: anything to show he was generous or popular.

But that is not what one looks for in the self-portraits, especially not the late self-portraits with their troubled conscience, their disappointment, resilience and doubt. You don't go to these paintings for a mellow account of old age, no matter how inspiring they are. Rembrandt is just as likely to be irritable, proud and uningratiating as he always was, if occasionally more penitent and sorrowful than in the past. But he never grants himself full pardon. What's given instead is something more like charitable compassion. He is a sinner, a miserable soul, full of fault and resentment and lacking forgiveness, but at least the self-portraits know and honestly show it.

The quotation from Montaigne at the beginning of this chapter continues thus: 'All contradictions may be found in me ... Whoever studies himself really attentively finds in himself, yes, even in his judgement, this gyration and discord. I have nothing to say about myself absolutely, simply or socially, without confusion and without mixture, or in one word.'

There is a late self-portrait in which Rembrandt depicts himself, unusually, as a painter holding his palette; and yet he is dressed like a king, his presence overwhelming, commanding. The Kenwood *Self-Portrait with Two Circles* looks like the last word on Rembrandt the master, holding court in the kingdom of his studio, and a summary of everything he could do, from the immense variation of accents in that ambiguous face to the lightly scratched moustache, cloudy hair and flashing white streaks for a cap. A flurry of angular marks sketches in the palette and brushes, the fur is a judder of scumbles, and the famous circles sweep like skate blades on the canvas behind him.

These circles have made a Mona Lisa of the self-portrait for art historians – fragments of maps, references to the legendary free-hand circles of the great Apelles, worlds that have yet to be created? – but the man himself makes the enigma. The black eyes are withdrawn, sinking into a face as strong as the Ancient of Days yet painted in soft and unresolved strokes. What is the expression – stern yet sympathetic, undeceived but forgiving? And to whom is this mercy directed, mankind or poor old Rembrandt? The familiar face is inconclusive, no more the final account than any of the others. In this sense the self-portraits represent the pinnacle of his art, and its truth, that neither Rembrandt nor any honest man can sum himself up absolutely, or in a brushstroke.

Chapter Six
Behind the Scenes

'Painting is no problem. The problem is what to do when you're not painting.'

Jackson Pollock

Self-Portrait as La Pittura, 1638

Artemisia Gentileschi (1593–c. 1652)

It is a shock to come across this woman, this artist, painting for all she is worth, hidden away in a dark corner of Hampton Court Palace. It is not just the way the light casts a surprising glare across her forehead and bosom among the shadows. It is not just the flash of naked white forearm as she strains towards the canvas, although you can't help noticing how her sleeve falls away to expose an unexpected strength. It is the wheeling motion, the way her body kilters so dramatically, head tilting towards the mark she is so urgently making and all seen from a dizzying viewpoint. Which way up? The picture feels as though it could be displayed from any angle, even high up on a ceiling, as the artist's whole being rises to the creative moment. This is not just a picture of painting, but painting as live performance.

Artemisia Gentileschi is working with all her might, but what exactly is she painting? The canvas is bare, the workplace is empty and there are no visible models or objects to give a clue to her subject. The tip of her brush disappears into a neutral void. Whatever it is – whatever it is going to be – this offstage picture is wider than her arm's reach and higher than the artist herself, as if she might actually be at work on some enormous fresco. She could be making any kind of image for all we know; there is no need to narrow it down, Gentileschi has the bigger picture in view.

And how far-sighted she turned out to be, for *Self-Portrait as the Allegory of Painting* is Exhibit A in any history of women's art just as Gentileschi herself is arguably the most celebrated female artist in Western culture. Her self-portrait was the first by a woman to become internationally famous, one of the first to enter a royal collection (and perhaps even to have been commissioned by a monarch, Charles II of England at whose court she was employed) and certainly the first to make such a drama of painting as physical labour. Most self-portraits of artists at work make the act appear pensive, delicate, a matter of brain over brawn, but Gentileschi is seized with passion, conviction and an almost athletic force. Her fingernails are dirty, her hair is coming loose and she looks burly enough to weld steel, never mind dab at a canvas. Gentileschi resembles nobody else in art, except perhaps an artist of the distant future: she looks like an Action painter.

What a strike at tradition this picture represents. The artist could have painted herself doing nothing at all, or just sitting sedately before the viewer. She could have shown herself putting the finishing touches to some charming miniature as other women artists before her, eager not to overreach, or simply at work on this very picture. But all of these images of herself would have amounted to a kind of lie (even the last, but we will come to that quandary later).

Artemisia Gentileschi's story is in many ways the opposite of the Old Master tradition in which male artists are born in obscurity, die in poverty and become famous only after their lifetime. She learned from a successful father, the painter Orazio Gentileschi, became a follower of Caravaggio in her native Rome and had a forty-year career of her own in other Italian cities and abroad. Records show that she was well paid for her paintings of suffering but defiant heroines – Susannah being spied upon by the leering Elders, Judith saving her people by severing the head of Holofernes, St Catherine bound to her wheel – and that she was enough admired to attract envy and even the theft by another artist of her sketches. Even if she hadn't been famously hard-working by nature, life would have forced it upon her. Raped as a teenager by her father's friend and fellow painter, Agostino Tassi, and forced to endure torture and the inspection of her private parts during a public trial to establish the case against him, her reputation as a marriageable virgin was stolen from her too. A marriage of convenience hastily arranged for money failed, leaving her with a daughter to raise. She painted for more than art's sake, and more than herself.

There are those who want to believe that Gentileschi's extraordinarily violent compositions are a form of vengeance – Judith in particular, blood spatter on her breast as she decapitates Holofernes with all the efficiency of a farmer hacking the head off a live chicken – but that puts no premium on her originality. There is a scarcely a painting by her that does not turn the screw, ratchet the tension, involve the viewer as immediately and powerfully as the best of Baroque paintings with their extreme close-ups, weird angles and multi-action pans. *Self-Portrait as an Allegory of Painting* is no exception.

On one level, the picture simply enacts the title: self-portrait as the muse or embodiment of Painting. Gentileschi got the prototype from Cesare Ripa's standard iconography manual where Painting is described as 'a beautiful woman, with full black hair, dishevelled, and twisted in various ways, with arched eyebrows that show imaginative thought, the mouth covered with a cloth tied behind her ears, with a chain of gold at her throat from which hangs a mask and has written in front 'imitation''. It's all there aside from the gagged mouth, of course, but here the convention ends. Light strikes off her breast and the chain that dangles over her cleavage emphasizing its contours; it shows off the exposed flesh of the forearm, an arm as strong, we are to suppose, as her mind. If Painting can be a woman, then a woman can embody Painting.

Gentileschi wastes no time on eye contact, on social introductions, but gets straight down to work, and this is very much how she wanted people to see her; not as some passive allegory of art but as a vigorous force of creativity. Had she known she would become a heroine to women painters, and this very clever woman must surely have had some inkling, then no self-portrait could better have presented the artist as a strong woman painter, and not just a painter of strong women.

———

Why do artists paint themselves painting? One answer is the explicit identification of person with profession. I paint so I am a painter. It may seem excessive to drive home the point, of course, since the very existence of the self-portrait is surely evidence enough of one's professional gifts in the first place, and it could be such a limiting form of role-play just to show oneself hard at it. All those artists who portray themselves as having other roles – husbands, fathers, lovers, friends – or quite other talents such as playing the guitar or blowing perfect smoke rings manage to present many more facets of themselves while simultaneously displaying their talents as an artist. For vocation is implicit in the genre, every self-portrait confirms its maker's profession.

Or does it? Gentileschi raises the point.

Susannah and the Elders, in which Susannah is shielding her nakedness with a tremendous shudder of repulsion from the Elders breathing lasciviously down her neck, was painted by Artemisia Gentileschi in 1610. At least that is what it says on the canvas. But Gentileschi was only seventeen at that time and some insist that this must therefore be the work of her father, despite a clear signature. What is his and what is hers remain in dispute, if less so than in Gentileschi's day when a woman, and a beautiful woman at that, who was able to paint was considered rare enough to be a freak of nature.

For Gentileschi to portray herself in the act of painting was to present vivid documentary evidence of herself as both woman and freakishly gifted painter simultaneously. She is the embodiment of her own legend. Prints and copies of the self-portrait were mass-produced so that more people could see her doing it for themselves and a French artist even issued an image of her painting hand as if it had cultish properties; it is, incidentally, a prettified version of the capable original, cuffed with a frill and holding an impossibly fragile brush like a geisha plucking an orchid. But Gentileschi portrayed herself in the third person too: she is not looking at us and she is not working on this picture; to those unfamiliar with her art, or sceptical of her legendary talents, she could even be the subject of someone else's portrait. The irony is that this picture actually needs its signature to hit home as a certified self-portrait.

Still, the working self-portrait is the simplest form of positive identification, the easiest way to declare oneself an artist. A man or woman, generally dressed in dark clothes with one hand raised to the canvas or holding some brushes, a palette somewhere in sight and quite often a work in progress on the easel: this was the baseline self-portrait for centuries and it has its obvious attractions. It shows how paintings are made, and maybe even how this painting was made; perhaps how the artist felt about – or during – the work. It reveals the artist in context, in habitat, in the heat of the moment, and with a plausible sort of sleeves-up immediacy.

It also gives the artist something to do and *be* in a self-portrait that might otherwise lack obvious *raison d'être*; perhaps it even offers a pretext for painting a self-portrait in the first place. The shy or underconfident artist can justify this kind of image as a casual moment in the studio – just going about one's business – or as an acceptable advertisement: at its most mundane, a billboard; at its most sublime, a vision of one's ability to conjure a world and oneself within it, like Velázquez in *Las Meninas*. But this is the first of many pitfalls for the studio self-portraitist, the great Western tradition against which one may be unfavourably compared.

And here is another. The working self-portrait may look simple, straightforward, true to the moment, but it is an exceptionally difficult concept to pull off. Velázquez shows himself as a creator, but not in the actual heat of creation; Gentileschi, in so doing, pictures herself as she might appear in a portrait by somebody else. Artists aiming for absolute veracity – the moment of ignition where the brain carries the eye's knowledge directly to the hand with no perceived time delay between action and image – are extremely rare and their pictures often excruciatingly awkward.

Compare Gentileschi's painting with one by her contemporary, the long-forgotten Orazio Borgianni. The artist stands with the canvas before him and the mirror beside him – scrupulously accurate – trying to negotiate between the two versions of himself. He cannot manage the eyes he sees in the mirror and has even plunged one into shadow to dodge the problem; worse still, he cannot get the painting hand right at this tortured angle. There is no doubting Borgianni's true-to-life principles but his expression says it all, agonizing concentration and dismay at the contrast between the man in the mirror and the one in the picture.

Self-Portrait, c. 1615

Orazio Borgianni
(c. 1575–1616)

It is a poor painting but it illustrates some of the physical difficulties of showing oneself literally in the act of putting brush to self-portrait, not to mention the potential banalities, for such literalism generally stifles the spirit. It is no surprise, therefore, that most artists depart from the immediate truth to some extent when depicting themselves as working artists. But few have gone as far as the early women painters in terms of ingenuity and none quite as far, perhaps, as the shrewd and witty Sofonisba Anguissola who died nearly four centuries ago but remains among the most experimental of all female self-portraitists.

Born in Cremona, a city with no court or powerful patrons, Anguissola had the luck to have a father so progressive he paid for her to be taught by two male painters, encouraged Michelangelo to take an interest in her art and sent her self-portraits out with formidable testimonials to possible patrons throughout Europe until he finally got her a place at the court of Philip II of Spain.

Anguissola painted family pictures and self-portraits above all else and it is remarkable that she made such a career from the little kingdom of home. But anyone who has seen the marvellous painting of her three sisters called *The Chess Game*, in which the eldest checkmates the middle sister to the frank glee of the youngest, will know how vivacious and *inventive* are her small-world portraits. One senses a barely suppressed comedy in many of her paintings, and it was a drawing of a child trying not to giggle as she teaches an adult to read that first impressed Michelangelo. When he challenged her to draw someone weeping she did not depict sorrow but slapstick, a girl laughing heartily at a boy whose tears are caused by the crab he has pinched from a basket pinching him back in return.

But it was the long series of self-portraits from youth to considerable age – she died at ninety-three – that fixed Anguissola's reputation. She paints herself in miniature and the size of life; holding a book inscribed with her name and the fact of her youthful virginity. She paints herself actually holding up her own signature so that you should not be in any doubt that this is Anguissola, the artist by herself and, to reinforce that point, she became one of the first painters to depict herself actively painting. Seated in front of the canvas, in suitably sober clothes, she turns to the viewer while applying the lightest touch of the brush to the work in progress; not her own image but a painting of the Virgin and Child, for you are not to suppose that portraits are Anguissola's only talent. In this painting within the painting, Mary is drawing the baby Jesus's face to her own very tenderly with the tips of her fingers and one notices the same loving delicacy in the artist's touch.

But the most humorous and original of Anguissola's self-portraits is a unique variation – an early send-up, you might say – of the self-portrait of the artist at work. In this impudent picture her teacher Bernardo Campi is putting the finishing touches to a picture of his pupil, a great big portrait of Anguissola up on the easel with a telling expression of alertness.

This might sound like an act of almost masochistic humility: here is the man who taught me everything I know, the man who made me a painter; the man who made me a portrait. But Campi is no Pygmalion; the composition doesn't allow him any such status. He is sidelined to the left and subjugated in scale as well as height to the much larger woman who dominates the centre of both paintings. The talent Campi has nurtured is now bigger than he is and more glorious in her velvet and gold. She is such an animated presence that her left hand actually seems to cast a shadow across the easel as if breaking free of Campi's portrait. Even as he is painting her, Anguissola is taking over, showing that this portrait is by her too and that the teacher himself is just another one of her works. The wit of this self-portrait, in which the student appears to pay tribute to the master in ladylike fashion, is above anything by the forgotten Campi. He holds a brush and maulstick, moreover, like the manual labourer he is supposed to be whereas she carries a pair of expensive gloves for all the world like Dürer in the Prado self-portrait. Anguissola is on her way.

Why paint yourself painting? It observes a certain truth to the moment, of course, observing oneself in the act of observing oneself and getting it all down on canvas. Here the artist may even have a small advantage over the writer who cannot so immediately portray the condition of sitting alone at the desk in the computer's glow with forearms raised, mind poised or perhaps emptying fast, tapping away at the very words that convey these sensations. Obviously there are fiction writers who have done it; John Barth made a postmodern joke of his own writer's block in *Life-Story*, eventually relieved by the interruption of his wife; Don Marquis's cockroach Archy jumps the keys on the typewriter as fitfully as the typescript shows while keeping a sharp eye on Mehitabel the cat. One thinks of Captain Scott trying to keep writing to his wife as the ink freezes in his nib, 'dear it is not easy to write because of the cold – 70 degrees below zero and nothing but the shelter of our tent', a last love letter that would only reach his widow a year after he had frozen to death.

But consciousness almost always overflows the moment of creation. 'As I write,' the author tends to write, unable to keep his mind tethered to the act and fast sweeping away, 'as I write, the daffodils outside my window are in bloom …' And it happens, too, to the artist in the studio. The sense of one's self starts to succumb to the distractions of the material world. What were once banal or irritating become so alluring as potential subjects – fading light, congealing palette, the easel's bad leg, the litter of paint rags – that it is hardly surprising that working self-portraits sometimes become sidetracked by these details, allowing the artist to complain, moreover, about his dismal conditions; though it is surprising how little can be learned about the processes of art, the mysteries of the studio, you might say, from self-portraits. But in the sixteenth and seventeenth centuries, before Romanticism's *nostalgie de la boue*, the working self-portrait is still likely to be a more or less flagrant advertisement. And truth to the moment goes by the wayside here if it was ever really observed in the first place.

Take the action itself: since working self-portraits show bodies performing in time and place, perhaps they ought to observe some equivalent of theatrical unities? Yet they never do. Here is the painter in the middle of painting his self-portrait, but the picture we see is always finished. Here is the artist with the self-portrait visible behind him, still in the sketchy stages as if it was one he made earlier, or as if there were two.

Then consider the premise. If the self-portrait shows the artist at the easel, then surely he should be working on this self-portrait. But eighteenth-century artists don't care about such scruples at all and frequently show themselves painting another picture altogether, a magnificent Resurrection, a landscape, the portrait of a powerful patron, preferably a crowned head of Europe. There may be a huge physical discrepancy, moreover, between the finished self-portrait and the picture within it. Life-size self-portraits show the artist painting a miniature. Square self-portraits show the artist working on a rectangular canvas. And when one has gone so far, why not go even further? Paul Bril portrays himself at an easel on which rests one of the dark and whimsical little landscapes that made his name, but he has left off painting momentarily to demonstrate that he can also twang on the lute.

Sometimes the whole family will appear alongside an artist showing how well he can paint women and children and, not incidentally, what a beautiful wife and children he has and how calmly he continues to work in the chaos. The Italian artist Arcangelo Resani, briefly known for painting livestock, even surrounds himself with a menagerie of hens and chickens, dead grouse and a live goat to which he bears a pets-and-their-owners resemblance. Resani is pointing to himself by way of signature – I am he who made this – but he could just as well be trying to distinguish himself from the goat.

This picture exemplifies the continuity problems of working self-portraits to perfection, namely how to distinguish between two forms of illusion, the picture on the easel and the finished work. Without some sort of distinction – one may be sharper, the other more provisional, or as if viewed through a misty window – it seems the artist does not trust us to tell the difference between the two; and perhaps there should be no stylistic

Self-Portrait, c. 1713

Arcangelo Resani
(1670–1740)

discontinuity in any case. But Resani is so eager to show how well he can paint that he wants to make the grouse on the canvas look as real as the live birds in the room with the result that it is hard to tell what's what at first glance.

Artists paint themselves at work in the field, blending in with the very kinds of landscape for which they have made a name. They show themselves painting nude models, studying geological specimens, sketching by candlelight, pencils clamped between their teeth. There are job descriptions, and there are job applications that amount to a conflict of interest so obvious that one starts to question their status as anything more than vanity publishing by other means, devoid of intellectual probity or insight. And yet these self-portraits hold their private truths too: of artists trying to get a foothold, conform to convention, penetrate the social network.

Adélaïde Labille-Guiard's *Self-Portrait with Two Pupils* looks like the worst sort of PR, with the painter at her easel dressed top to toe in powder blue satin, the dress cut low, the straw hat plumed with high feathers. It is no stretch to imagine her parading through the Tuileries with the rich and famous instead of labouring in a fume-filled studio, and this is an insane choice of outfit for the filthy business of art, as mad as Nigella Lawson frying offal in cream suede on television. The satin would be ruined by the oily maulstick were this scene remotely plausible, instead of the florid fantasy it is.

What Labille-Guiard is painting is unknown since the shape of the canvas isn't specified, but it hardly matters in any case. The two pupils leaning over the back of her chair are bathed in its reflected glory, their faces lit as if by a supernatural glow. One smiles in admiration, a handmaiden as devoted as the bust of a vestal virgin pointedly placed behind her, worshippers at the flame of the goddess.

Like her supposed rival Elisabeth Vigée-Le Brun, who entered the French Academy on the same day as one of only three female members, Labille-Guiard was a divorcee with a good head for commerce. She adapted her output according to the radically changing tastes of the times, from miniatures and history paintings to informal portraits and genre pieces, and she even survived the transition from the Ancien Régime to the French Revolution sufficiently to paint Robespierre without losing her reputation when he lost his head. She also opened an academy of her own, teaching up to nine female pupils at a time, two of whom appear in this glorified prospectus.

It is a preposterous painting since nobody could possibly believe this was how things really went on an average day in the studio, but it fulfilled its purpose as propaganda. The self-portrait was exhibited at the 1785 Paris Salon as being by a Painter of Ladies – Labille-Guiard painted portraits of the aunts

and sister of Louis XVI, so not any old ladies – just as she was arguing, successfully, for female artists to be admitted to the Academy. It would be a long time before women stopped portraying themselves at work to prove they too could be painters; but by the end of the eighteenth century the self-portrait would in any case be valued less for showing the conditions of its own making than the human condition itself.

A man at a desk, writes Italo Calvino, arguing that writers should remain loftily invisible, resembles every other man at a desk. So do many artists at the easel. Or rather, the resemblance is very great among all those artists who paint the standard working self-portrait – the two verticals of easel and self, tidily framed – that tells the bare truth of their situation, namely that they are alone with the mirror and the picture. The discrepancy between the face that appears in each may bring on ill-concealed disappointment, though some artists appear perfectly self-satisfied in both respects. But the most inquiring self-portraits often display a cool detachment almost to the point of impersonality. These are the real backstage revelations, where the painter's high seriousness and insight are as palpable as the flaws exposed by these virtues.

Self-Portrait in the Studio,
1790–5

Francisco José de
Goya y Lucientes
(1746–1828)

Goya in his studio is dressed like a matador or *majo*, a wideboy, a mistake as he himself owns: his jacket is too tight and the trousers are straining around his bulging thighs. At nearly fifty he is too old and too stout for such clothes, as he very well knows, for in letters to his boyhood friend, Martin Zapater, Goya periodically laments his snub nose, and increasing girth. Yet he chose to paint himself in the least flattering position – side on – and the worst possible light, silhouetted against a whiteness so shattering that every contour is emphasized. He might as well have stood there naked.

It is high noon in the studio. The light is so bright that nothing is visible beyond the window as reflected in the mirror, and you need to squint to see this man of darkness. The brim of his hat is ringed with candleholders; according to his son Javier, Goya preferred to paint in the clear morning light but give 'the final touches at night in the artificial light'. He may not have been the only painter to get a close glow by turning his hat into a lampstand but he is the only artist to paint himself wearing one of these candle-hats and thus revealing a trick of the trade. Presumably it is acting as an eye-shade at this moment, though he could have taken it off in the final painting for the sake of vanity, this cumbersome pot that's too tall for his head. But size is a running gag here. Look at the tiny brush he is using to prod away at a painting so big it makes the artist look even smaller beneath his outsize headgear (matador and bull), a painting that is too large to correspond to this one for the self-portrait is surprisingly small – not quite two feet tall.

So small and yet strong enough to carry the full force of the scene, the stark light and the stark disenchantment of a man who turns upon himself very suddenly out of a spell of protracted thought. Just as in his portraits of the Spanish royal family – like the corner barker and his wife, as the French writer Théophile Gautier once described them – Goya doesn't lay a gloss upon the facts. He is a fat man, quite probably a small fat man, tousled, unshaven, unsuitably dressed and able to see the truth quite clearly. That is what his look declares: I see how I look, I know what I am doing and who I am in this world.

Goya was probably stone-deaf by the time he painted himself in his studio at number I calle del Desengano, Madrid, the final cruelty of a long and mysterious illness. And the world is shut out of this picture, the window a white-out, the artist all alone in the little kingdom of his studio. The solo studio – as opposed to the buzzing workshop or atelier – was still quite a recent luxury in Goya's day, only just becoming a place of withdrawal. It plays its part in the history of self-portraiture not just as a room of one's own, or a refuge from society, but as the cell that throws you back on yourself and your misfortunes.

In the seventeenth century Gentileschi would have been working in a corner of a workshop, Labille-Guiard, in the eighteenth century, in a busy atelier with her pupils. Artists didn't get the splendid isolation of their own white-cube studios until they finally stopped having students. So many pictures that one poetically imagines to have been painted in sessions of sweet silent thought came straight out of noisy factories. David Teniers the Younger, at the easel around 1645 in Holland, is working so close to the next man it looks as though he is attending an oversubscribed evening class. A few years later, Adriaen van Ostade widens the screen to take in not just the artist and all his pupils but the colour-grinder hard at it in the corner; a drawing of Rembrandt's workshop shows not one but six artists crammed into a room so small it is practically impossible to get a decent viewing distance between them and the (unusually) half-nude model.

Was Velázquez ever really alone? There are eight other people with him in *Las Meninas*, not counting the implied presence of the king and queen; and he paints himself, as we shall see, in something less isolated than a studio. Van Dyck is said to have kept up such a beguiling flow of conversation while painting, and been so eager to have his patrons and their hangers-on stay on for dinner, that his house at Blackfriars was regarded as an upmarket salon. In the nineteenth century, when other painters are concentrating on the crumbling walls of their minds and garrets, Gustave Courbet boisterously depicts his studio in L'Atelier as a return to the milling workshops of the Old Masters, vast and visited, as he boasted, by all the world.

If the use of the solo studio from the late seventeenth century onwards has any measurable effect on art – the rise of the still life and the corresponding decline of the multi-figure history painting, it has been suggested[1] – it is undoubtedly pertinent to self-portraiture. Studios bring peace and privacy, a bare stage for an artist's performance, and it seems reasonable to suppose that the seclusion and freedom they represent has probably been responsible for inspiring some exceptional self-portraits, just as the status they confer – I have a studio = I am an artist – must have produced many mediocrities.

Eventually studios become places of pilgrimage, the rooms in which artists spent all the working and perhaps even waking hours of their lives. Eugène Delacroix's Paris studio, which he scarcely left and where he painted his self-portrait, is an austere affair now expensively decorated by florists ('a volcanic crater artistically concealed beneath bouquets of flowers' was Baudelaire's description of the painter himself). Cezanne's studio in Aix-en-Provence is in a secret garden behind an ivy-clad door. In Texas, the sculptor Donald Judd bought the entire town of Marfa, building by ramshackle building, as a total environment for his Minimalist art and it feels exactly as it should, simple as a Shaker village out there in the silent desert. But who isn't surprised by the studio barn in the East Hamptons where Jackson Pollock worked his action paintings on the floor – a place so small he hardly had room to move around the edges of the canvas.

The studios of the Abstract Expressionists are regarded as places of the mind, sites of pioneering struggle. Mark Rothko, defeated, slit his wrists and overdosed on barbiturates in a vast pool of blood in his New York studio. Clyfford Still's loft had to be more than fifty feet high to take the mountainous crags of his works. Arshile Gorky went out to his studio in Connecticut on a summer's day, chalked a suicide note on a picture crate and hanged himself from the rafters. The terrible seriousness of these lives and deaths, this fateful sense of mission and heroic labour, is by now so closely associated with the night studio and the naked light bulb that it is hard to imagine these artists as social beings garrulously hammered in the Cedar Tavern.

The grand tradition of the self-portrait at work is in decline now that studios are more like well-staffed workshops and contemporary art is less a sacred mystery than a billion-dollar enterprise. But it does have one last great farewell in a work by a painter who quit a most ethereal kind of abstraction – Abstract Impressionism, people called it – for unfashionable figuration. This is Philip Guston's tragic-comic masterpiece, *The Studio*.

The artist is painting a self-portrait, a smaller version of this larger self-portrait, so we know he is the painter, and this is just as well since he has his head in a bag, got up like a spoof ghost or a Ku Klux Klansman. There are slits for the eyes and the two huge fingers of one hand, toting a cigarette, while the other is getting down the self-same image, stitch by stitch and slit by slit. The clock ticks, the blind is half-drawn and the bulb dangles naked and bright as if the long day was beginning to fade. But the artist keeps stoically at it.

What a fierce cartoon *The Studio* seems, lumpen, self-satirizing, wilfully awkward, full of cunning humour. There is the droll joke of an artist painting his self-portrait with a hood over his head and the equation of smoking with painting, cigarettes with fingers, fingers with brushes. The cigarette sticks out horizontally from one hand as the brush sticks out from the other, the brush paints as the cigarette smoulders, but where is the smoke coming from – which is the greater addiction, fags or painting?

Caught red-handed: the painter at work. The biggest attribute Guston gives himself is that stubby object, fingers cocked like a gun, the big bad hand at the heart of the work. It is always there in front of him, this creature, this tool the brain uses to articulate itself in writing, painting, music, drama, in all of the arts. But in painted self-portraits as nowhere else the hand becomes an object. For the painter must come to terms with the very hand with which he paints, and possibly in the very act of painting. One imagines that it could involve a most peculiar state of consciousness, eye, brain and hand decoupled, as it were, like that frightening moment in William Golding's *Pincher Martin* where Martin, stranded on a bare rock in the North Atlantic, watches with calm curiosity the movements of a strange pink sea-creature a few inches away from him before

realizing with startling horror that it is his own waterlogged hand.

What should this object look like in a self-portrait where the artist is at work? Rembrandt, in the late Kenwood self-portrait, amalgamates palette and hand as if they were organically fused. In *Las Meninas*, Velázquez paints his tapering fingers as if they were brushes themselves, quick as the sliver of vectoring whiteness with which he is just about to apply a point of light to the canvas. In a marvellous drawing by the German artist Käthe Kollwitz, the fingers narrow to hold the charcoal as a pencil holds its lead and the drawing arm is described in a long black zigzag issuing from the charcoal's tip. An unbroken circuit, a live current that flows from mind and eye to hand and charcoal, it is a most expressive continuum. 'Drawing,' Kollwitz wrote, out of the poverty and hunger of war, 'is the only thing that makes my life bearable.'

Guston's stubby hands, holding butt and brush as if there were no difference, are glove-puppet hands, Disney hands, blunt instruments. Once they might have been delicate, the hands of a mountain-top sage with an instinct for Zen Buddhism, serial music and Chinese calligraphy, whose exquisite abstracts looked like spectral forms furled in mist. 'Such a beautiful land,' sighed his friend John Cage, regretting its passing. But now, by the late 1960s, Guston has become the artist of a horrible lower world, a real world outside the studio. 'What kind of man am I,' he had asked himself, 'sitting at home, getting into a frustrated fury about everything and then going into my studio to adjust a red to a blue?'

The Studio is a revolt against all those other studios in which artists proclaim their status while promoting their art. Guston is the anti-hero, the cruddy, slovenly hood who can't come up with anything but this near-cartoon. Yet everything here is filtered through high art. The red swag curtains are from Jan Vermeer's *The Art of Painting*, the light bulb from Picasso's *Guernica*, the pots supposedly sitting on the bottom 'ledge' of the painting echo the way Renaissance artists lean on the bottom edge of the painting in their self-portraits. The silvers, greys and pinks are the colours of Velázquez's portraits and you can see them isolated in pure form on the palette too, just the way the dabs of raw pigment used in the creation of *Las Meninas* appear like tiny emblems on Velázquez's palette. Art makes art. It is a most conscious, and perfect, construction.

Philip Guston got through three packets of Camel a day and the smoking paintbrush is only half a joke. But this obdurate, humorous image of the artist puffing away at his cigarette and his picture, oblivious to society, his health and anyone else's opinion, can't help being heroic despite itself, the epitome of the artist who labours against the times to make his own world. Why paint yourself painting? This scene gives the best answer, assembled as it is piece by piece from everything this painter knows and loves about painting. He is not separate from the art but a part (like the brushes, like the palette) of its working tradition.

Chapter Seven
Velázquez

'Golden lads and girls all must,
As chimney-sweepers, come to dust.'

William Shakespeare, Cymbeline

Las Meninas, c. 1656

Diego Rodríguez de Silva y Velázquez
(1599–1660)

You are here. You have appeared. Their eyes announce your arrival, all these people looking at you out of the shadows. The little princess and her maids with their ribbons and bows and shimmering clothes, the tiny page and the tall dark artist, the massive dog and the lady dwarf, the courtiers whispering, rapt, or poised ready in the doorway at the back: all are gathered here for your presence. They were waiting to see you and now you have entered the room — *their* room, not the real one around you, as it mysteriously seems. This is the first sensation when you walk into the gallery in the Prado where *Las Meninas* hangs, a picture the size of life and fully as profound, that you have walked into their world and become suddenly as present to them as they are to you. And the impression is defined by light, for these brilliant children, the princess and her attendants, live in a pool of sunshine at the bottom of a monumental volume of shadow, brief and bright as fireflies in the sepulchral gloom. It is the most spectacular curtain-raiser in art and it sets the whole tenor of the painting.

You could stop there, stunned, at a distance. Many people do, struck by these people assembled like the guests at a surprise party who are trying to keep still and silent in advance of your arrival. Everyone in the picture has ceased whatever they were doing except the page who nudges the drowsy dog with his foot; everyone has stopped speaking apart from the nun just reaching the end of her sentence. The scene is motionless except for the movement of air and sunlight stealing through the unshuttered window and fluttering across the lustrous blonde hair of the princess, who is staring at you with the unembarrassed curiosity of a child at the centre of a painting that is itself completely attentive. The maidservant on the left is kneeling to her diminutive mistress; the one on her right is pausing in the dip of a curtsy in your honour. The dwarf gives you her full and frank consideration, hand on heart, and behind her other courtiers are observing you all the way to the man in the doorway at the back who hovers on the threshold of this enormous room, perhaps waiting to usher you into the next. And at the very front on the left, but turned against you, unlike the rest of the scene, is the most famous canvas in the history of painting — the blank back of the picture the court painter is making, twice as high as he is and more, and from behind which he appears, the magician revealed: head tilted and looking fixedly at you.

Pictures, if they wish, can slip time and take the viewer anywhere. That is in their scene-shifting gift. But *Las Meninas*, Velázquez's last masterpiece, gives more than just the illusion of a fragment of time held perfectly intact down the centuries, an actual moment in which these people in their queer archaic clothes, their slashed sleeves and panniered dresses and scarlet wrist rosettes, were all together in this grand room of the Spanish palace working and painting and possibly posing, perhaps having a drink, watching and waiting and quietly talking and trying to rouse that laconic dog. At the very least the painting makes you feel you were there at the court with those people right then, but it is the praise you could give a thousand time-stopping pictures and *Las Meninas* is more advanced than all of them for it also reverses that proposition, creating the illusion that these people feel you are there with them too, that their scene is fulfilled, completed, by you. Velázquez, supreme conceptual dramatist, invents a new kind of painting: the picture as living play, with a composition that seems to open into our space and a plot that gives a part to every viewer.

The picture opens up like a stage set, the tiny black figure against gold at the back, the mid-scene characters, the artist edging towards the wings, the stars at the front who might equally well bow were they not in the act of curtsying in response to the spectacle we present them, as they to us. And where precisely does one begin or end? We are all in this play of life together.

All of this registers in a single instant as you pause at the door of the gallery, on a threshold that corresponds with the one in the picture, before the painting starts to yield up its strange singularities – the way the scene continues outside the picture, obliterating all the old boundaries of art; the way the mirror in the back glows like a nocturnal television set; the blocking of the characters like chess pieces, receding all the way to the enigmatic man in the doorway who haunts the whole picture, so dazzlingly silhouetted and yet so opaque; above all the poignant glory of the scene. For although it is an interrupted moment, a freeze-frame in cinematic grammar, somehow it continues to reverberate as if nothing will change, time will not happen and childhood will continue for ever.

Velázquez is somehow able to make you, and all before and after you, feel as alive to these people as they are to you and that they will not die as long as you are here. This little girl and these courtiers and the dwarves, all dead and gone so long, nearly four centuries in their graves, are transfixed in the here and now by every single viewer stretching on into the future. The knowledge that this is all achieved by brushstrokes, that these are only painted figments, does not weaken the illusion, indeed it only deepens the enchantment of this stupendous painting. The whole surface of *Las Meninas* feels alive to your presence.

———

Las Meninas was made in 1656, towards the end of Velázquez's life, and it shows a room in a palace that is also long gone, destroyed by a fire from which the painting was only just rescued. This room is not where Velázquez generally worked, which was on another floor in another wing of this immense edifice, but it is the painter's realm to an uncommon degree for he designed it himself, acquiring and arranging the paintings on the walls for his monarch, Philip IV of Spain, and later adjusting its windows, shutters and doors to arrange the best light in which to paint its representation. It is not a studio so much as a royal apartment of Velázquez's own creation, twice over – and the very apartment, of course, in which it was originally shown.

The mind rushes like mercury into this conceit: how perfectly the illusion must have fused with the reality when the picture hung in that room, the two sides of the chamber, real and depicted, presumably appearing seamlessly connected, dovetailing as invisibly as life and its looking-glass reflection.

To walk in and find these people waiting there must have been astounding, perhaps as if one had chanced upon a flickering projection of reality quite unimaginable before the invention of film. And anyone who stands there now, held fast by their gaze, is positioned exactly where all these generations of viewers once stood. This is part of the picture's content. It elects you to the company of all who have ever seen it, from the princess and her maids who must have rushed round to see themselves the moment it was finished, to the king and his courtiers and all the citizens of Madrid who finally got to see it when fire liberated the painting for public viewing outside the palace, and on through the many artists from Goya to Manet to Picasso who have studied it first to last. We stand in history, and the painting embraces us in its democracy.

The first viewers are all identifiable figures. From Maribárbola the compellingly level-eyed dwarf, to the moon-faced nun in charge of the princess's education and Nieto, the black-clad chamberlain at the back, every identity, age, court position, dress colour and professional duty is recorded. The scene is precise in its detail and each is a matter of historic fact, from the master-key tucked into the artist's belt with which he could unlock every door in the Alcázar (the freedom of the palace, highest honour) to the *gollila* collars worn by Velázquez and Nieto that were made of cardboard and supposedly helped Spain's ailing economy by remaining stiff for months and thus saving on the production of starch. No matter that the country was in political and military decay, its empire crumbling, the court was maintained as a magnificent theatre with a cast of hundreds, daily life as ritualized as a masque; *Las Meninas* indicates precisely the royal progress through the court. Ten thousand books, a writer once said, could not tell you as much about this particular place at this particular time as Velázquez's great masterpiece.

Historians study it as conclusive evidence of protocol and politics in the reign of Philip IV, father of the little infanta in her gleaming white dress. Art historians compare it to the densely detailed Dutch interiors of the period, as if it was similarly bent on offering a meticulous inventory. Economists, social historians, scholars of costume and custom treat it like a photograph to be scanned for evidence. Novelists think of it as a pictorial novel – all these characters, the relationships between them so carefully plotted – and playwrights as a brilliantly complex tableau. But *Las Meninas* is neither photographic nor cinematic, and it is not precisely literary or historic in nature. Perhaps it is nearer to philosophy; and philosophers have certainly prized it above other pictures; perhaps because, in the words of a fellow painter, it represents 'the theology of painting'. What Luca Giordano meant by this phrase was that *Las Meninas* told the truth about life as theology tells the truth about God, and that its truths were conclusive. But the nature of its depiction, how the painting acts upon us – like an illusion, a hallucination, a vast reflection of life – remains mysterious, caught between reality and a waking dream.

The tale is told of a British artist being led blindfold on to a plane to Madrid, and then by taxi to the Prado, his eyes still covered, through the galleries and up the staircase to the room where *Las Meninas* hangs. The blindfold was removed and he beheld the masterpiece until the gallery closed, whereupon he returned, once more blindfold, to London. It sounds like a parody of preciousness, and the story is possibly apocryphal, but on the other hand this is how many people hope to experience the wonders of the world, with their minds clear and their vision unsullied, someone else's hands over their eyes until they see Venice over the waves or reach the edge of the Grand Canyon. And *Las Meninas* is a wonder; one of the very few paintings in art that one experiences as if it were part of the living world. By arriving in complete darkness, having seen nothing, depicted or otherwise, for so many hours, the blindfold artist perhaps hoped to discover how it would strike the eye. Would it seem like art, or a reflection of life?

Las Meninas imitates the characteristics of a mirror – one looks into it and is seen in return – but it has the semblance of a mirror as well, especially the misted brilliance of mirrors made long ago in which the world appears so much more gracious. The light filtering through the window turns white clothes silver and blonde hair platinum, transforms the narrow edge of the canvas into a shaft of gold, ignites the bright nails of the stretcher. A pool of light on the floor has its distant reflection in the ceiling. The painting glimmers. The mirror on the back wall, reflecting the king and queen in miniature and with the softer haze of distance, its bevelled edges catching the room's sharper light, is like an emblem.

If *Las Meninas* carries the moment's reflection in a flash upon its surface it hardly seems necessary to emphasize the comparison. Yet the directors of the Prado used to display the painting opposite a mirror of exactly the same size. People who saw it reflected said that it was like looking at shadows turned solid, or actors hovering on a darkened stage, or living figures seen through a camera obscura. The implication was that the illusion, large as life and mirror-bright, actually came supernaturally alive when it was itself reflected. It sounds far-fetched and yet this is exactly the experience anyone can still have at the Doria Pamphilj Museum in Rome, where the first glimpse of Velázquez's deathless portrait of Pope Innocent X is not the canvas itself but his frightening face looming round the corner in a specially angled mirror. It is a sight to make anyone flinch: Innocent's merciless intelligence glaring right back at you; who hasn't been momentarily deceived? Obviously one's own continuous eye movements and the mirror's slippery volatility abet the illusion of spontaneity, of a face suddenly appearing at a window by night. But even without a mirror Velázquez's portraits have been taken for living people.

During his lifetime, the art of Velázquez was often described as some form of magic. In an age when the only available images of people were paintings, his realism was exorbitantly prized as if a speaking likeness was his uppermost talent. Philip IV himself is supposed to have rebuked one of Velázquez's portraits – 'What – are you still here?' – mistaking it for a courtier in the evening shadows. A Vatican aide, confusing Innocent X with his portrait fleetingly seen through a doorway, warned everyone to keep the noise down because the Pope was in the next room, although Innocent's own comment is far more telling. Of this devastating icon of ferocity, he simply conceded 'Troppo vero' – too true.

Too true to the inner as well as the outer man: that is what we nowadays understand Innocent to have meant; that Velázquez's truth was too piercing. The aide's confusion of image with reality, by contrast, is just a meaningless cliché applied to any kind of mimetic art all the way back to the Ancient Greeks. But his mistake, or his claimed mistake, presumably sounded to his colleagues like the highest form of praise.

In Rome, Velázquez also painted a portrait of his black assistant, Juan de Pareja, and sent him round town to show it off in high places. This exercise in compare and contrast, no doubt intended to drum up commissions, only yielded the same old clichés. The Romans politely exclaimed that they didn't know which of the two heads was more likely to talk, that they found themselves delightfully confused, which might have satisfied the quick-fire portraitists who hung around the streets even then, but was no praise at all to Velázquez.

For his is not an art of flawless illusion, intent on simple deception. It is not an art that conceals itself in order to deceive. Every one of Velázquez's special effects is created by strange and singular brushmarks laid out in full public view and you are meant to notice them, to marvel that Velázquez makes it possible for you to be astonished by his realism while simultaneously aware that it is entirely conjured from specks and slashes, dots and flecks, and other illegible dabs of paint. The amazing veracity arrives out of incomprehensible chaos: it is vital that his people *should* look like paintings.

The art historian Kenneth Clark tried to identify the precise moment where one becomes the other, where the chaos of brushmarks coalesces into an image. He had been looking at *Las Meninas*. 'I would start from as far away as I could, when the illusion was complete, and come gradually nearer until suddenly what had been a hand, a ribbon and a piece of velvet, dissolved into a salad of beautiful brush-strokes. I thought I might learn something if I could catch the moment at which this transformation took place, but it proved to be as elusive as the moment between waking and sleeping.'[1] Somewhere between waking and sleeping, between consciousness and dream: that is where *Las Meninas* lies.

Detail of *Las Meninas*, c. 1656

Diego Rodriguez de Silva y Velázquez (1599–1660)

A hallucination, a vision, a work of magic: the painting is often described in such mystical terms perhaps because it is commonly felt to be the most mysterious of pictures. Velázquez gave it no title, nothing to seal its meaning. In palace records it first surfaces as *Her Highness the Empress with Her Ladies and a Dwarf*, later as *The Family of King Philip IV*. The servants did not rise above their masters — *Las Meninas*: The Maidservants — until the 1840s, a decade of revolutions, when the painting was given its present title in the Prado catalogue. Perhaps it does represent a world turned upside down, with the servants becoming the protagonists in a royal portrait, but that depends somewhat on whom one believes to have been present that day in the palace.

It seems straightforward. Their names are all on record, from Maribárbola in her rustling frock to the two maidservants. The mirror on the back wall reflects Philip IV and his second wife Mariana standing at the other end of the chamber, their majesties having arrived either to watch or pose for Velázquez at work, causing this chain reaction. Or so one might think, namely that the point of the mirror is to imply their presence, make them cunningly there and not there, present in the room but not directly in the painting, since such exalted personages could not actually suffer themselves to be depicted in the company of painters. From Titian and Van Dyck to Lucian Freud in his queer little head of Elizabeth II, this etiquette is rigidly upheld, and it is hard to think of an artist inveigling himself into a royal portrait other than Goya, whose group-shot, *The Family of Charles IV*, in which he appears as a shadowy sceptic in the wings alongside the gauche and devious Habsburgs, is in any case a wily sequel to *Las Meninas*.

Yet from Velázquez's first biographer onwards, many writers have insisted that the mirror does not show Philip and Mariana. Rather, it merely reflects the portrait that Velázquez is painting. So the back of that enormous canvas – representing the opposite of a painting but such a marvellous painting in its own right, the hessian rough-grained on its towering stretcher, the light shooting up the frame showing the scissor-scalloped edge of the fabric, as vivid a presentiment of forthcoming revelations for anyone who loves art as the lights going down in a theatre – is nothing but the humdrum reverse of a double portrait, carrying no secrets, promising no mysteries or marvels. By this account, the picture is just another self-portrait at the easel, with unusual company.

To argue that this whole scene has been conjured to show nothing more than the objective reality of the artist at work – close to the little infanta and painting the king's portrait, once again, as if Velázquez was awfully keen to be seen touching the royal hem – is to go against the evidence of Velázquez's genius. The mirror in the back becomes nothing more than a way of showing a picture within the picture; a banal device that other artists had already made trite.

Velázquez, who numbered among his many offices the administration of the royal art collection, was deeply acquainted with one of Philip IV's most precious possessions, *The Arnolfini Marriage*. He knew its ingenious use of a mirror to draw the rest of the room outside the scene, including Jan Van Eyck himself, into its depiction. It is not to be supposed that Velázquez, most intelligent of painters, would have conceived of anything less remarkable. And if the mirror reflects the presence of the king and queen indirectly – another in its chain of conceits – then its gives deeper resonance to that first double take, implying that you now stand where the monarchs once stood; that you, like they, are both audience and subject. Time telescopes, and you too are contained in the vision of the artist.

If the mirror only reflects a picture then *Las Meninas* loses its transcendent ambiguity and deflates into a conventional self-portrait of the painter as portraitist. One objection to this theory, admittedly as pedestrian as the theory itself, is that no such double-portrait is known to have existed. Another is that the canvas on which Velázquez has been working, or is about to work, is proportionately large enough to correspond with *Las Meninas*, and occupies such a large expanse of the picture as to make a drama of itself. But the most pedantic objection is that Velázquez is standing between canvas and mirror, thus blocking the reflection; and come to that, wouldn't Velázquez be tripping over the maidservant's skirts every time he tried to make a mark on that canvas? This is the kind of literalism that besets such drastically limited and limiting interpretations of the painting. Yet the premise they share is in some ways understandable: *Las Meninas* is so persuasively real it must be bound by the reality it represents.

The idea that sightlines, reflections and perspective must be accurate and therefore subject to logical analysis was taken to its *reductio ad absurdum* by the Spanish architect Ramiro de Moya in the 1960s. Moya reconstructed the room, windows, mirror, canvas, figures and all according to their positions, as he supposed, on the day that *Las Meninas* was painted. Thus he claimed to *solve* the painting, establishing to his own satisfaction that the mirror can only reflect the canvas and not the monarchs, because the monarchs simply weren't there; or rather, they had to be standing where Velázquez stands in the picture, on his side of the canvas as it were. For Moya believed that Velázquez could only have painted the masterpiece by observing the whole scene, princess, servants and all, from a position outside their space using some kind of mannequin as a stand-in for himself and adding his features, from a mirror, later. The roles are reversed: he observes the monarch from outside the picture.

Poor Moya, one feels, can only have been blind. Blind to the stupendous and manifest staging of *Las Meninas*, to the painting's conceptual drama, to all of its reflections on art, mortality and time or simply to the fact – and this is part of the picture's own wisdom – that the laws of perspective do not apply to the human eye. The picture is painted, so to speak, both in and out of focus. Velázquez understands that the eye shifts continually, seeing sharply only what it focuses upon for a second, and that it cannot possibly take in the entire scene in an instant. So the painting runs all the way from solid description – the wooden stretcher, the coffered door – to the little boy's flurried movement on the right, not much more than a brushy blur, even to the nearly imperceptible frisson of circumambient air. The execution is a marvel, conveying the actual movements of our eyes while baffling our minds. For how could Velázquez know where to place that speck of white that ignites such flashing glints across silk, how to convey the stiff transparency of gauze with a dab of blue on grey, or the gleam of the infanta's hair with a nearly impalpable wash of white? The methods are laid before you, freely declared as special effects, and yet you cannot break free of the illusion of life.

And the mystery of Velázquez's art is not just that his pictures are both dazzling and profound all at once, but that these apparent opposites coincide to the extent that one feels neither can exist without the other. The theology of painting, the mortal truth, has to be set down in a flash of brilliant brushstrokes always on the verge of dissolution.

Moya's interpretation, like so many others, is entirely dependent on perspective, but perspective was never Velázquez's strength in any case. Throughout his career, from the early masterpieces made when he was barely seventeen in Seville to the allegories and the late portraits, there are lapses in many of his works. Saints don't quite stand firm, landscapes buckle, black and white tiles don't accurately measure a space. It seems quite improbable that Velázquez would have allowed the meaning of his greatest masterpiece to rely upon what might be described as his only weakness. He is an artist, after all, and can do whatever he likes, make a king and queen appear and yet disappear, cast the whole world as part of his spectacle.

Moya's reconstruction, incidentally, was challenged first by one architect and then another until it became obvious that the perspective could be redrawn to produce any number of contradictory scenarios, which ought to have exposed the flaws in this idea of the painting as having the relationship of a photograph, a mirror or indeed a blueprint to reality. And yet this urge to make models of *Las Meninas* is not hard to understand because the picture is so fascinated by architectural space, by the bare stone floor, the shuttered windows receding all through the austere chamber to that luminous rectangle at the back, the door that leads out of the room, and out of the picture, analogous to the mirror that hangs beside it, which in turn reaches forward to the other end of the room. Step through the looking glass, enter the dream: this is one of the invitations extended by the picture, or rather the painter.

For all avenues of interpretation must eventually lead back to Velázquez and his self-portrait in the shadows behind the canvas, a figure so distanced and dark as to be almost overlooked by most writers. This is surely how he ordained it – not to be the subject of the painting but its master, its source, visible only as its creator.

But without Velázquez none of what philosophers and scholars dispute in the painting would remain. Minus Velázquez, the vast canvas becomes a riveting but empty prop; the mirror becomes nothing more than an optical trick, the relationships between viewer and viewed are abolished, along with the openness to all. If Velázquez had not included himself, the picture would still be exceptional but its emphasis would be thrown: a princess, some maidservants, the family of Philip IV (no title ever acknowledges the artist's presence), but an end to that unique cycle of connections, and reversals, between us and them. Our participation would no longer be required and the never-ending transmission between us would cease. Since this is central to the painting's complexity – and Velázquez must surely have meant to make his masterpiece as complex as he could, this meditation on art in which he finally reveals himself as an artist and a courtier, a poet and a philosopher of the human condition – the self-portrait, taciturn, remote, is the linchpin.

Detail of *Las Meninas*, c. 1656

Diego Rodriguez de Silva y Velázquez (1599–1660)

Velázquez's only world was the Spanish court. He was twenty-four when Philip IV hired him as court painter in 1623 and except for two hard-won trips to Italy from one of which he attempted not to return, the remaining forty or so years of his life were immured in the royal palace.

Philip described his painter in a letter as phlegmatic, meaning that he had a detached and unhurried cast of mind. According to a contemporary poet he 'breathed dignity'. Even if one could not tell it from his self-portrait, Velázquez was regarded as silent and watchful although not, perhaps, by the dwarves and jesters and other servants he portrayed at the

Infante Carlos Baltasar in the Riding School, c. 1640–5

Diego Rodriguez de Silva y Velázquez (1599–1660)

court, considering the mutual empathy that radiates from these infinitely humane paintings.

The very few recorded sayings are resonant: that he thought painting began with Titian and not Raphael; and, when his scenes of working-class Seville were rebuked for being too low-life, that he 'would rather be first painter of coarse things than second in a higher art'. By the time he reached Madrid, where his subject was the court and his art would become extraordinarily evanescent, he was, of course, first in every respect.

Velázquez was one of more than a thousand courtiers bound by hierarchies and rituals so elaborate that life seems to have proceeded like an interminable masque; and the artist, who would eventually design the royal entertainments, invented new ways to dramatize the royal portraits in turn. His painting of the king's son, *Infante Baltasar Carlos in the Riding School*, overturns the conventional equestrian portrait not least by putting a tiny boy on a charger, a child shown rearing up at the very edge of a space so foreshortened he seems about to leap toward our world. Courtiers and dwarves observe from the heat and dust behind and away in the distance, high on a balcony like an opera box the king and queen preside over all. And behold! Everyone turns our way. As an allegory of watching and looking, of society as spectacle, it prefigures *Las Meninas* two decades in advance.

———

'The diligence of a bee,' wrote Antonio Palomino in his early biography of the artist. Velázquez's industry as a royal servant is distressing to this day since it speaks of all the pictures he never painted. How can one not think of him as shackled by protocol, perpetually unfree as he ascends from Privy Chamber to Wardrobe to Superintendent of Private Works and eventually to the keys to the palace? 'Palaces are tombs,' wrote his contemporary, the playwright Lope de Vega, 'and if they had feelings, I would be sorry for the very figures in the palace tapestries.' Yet the truth is that Velázquez aimed for social advancement. He must have known he was a great painter but he struggled to become a great courtier instead, angling year after year for the very knighthood the king so glibly gave Rubens when the painter was in Madrid on a diplomatic visit.

For all this scaling of the rungs Velázquez scarcely surfaces in the royal archives as a person as opposed to a job title, and when he does it is always poignant: the one line he was given in the palace masque in 1638 (a mock wedding between the Marquis of Cauliflower and the Countess of Parsley); the demeaning seat in the gods at the royal bullfight; after nearly twenty years at court, Spain's greatest painter alongside the barbers.

Palomino also says that Velázquez was 'pursued by envy even after his death …by malevolent people trying to deprive him of his sovereign's grace.' That there was a bond between them is palpable even in the portraits of Philip IV as an uncertain young emperor and especially in the late painting of him as a sunken old lion, the full grief of his life's experience discreetly expressed. Legend has it that the king himself added the red cross, emblem of the Knights of Santiago, to Velázquez's breast in *Las Meninas* when the artist was finally elected to the Order. Philip certainly went to some lengths to get him in, but not without anxious prompting from the painter who spent years espaliering the family tree to prove he had enough class to join the aristocrats, besides which the cross is as virtuoso as everything else. Even as Velázquez was working on *Las Meninas*, jealous bureaucrats were thwarting his hopes by the day so perhaps his addition of the cross, three years later, was somewhere between vindication and retort. How apt that Velázquez, ennobled by his paintings far above any title, should speak triumph through the silence of art.

One senses a high Spanish pride in the scant anecdotes about Velázquez and his art. He must have hoped for a wider audience than the shuttered Alcázar or the gloomy Escorial outside Madrid which was his only other home, for he went so far as to display some of his paintings in public. One picture was set up outdoors in the Plaza Mayor, buzzing epicentre of Madrid. Pareja's portrait was carried through Rome. *Innocent X* was exhibited to stunned acclaim by Italian colleagues, pleasingly alongside a Raphael, under the dome of the Pantheon. Artists were his best judges, never courtiers. When an equestrian portrait of Philip IV was presented at court and actually *censured*, Palomino says, 'for being done against the rules of art but with such contradictory judgements that it was impossible to reconcile them, Velázquez, annoyed, wiped out the greater part of his painting'. Not in compliant acquiescence but quite the reverse: to show that the same power that created this world could destroy it. On the canvas his superb reply was painted: 'Didacus Velazquius, Pictor Regis, Expinxit' – Diego Velázquez, Painter to the King, Unpainted This.

———

Picasso, obsessed with *Las Meninas*, went in and out of that room for years trying to take its mystery apart in over forty prints that are on the level of a cartoon by comparison. But he does isolate some of its singular elements: the great weight of darkness, the activity of light, the solitary figures in their different planes of reality, the queer relationships and obsolete shapes. Yet when it came to the self-portrait, Picasso drew a blank. His Velázquez is a towering crag of geometries, an unreadable abstraction unlike everything else; unknowable, yet the *sine qua non*.

Even Picasso was not completely immune to the lure of perspective, but his sense of the painting does not hinge upon it as most 'solutions' do from the earliest biographers to the philosopher Michel Foucault, whose essay on the painting in *Les Mots et les Choses*, with its famous conclusion that *Las Meninas* is nothing less (and perhaps nothing more, for him) than 'the representation of Classical representation, inaugurated whole schools of interpretation.

What Velázquez is painting, who he is looking at, who *we* are, as it were, why and how we are so compellingly bidden by the painting: *Las Meninas* accepts as many answers as there are viewers and part of its grace lies in allowing all responses and interpretations to coexist, no matter how contradictory, by being such a precise vision of reality and yet so open a mystery. Mystery is surely part of its content, the mortal mystery it represents and transmits.

The Art of Painting,
c. 1665–6

Jan Vermeer
(1632–75)

But of course it speaks of art's mysteries too and a more appropriate title than *Las Meninas*, perhaps, would be that given to Vermeer's portrait of an artist: namely *The Art of Painting*. Both pictures were painted within a single decade; both show, and show off, the work of the artist; both put the viewer in an especially unusual position; and both include, as a matter of overwhelming significance, a picture contained in a picture.

Vermeer reverses Velázquez's conceit. His artist is seen from behind, whereas the model and the image he is making of her are both in plain view. You watch over his shoulder, alternating exactly as he must between looking at her and the canvas, sensing the continuity between this little work in progress and the larger painting, both conceived, *invented* by Vermeer.

Invented, because his canvas shows that the artist is not just painting but transforming his model into a muse, making her the Muse of History. He has only managed to complete a few of her laurel leaves but one sees that he intends to include her emblems, her musical instrument and her heavy book, and that everything else in the studio where the model stands is to be excluded. History will have her own pictorial milieu, just as the extravagantly dressed artist has his studio, both brought into being by Vermeer.

The light that navigates the map on the wall, sheens the chequerboard floor, glancing from the sketchbook on the table to the canvas on its easel, eventually reaches the hand that holds the brush. The picture irresistibly proposes its own making as a subject. Yet the artist has his back to us, revealing neither his face nor his thoughts, and his hand merges with the picture he paints as if he too were a figment. Vermeer keeps his distance, remaining behind the arras. He paints a masterpiece about a master painter and then slips away, like the conjuror who makes himself vanish.

While Vermeer does not reveal his identity, Velázquez steps free of the canvas so that his self-portrait, no matter how reserved, visibly declares that this world is all his. That the brush with which he made everything from the physical to the philosophical truth should be no more than a streak of white – the one mark that is scarcely legible at *any* distance, yet so sharply itself – feels like the subtlest of quips. The whole cycle of representation – light, reflection, eyes, palette, canvas, picture – is set in motion by its delicate tip. Perhaps there is a hint of the conjuror here too, but to modern eyes the tall figure of the black-clad artist, set apart, rising watchfully above it all, sombre in his knowledge, has more affinity with Prospero, the dramatist-magician who brings the action of *The Tempest* into being and then breaks his wand at the play's end, revealing the secrets of his art. The secrets of Velázquez's art are all on show, yet their mystery does not melt into thin air. No other artist before or since has made the paradox of painting so visible: the idea that three dimensions could be convincingly portrayed on a flat sheet of cloth; or, in his case, that fixed pictures could represent the mobile, ever-changing world and yet themselves seem to dissolve into flux. Even the little dots of pigment on the palette, echoing the chain of faces in the room, repeat the central compositional truth that the artist, and only the artist, is responsible for everything you see in the room; that although these people will one day disappear, unmade by death, they continue to live for ever through Velázquez.

———

Ars longa, vita brevis. You only have to look at all the amulets dangling from the belt of the infant prince Philip Prospero in another of Velázquez's portraits to sense the desperate fear of death at the Spanish court; the child was dead at the age of four. Philip IV's first wife died young. His two sons and youngest daughter all predeceased him. His second wife would have been his daughter-in-law, had not the son for whom she was intended died before the wedding. Velázquez himself was carried off by a sudden fever, caught during a royal betrothal ceremony he had designed down to the last collar and dinner plate. He was buried in a church later ransacked by the French during Goya's tenure as painter to the court of Spain. Nobody knows where, if anywhere, his body now lies.

The king's face in *Las Meninas* is a hazy blur. These are the twilight years of his reign, the high summer of the Spanish empire is over and war with France is bankrupting the government. By 1657 he will not be able to get credit even for food. A few years later he will be dead, followed with terrible swiftness by the tiny princess.

Of course, it is thanks to Velázquez that Margarita's youth and charm survive her. But *Las Meninas* is more than an arrangement of beautiful portraits; more than the sum of all its interpretations and more than a meditation on painting.

It is well said that Velázquez's brushstrokes reveal a true freedom of spirit. In this masterpiece they also release something equivalent in the people he portrays, so alive and unique, and in every viewer who comes before the picture. *Las Meninas* is piercingly sad in its representation of these lost children in their obsolete clothes, dead and gone for centuries, and the painting makes its elegy for what must come in miniature at the back of the room, where the chamberlain waits to lead us onwards into that other light, hovering between this world and the next.

But he does not go and they do not fade, kept here by our presence and Velázquez's art. The golden haze remains bright against the monumental darkness above. The figures of the past keep looking into our moment, our present, as long as we keep looking back at them. Everything in *Las Meninas* is designed to keep this connection alive and merciful for ever; that is Velázquez's gift, and his consolation, to us all. We live on in each other's eyes and our stories need never end.

Chapter Eight

Mirrors

'Mirrors: no one has expressed in rhyme
the life you really live
you strange loopholes in time
as full of holes as a sieve.'

Rainer Maria Rilke

Self-Portrait in a Convex Mirror, 1524

Parmigianino (1503–40)

A self-portrait made his name, very suddenly, in the space of one day, and it was painted when Parmigianino was not yet twenty. It shows a teenager so young he could still be a boy, his smile not fully formed, looking out of a room lit by a small latticed window. There are no brushes or palette, but he makes a great exhibition of one hand, laying it out before him like a still life at the front of the picture. It is a work of art — and of this worker's art, for you could scarcely mistake the gesture. The artist's own hand is enlarged and displayed as an advertisement for his gifts, including the novelty of this *circular* self-portrait.

But it is not just circular. Seen in reproduction, this picture of Francesco Mazzola, better known as Parmigianino, the little painter from Parma, looks flat even if the scene is queerly distorted. The room swoons, the walls bow and arch up to a diminutive ceiling, the painter's head is small and remote, as if this were a fantasy circling in the mind's eye, or an apparition in a crystal ball — and that is what the painting itself actually resembles, for it takes the form of a hemisphere.

Parmigianino's exact subject is, in fact, the object that contained his reflection, a convex mirror likely borrowed from a barber. Barbers used convex mirrors in the sixteenth century because flat ones were not yet cheaply available, in order to display their scissor-work. Parmigianino would have been able to inspect his girlish trim in such a hemisphere of glass, and to see the world magnified and miniaturized in its surface; which illusions, Vasari tells us, so fascinated the youth that he set out to reproduce them precisely. Parmigianino had a ball of wood turned on a lathe and sliced in two by a carpenter to produce a hemisphere of identical proportions to the original mirror: a counterpart on which to paint the facsimile of that mirror.

If you are lucky enough to come across it by chance, this quasi-mirror appears very eerie, as if it had been empty until you walked by and then suddenly flashed up an image. There is a sense of something present within its shadows that stops when you stop, looks when you look, very much as it seems with a real mirror, that blank thing that is empty and waiting until we come along to bring it to life, and give it some *raison d'être*. The illusion is short-lived, of course, no more than half a second if it happens at all, although it may have been longer for Parmigianino's contemporaries, for whom a convex mirror was commonplace, instead of a queer archaism from another world. You can see how the faint blurs and silver-grey glimmers within the painting are meant to sustain the illusion and how the advance into three dimensions is supposed to work. At a distance, the play of light across its swelling contours certainly announces a round object instead of a flat picture, an object moreover that is so dark and small — not ten inches in diameter — that you have to get up quite close to make out the face in the mirror.

That it is not your own is obviously no surprise. What surprises instead is this other person's presence, the sense of someone else having slipped into the mirror, who is now looking back at you through all its optical distortions. For this is not the glassy-eyed stare of an artist trying to see and paint himself in the mirror, even though the challenge must have been severely complicated by this particular mirror's convexity. Parmigianino intercepts your gaze and returns it as if he had been expecting the encounter all along and was just waiting to take you unawares.

The second surprise is that the creator of this sophisticated conceit looks more like a child than a man, and more of a girl than a boy. Pale, pretty, sweet-faced, with a delicate nose and a beardless chin, he would be perfectly cast as the boy actor who plays Viola playing a boy. In his fur coat and a cambric chemise, gathered at collar and cuffs, he looks dressed for something cleaner than painting. Though he is not painting, so much as keeping fantastically still – one false move and his reflection will slide across the mirror like mercury. The hand is a ballast, an anchor that tethers this weightless reflection, keeping the conceit from drifting away. It lies motionless at the front of the picture, a reclining nude, a body at rest, fingers like elegant legs.

Or perhaps, as John Ashbery has it in his melancholy poem 'Self-Portrait in a Convex Mirror', it is more monstrous, this great white shape, more like a creature from the deep:

> (Big, but not coarse, merely on another scale,
> Like a dozing whale on the sea bottom
> In relation to the tiny, self-important ship
> On the surface.) But your eyes proclaim
> That everything is surface. The surface is what's there
> And nothing can exist except what's there...

Parmigianino's image, writes Ashbery, is trapped in this surface, 'glazed, embalmed, projected at a 180-degree angle'. The hand looks big enough to break free, you might think, to smash the sphere that detains it; except that all that exists would then vanish. And the gesture is so ambivalent: an expansive greeting in one respect, but wary as well, like a player guarding his cards, or a schoolboy shielding his homework. The hand is in cahoots with the mirror, pushed so close to the surface that one's impulse is to reach forward and touch it as if the mirror, like Alice's looking glass, was nothing but thin air and opened straight into another world.

But it is there all right, a permanent barrier that cannot be breached; you can never reach Parmigianino, and he can never reach you. The glass always intervenes – a solid object, burdened with surface reflections – and that is what the hand is telling you. Vast, elongated, so much bigger than the head, it is the mirror's most outlandish distortion. The face with its ghostly smile is far enough away to escape extreme deformation and could almost pass for a regular portrait. It is the hand that makes the mirror manifest, coming so near and yet swerving away, fending off the viewer, bending to the mirror's curves. Parmigianino cannot quite touch the glass because his hand would no longer be visible as a distinct reflection, although he gets as close as he can. The hand obeys the rules of the mirror.

————

Nobody really knows quite what he or she looks like. That privilege belongs to other people. All we have are the camera's partial images and the intangible reflections of mirrors. And mirrors can only give as good as they get, after all, which is whatever we choose to give them: a face arranged to fit the mood of the moment, perhaps, to make us look as we feel, or would like to feel. A face marked by the effort of looking, or pretending not to look, or the effort of keeping still. A fact-checking face, paying close attention to detail but missing the bigger picture – which can't be seen all at once, alas, and which never stays still for a second; the eye moves, its reflection shifts; we are altered by our viewing conditions.

Parmigianino's self-portrait conveys this slippery relationship as no other before it and very few since. A great many self-portraits express unease in front of the mirror but the unease is circumstantial. The drawing Dürer made of himself frowning in a mirror, head in hand, eye and cheek squashed, might look like a man with much on his mind and it has been hailed as the first modern self-portrait for depicting not just the outer man 'but also his unique inner self'. But is the artist facing up to himself – self-analysis – or his own fugitive features, the hand there just to steady the head? Dürer complained of 'an unrest in painting' caused by the mobility of his own gaze, to and fro between subject and picture, and now even the subject is not still either.

Dürer, like Parmigianino, may have been using a convex mirror (although there were already some master mirror-makers in Nuremberg working on flat glass). They are often listed in studio inventories after an artist's death or on auction lists if he had fallen on hard times. Until the sixteenth century, most mirrors were either made of prohibitively expensive polished metal or cheaper convex glass formed by pouring lead into blown glass balls and slicing them in two. Ingenious Venetian mirror-makers on the island of Murano developed a method of backing sheets of glass with tin and mercury to produce mirrors that were internationally prized because they were both large and flat. In an act of early industrial sabotage, the French bribed these mirror-makers to come to Paris with their wares and then terrorized them with threats and even poisonings until they got the formula.[1] One prodigious result was Louis XIV's Hall of Mirrors at Versailles.

It is an ordeal to portray oneself in a convex mirror, circling around, shifting to catch another fraction or two of one's appearance as it slithers about. The reflection has to be spread flat in the mind like a handkerchief; the representation has to be partly deduced and partly imagined. Not much of oneself is visible, which is one reason why early self-portraiture is mainly head and shoulders, and even when flat mirrors come on the market an artist has to be very rich to buy one big enough to show very much more. More self-portraits than one might guess are made with small rectangular mirrors reflecting nothing but the artist's face, the rest of the body extrapolated from common knowledge and memory.

How the mirror is used – or first used, for those who believe she is the earliest self-portraitist – is the subject of the beautiful miniature 'Marcia in her Studio'. Marcia, like her fellow Greeks Phidias and Apelles, is known only by repute, an artist praised in classical literature none of whose works have survived. But here she is in this illuminated manuscript of Boccaccio's *Concerning Famous Women*, doing exactly what made her famous. In one hand she holds a small oval mirror, with the other she touches up her lips in the larger image in front of her that looks like another looking glass. It is not, of course, but there is the hint of a toilette in the paraphernalia that surrounds her: the hand mirror, the dressing table, all those little pots and brushes, and Marcia painting her face.

What this imaginary portrait makes clear is just how much Marcia has had to make up. If she copied her reflection precisely, it would be small and

Marcia in her Studio
(St Marcia, d. 632)

From *De Claris Mulieribus* by Giovanni Boccaccio (1313–75)

cramped and not much bigger than a miniature. The mirror looks convex, but the self-portrait is flat and free of distortion. It also shows far more than the looking glass gives her. Marcia has painted her shoulders and dress and a rich blue background, none of which she can see in the mirror, and she is no longer looking herself in the eye. It's a departure, a better image than the little one in her hand. There is no question of setting things down exactly as the mirror dictates; this is not stenography, this is art.

Parmigianino's conceit is to be far more literal and yet fantastical; literal in showing only and exactly what he could see in the mirror, nothing made up; fantastical in duplicating the spherical reflections in spherical dimensions. His self-portrait is not meant to look like a painting – a mirror of life – it is meant to look like a mirror. He made it to impress Pope Clement VII, who is known to have been gratifyingly amazed, and amazement seems to have been the prescribed response for centuries. It was a sensation, a 'cosa rara' that tourists would take detours to visit, and it had an exceptionally large audience in an age before public museums. But time passes, tastes change and Parmigianino's double act with the mirror now seems less astonishing as an object than for its mysterious reticence as a self-portrait. The painter is so near and yet so far; not a strong presence, just a fragile reflection in a shadowy room, something he once saw, and then painted, because the mirror allowed it, something that would vanish if he didn't keep his distance.

———

The mirror is vital, essential, the main thing needful for the artist's self-portrait at least until the advent of photography. It is the quiet accomplice always there with an image from which to work, helpful and non-judgmental. One mirror may be needed, possibly two for a profile, sometimes more for a sculpture, but few are ever acknowledged in the finished work. Most self-portraits make no mention of this necessary aid, this bit of treated glass, which is after all only a tool.

Perhaps this has something to do with the way the mirror *contains* the self-portrait. In portraiture, the artist looks outwards at other people in the wider world; in self-portraiture, the mirror narrows this world to its own dimensions. The eye the artist is trying to paint is the same eye that is directing operations. What is outside the field of the mirror is scarcely noticed or noteworthy compared to the person reflected in this frame on whom the artist concentrates, so the mirror equals the picture.

This is one reason why Edouard Vuillard's *Self-Portrait in a Mirror with a Bamboo Frame* is immediately striking, quite apart from the fact that Vuillard has blanked out the eyes. It is as if the camera has panned back to show the film set in its true surroundings, a flimsy box in the real world of the studio. The

physical characteristics of the mirror are beautifully described, its quicksilver
surface alive with slippery motion, the light from the attic window reflected in
blurry halations. The painter, you feel, has been right up close to examine the
varnishy sheen of its bamboo frame, bright against the matt wallpaper. In fact,
the picture puts you closer to the mirror than Vuillard himself, who stands
further back, a more remote reflection. He can see, or know, more about the
mirror than himself, the painting implies; for what can one discover about
oneself from a mirror?

Another reason that mirrors, despite being so crucial, rarely appear in
studio self-portraits may be their peculiar insubstantiality as objects. Without a
frame to draw attention to their limitations, one barely notices their form at all.
They become what they are — invisible surfaces.

Mirrors are there and not there, surfaces that only become visible because
and when they make other objects visible. It is no surprise that Western art, so
fascinated by the look of things, and by the experience of looking, is so
interested in depicting the mirror in other genres of painting. The mirror is an
optical illusion, another kind of picture, a way of magically extending or
multiplying images. It is a symbol of vanity, or self-knowledge, the transience of
life or beauty. It can reveal what is hidden, or what lies offstage; it can show the
world in reverse, and it can show the world outside the painting like *The Arnolfini
Portrait* or *Las Meninas.* But it is still only an optical device, and one can pay too
much attention to its role in a picture. Any view of art that takes so much
interest in the way the mirror works in *Las Meninas* as to interpret the entire

masterpiece according to mechanical reflections is probably likely to be just as interested in the optical illusions of M. C. Escher. One of Escher's self-portraits, incidentally, shows him looking in a shaving mirror. His trick is to make the mirror look fantastically real and then breach the illusion with a signature that appears to be reflected in its surface, but is not reversed, as it would be in a mirror: so you are reminded that this is a picture (you dolt) not a mirror.

Some say that self-portraiture has to be a complete fiction from the off because artists are always adjusting the mirror's reflection of left as right, and vice versa. Much is made of the fact that in the Kenwood self-portrait, Rembrandt corrected the switch, that is to say, he put the palette in his left hand since he was right-handed; X-rays of the underpainting show it was in his right hand originally.

But who cares about mirror reversals? Rembrandt aside, they cannot matter much to most artists, whose only way of seeing themselves, after all, with the exception of photography, is in a mirror. I draw myself from the mirror; I look exactly on the page as I look in the mirror; which is the only image I have of myself in any case. Why would I care if you think I am left- or right-handed?

Self-Portrait, 1925

Lovis Corinth
(1858–1925)

These switches are trivial; what may be more significant is the lateral vision we have of one another.

At New York's 2008 Whitney Biennial, John Walters set up some of his non-reversing 'true mirrors' – unlabelled – in the washrooms. Looking into them, one sensed that something about oneself was not quite right, and eventually that everything was the wrong way round. Anyone can have this experience by standing next to a close friend in a mirror and seeing them – peculiarly altered – as they appear to themselves. Perhaps laterality matters because of the hemisphere specialism of the brain; if a facial feature appears on the right, Walters thinks, we may interpret it differently than if it occurs on the left.[2] Certainly, if you look at a portrait in a mirror, the character of the sitter seems to change; and the same is true of our artists, their self-portraits a reversal of life.

Mirrors may be a *sine qua non*, but they are used and removed, returned to invisibility time after time, deleted from the final self-portrait. Rembrandt never shows a looking glass. Van Gogh paints every other object in the room. The German painter Lovis Corinth produced countless self-portraits, quite possibly more than Rembrandt, using a mirror wherever he went. He lugged it outdoors, to the garden, the seaside, to the Austrian Alps in the 1920s and on summer holidays to the lakes of Bavaria. He posed in front of it with a skeleton, with his models, his mistress, his wife, even half-naked, garlanded with vine leaves and more than once in a suit of preposterously self-aggrandizing armour. Several times he raises a brimming glass to his own image – his own reflection; but it is still no show for the mirror.

For how could this bric-a-brac possibly intrude into the great drama of being Lovis Corinth – man and superman, maker of his own destiny, Nietzschean to the very hilt? The mirror is a nonentity. And yet it does appear, once, and significantly, in one of the few paintings where Corinth's self-certainty visibly weakens.

It is not immediately clear where the mirror is in this picture. It looks as though Corinth is following the old painter-painting-this-one convention, body facing canvas, head turned front towards the mirror. But then there is that other image in the background, as if he was working on two different portraits, which turns out to be more than literally the case. The background Corinth is obviously meant to be a mirror reflection, but the optical relations are all wrong and he seems a stronger and more resolute man than the wavering soul who looks our way, searching for himself in the mirror. Here, in his last self-portrait Corinth is not a robust hero to himself any more and notices the instability of his reflection as well. The mirror responds. He appears doubled but also divided.

———

That mirrors are in some ways like pictures is a truth most artists think too obvious to point out (though not Escher). The differences are surely more intriguing. In self-portraits one sees them pitted against each other sometimes as a matter of a professional pride, sometimes as a kind of schizophrenia.

Johannes Gumpp, an Austrian artist about whom so little is known that his self-portrait seems to be almost the only proof of his existence, produced a quirky stand-off to go with his comedy surname. Gumpp is painting his self-portrait from a mirror. But how is he to make it look like a mirror and not another painting? There is the distinctive shape, the metal frame and the telltale size of its reflection – mirrors, no matter how large, or how close we get to them, always make us look smaller. But the Gumpp in the mirror looks a little static whereas the Gumpp in the portrait has a more animated turn of head, more vitality in his face and a brighter glint in his eye. It's a highlight, in fact, the very artifice with which an artist makes an eye look round and shiny and plausibly real, and which he has craftily omitted from the mirror's less life-like reflection.

The picture invites you to switch back and forth between these two Gumpps, seeing the eyes shift, the head move, as if turning the pages of a cartoon flick-book, and then it wants you to notice the mocking sub-plot. For beneath the mirror is a cat, beneath the portrait a barking dog, staging a little pet-fight that sends up the contest of illusions supposedly won by art. But a third Gumpp intervenes, a middle man between the others, conducting the

Self-Portrait, 1646

Johannes Gumpp
(1626–1728)

performance with his back to the viewer. Which is the real Gumpp? His identity, you feel, will only be revealed if this third man turns round and declares himself. But he never will. Who he is cannot so easily be revealed in a painting.

Or in a mirror … Mirrors eventually became so cheap and ubiquitous after the Renaissance that their mystique faded away; after all, what is so special about an object that just sits there dumbly echoing the world? The old conventional praise, in which admirers were always comparing pictures with mirrors, as if they had identical functions, also dies out. Just to be able to fool the eye, create an illusion like a mirror, may have been all the world once wanted of art, but art had long since exceeded that function.

It is just possible that Norman Rockwell had Gumpp in mind when he painted his triple self-portrait, for Rockwell was steeped in art history. Not that his public necessarily knew it, for as has often been remarked, Rockwell was thought to produce *pictures* not paintings, namely sixty years of covers for *The Saturday Evening Post* that made him America's favourite twentieth-century artist.

That they were paintings and not just pictures might have become apparent to anyone who looked closely at the issue dated 13 February 1960. That week's cover showed Rockwell seated in front of a large canvas working away at a self-portrait in oils. He has a maulstick, a palette, a good handful of brushes and a sheet of working sketches pinned to the canvas, which has already been signed in upper and lower case. The name is printed, in fact, just as it always appeared on the magazine's cover except that here it doubles as the signature to an oil portrait. It gives Rockwell's name, as usual, and announces that this portrait is his, but it is also his modest way of indicating that these covers were always paintings in the first place.

Not that he described himself as a painter. Rockwell, if asked, would say he was more of an illustrator. The artists of his time – he was born in 1894 – did Cubism, Futurism, Abstract Expressionism; he had been to Paris to try it out, unsuccessfully he said, before returning home to good old representation. His was an America of soda-fountains, proms and mountainous Thanksgiving turkeys, of avuncular cops, family doctors, young love and long marriages. Not the kind of thing Picasso painted and nothing the critics would admire – 'the Rembrandt of Punkin Crick', sneered the *New York Times* – until Rockwell's reputation was dramatically upgraded in the 1990s. His view of life excluded the sordid and ugly, he said, because 'I paint life as I would like it to be.'

This is how Rockwell shows himself in the *Triple Self-Portrait*, improving on the reality in the mirror. Things really look up between the reflection and the canvas – the expression brightens, the drooping pipe becomes erect, the spectacles disappear. The head becomes larger, especially compared to the rear-view head beside it, craning into the mirror, in which it appears once again even smaller: all part of the comic self-deflation. Above the portrait is an old-

Triple Self-Portrait, 1960

Norman Rockwell
(1894–1978)

fashioned hero's helmet, but mock-heroic, wry, and no more a reference to himself (it's European, as opposed to the all-American eagle above the mirror) than the reproductions of famous self-portraits tacked to the top-right of the canvas. These are by the artists he admired and to whom he made deft allusion: Dürer, Rembrandt, Van Gogh and Picasso, pin-ups for the humble illustrator, who has, by way of rueful comparison, posted his own quartet of self-portraits on the left, thumbnails of Norman Normal and his oversized pipe.

Perhaps Rockwell would have liked to have taken himself more seriously. 'Just once,' he confided to his youngest son, 'I'd like for someone to tell me that they think Picasso is good, and that I am, too.'[3] Many Americans thought him far better. The reproductions he so skilfully miniaturized on that cover might have been instantly recognizable, but so was a Norman Rockwell.

Rockwell himself would never have been spotted outside the small Massachusetts town where he lived. His self-portrait might have become familiar to millions of readers, but it didn't pluck him out of the crowd and was never meant to because Rockwell made himself look like anyone else. It was part of his modesty to portray himself as a lanky guy in sensible shoes, slightly stoop-shouldered, as ordinary as the next man — as ordinary, and just as complex. For there are three Rockwells to choose from, and more if you count the pencil sketches. The man with his back to the viewer is entirely subsumed in his work; the face on the canvas is a self-deprecating joke; and the man the mirror purports to reveal is shyly concealed behind those blindingly reflective specs. What Rockwell looked like in the mirror was not what he was. But what he makes of himself in this definitive self-portrait – an expert narrative, transparent, inclusive, gently humorous – was the essence of his art at its best.

That paintings are objects as well as images, and in this respect like mirrors, is a truth Parmigianino made doubly apparent. His mirror portrait is such a perfect simulacrum, both as image and object, that as with few other paintings you want to pick it up, measure its weight, feel its material substance. Paintings are as portable as mirrors. Taken together, a canvas and a looking glass can place the painter in Tahiti or the Austrian Alps, and portable mirrors, having no fixed view of the world, can shift the scene moment by moment, altering the angles, transforming the perspective, showing the artist in a sudden new light.

Lucian Freud lays a mirror at his feet, looks into it and sees a towering inquisitor bearing down on himself and the viewer, the light above him like an interrogator's bulb. He arranges three mirrors at different angles, a concatenation of views in which to trap himself unawares, aiming for a glimpse of how he might look when glancing at some other person. Is he self-surprised? It is impossible to tell. Hawk-eyed and suspicious, he breathes heavy concentration as he looks in the mirror, over and again, and then paints his looks. A fine mist furls these shifty reflections.

Self-Portrait, Man's Head, Portrait III, 1963

Lucian Freud (1922–)

Even by wedging a mirror in the window frame and standing with his face to the light, Freud cannot get a clear look at himself in the brightness of day. He moves to look, and the image shifts. He narrows his eyes the better to focus, and they shrink from the mirror reflection. He is too active to be a passive subject, too busy to be his own sitter, and this is a distinct conundrum for self-portraitists. Freud knows his own face very well, has painted his mirror-image many times, could probably do it from memory, but instead he sees, and transmits, the indeterminacy of himself as a reflection; something you might see daily, even at the same time and place, without ever getting used to it, without ever feeling the mollifying comfort of familiarity.

Everyone's mirror is the site of repeated stand-offs between hope and disappointment, confidence and frank incredulity, between yesterday when things were looking up and the cold light of today. This unsteadiness is not just a function of the mirror, of course, for it occurs within our selves. But the mirror becomes a metaphor for this appalling mutability, its slipperiness reflecting our inability quite to grasp, or even clearly see, our ever-shifting selves.

At Pierre Bonnard's house on the Côte d'Azur, the mirrors are still exactly where they were when he died in 1947. Nothing has changed; and nothing ever changed in all the years he lived there. Pilgrims to this shrine will know from his paintings the exact position of every fixed mirror: the one in the upstairs sitting room where he sometimes appears, a discreet blur, watching his wife Marthe at breakfast; the mirror in the bathroom where she washes incessantly; the one in his bedroom that reflects nothing but an expanse of bare cupboard and occasionally his own face in the final bleak years.

Bonnard bought the house in 1926 when he was almost sixty. His neighbours in the village of Le Cannet were lawyers and bankers who had retired to the Southern sun and in photographs he looks very much like them: neat suit, pressed handkerchief, spectacles and trim moustache, a sun-hat when out in the garden. But Bonnard was not in retirement. He had never had a public life and his neighbours did not know who he was. His subject was always privacy and at Le Cannet he painted more than three hundred images of his domestic life with and without Marthe in which the official Bonnard never makes an appearance.

In his lonely self-portraits, Bonnard only ever paints himself as a reflection in the mirror, never free of its surface. And freedom seems to be at issue for Bonnard always looks trapped, as if he longed to leave but found himself locked in the mirror's precincts. In his vest in the bedroom, he approaches the glass with undisguised dismay. Light lavishes the pale yellow cupboard behind him and throws a shawl over his shoulders (something to celebrate). But between the face and the mirror falls a shadow. Bonnard can hardly make himself out except as bare and blood-red as if flayed, a raw thing exposed to the looking glass.

In the bathroom, he checks to see how bad things are, noticing his own apprehension. There are the opalescent tiles to praise, and the little congregation of brushes, soap and shaving stick; light sometimes dabs his nose like shaving foam. But he is a ghost behind his spectacles, and without them his eyes are dark slits in the bald head. Dressed in an orange kimono he looks like a Noh tragedian, or a grief-stricken Buddhist monk.

Estrangement is the condition of all his self-portraits. It is as if the mirror removes Bonnard from himself, or presents him with some other being. Like Parmigianino, he gets up close to look at his face, but draws away from the one in the mirror; like Parmigianino, he is near and yet profoundly remote. But these are not showpieces for a public audience. Some of them hardly seem like independent self-portraits at all – here I am – so much as paintings of mirrors in which Bonnard just happens to appear, dispirited to find himself present. Sometimes he even puts up a half-hearted resistance, a puny figure flailing at the mirror with his fists, boxing his own reflection, knowing that this is the only way to view and paint himself but conscious that all he sees is a shadow; not a self, not *himself*, for the mirror can never give that back, but an incorporeal figure.

At the end of his life, Bonnard painted the most mysterious of all his self-portraits in which he appears shaven and stripped before the mirror; nothing concealed, but nothing revealed. A pale, bald creature of completely indeterminate age, according to the mirror's report, who or what he is can no longer be described. He has become a space man, alien even to his own eyes.

Self-Portrait, c. 1940

Pierre Bonnard
(1867–1947)

Chapter Nine
Performance

'Every person lives in a world of social encounters. In each of these contacts, he tends to act out what is sometimes called a line. Regardless of whether a person intends to take a line, he will find that he has done so in effect. The other participants will assume that he has more or less willfully taken a stand.'

Erving Goffman, 'On Face-Work'

AVT TACE,
LOQVERE MELIORA
SILENTIO.

Self-Portrait, c. 1645

Salvator Rosa (1615–73)

The painter has something to say and has decided to say it in words. Since he cannot speak for himself he has overcome this obstacle by giving his lines to a stone: unless your conversation is better than silence, shut up.

This is exactly what Salvator Rosa is not doing, of course. The artist can look as brooding and stony as he likes but by painting these words he is effectively talking, and what he has to say manages to communicate on several levels all at once – philosophical yet bossy, boastful yet droll given that he is so clearly disobeying his own injunction. And in so doing, Rosa is being exceptionally true to himself for it is generally agreed that he could never shut up.

Salvator Rosa is famous for inventing a new kind of landscape in the seventeenth century in which nature becomes thrillingly wild. He was a master of the plunging gorge and the portentous sky, of hair-raising cliffs and lightning-struck trees in forests infested with hermits. In the centuries after his death, his art became such a byword for extreme nature that the writer Horace Walpole only had to cite his name to sum up the horror of crossing the Alps: 'Precipices, mountains, torrents, wolves, rumblings – Salvator Rosa.' An artist for whom nature is all emotion and turmoil, nothing like the well-ordered Edens of his rival Claude Lorrain, Rosa has come to seem a true proto-Romantic and his self-portrait as a doom-dark soul, alone against the gathering clouds, seems both to prefigure and parody what is commonly imagined to be the typical Romantic self-portrait.

In fact, it is a one-off, a most singular performance, and as original in its outrageous way as Rosa's other compositions. For he painted *portrait*-shaped vistas, where the eye is led up and down the picture and not from side to side, as is intuitive with landscapes. Rosa would split pictures in two, show towering scenes from way down below, plunge half a landscape into visible darkness. He aimed to disorientate, to strike the mind's eye and very often to put across a searing moral message as well. And so it is with this stern self-portrait: the artist instructs you to show stoic restraint (put up or shut up is the subtext here), while bearing down on you like a vast black crag.

You see Rosa from just below the waist rising steeply to the peak of his hat. He is the dominant – indeed the only – feature in this landscape. There is no ground, no foliage, nothing to tell you where he might be standing, only this powerful shape silhouetted against the darkening sky, face pale as the moon at midnight. The viewpoint requires you to look up to the artist and like a mountain he blocks the way, standing sentry over the space of his lofty painting. This is not the picture as a window freely opening on to another world but something more like an impasse. There is no going beyond this point.

It is amusing to learn that this smouldering loner was in real life a terrific comic actor and satirist, a lively poet and musician, a bon viveur whose house was once described as 'an abode of mirth and the marketplace of gaiety'.

Never mind keeping silent, Rosa held salons, wrote magnificently self-regarding letters and lengthy plays mocking his professional rivals. It seems he even had to relocate from Rome to Florence after insulting the theatrical productions of his more powerful contemporary Bernini. Insisting upon his own artistic independence, he was an unusually free spirit for his times who seldom met deadlines and always selected his own subjects. 'I do not paint for money but for my own satisfaction,' he informed one dispirited patron, 'so you must allow me to be carried away by the power of my raptures, and to wield my brushes only at a time when I feel myself to be ravished.'[1]

The rock star pose goes with the cult of Salvator, as he used to be known. A century after his death Rosa would become what Caravaggio is to our day, a genius with a mysterious past. He came from Naples, city of dangerous shadows, and had a reputation for recklessness cherished by the aristocrats who bought his wild landscapes. There were stories of running away with roving bandits as a teenager, serving in the Neapolitan Death Squad during the Spanish invasion and joining the bandits all over again in middle age.[2] As John Constable sourly remarked, 'Salvator Rosa is a great favourite with the novel writers, particularly the ladies.'

Rosa's self-portrait is tightly plotted, word to character to backdrop. He presents himself as the embodiment of his own lines, tight-lipped in the face of fortune's storms, playing the part of the silent Stoic (his chosen philosophy) to the extent he looks fit to burst. And if you didn't know that he was, in fact, quite unable to contain himself, that he seems to have put up with very little that did not suit him in life, you might also infer a knowing element of humour, after all a man holding up a placard that effectively says don't say anything at all is performing, at the very least, a sight gag.

A true Stoic, believing that silence is golden, might approve of painting's ability to address us without ever speaking louder than silence; a true Stoic rises above the temporal world. Although he may have an eye on the ladies, and this self-portrait thrilled them even when reduced to a modest black and white print, Rosa does not simply come on like a matinee idol. He takes his position very seriously, drawing himself up and away from this buzzing world, taking a stand as a crag of a man alone beneath the shelterless sky.

———

Where do you stand? What is your position? Life's questions apply to art. To be seen in a self-portrait is to make an appearance; to make an appearance involves striking an attitude, arranging a face, holding the two together (or showing them wilfully opposed). The body takes on the language of thought and belief as much as the face, even when the pose is only half-conscious.

People in portraits may hope to hold their own, to choose their own stance, but they are far less free than artists in self-portraits. Ingres, for instance, was a despot with his sitters, agonizing for months over the pose for each portrait (years in the case of Madame Moitessier, finger to temple, impassive as marble). But when it came to painting himself, he simply sat in a chair, slightly angled to avoid head-on confrontation, a choice evidently made in moments.

The narrowness of that choice – standing versus sitting, angled versus frontal, painting or at ease – is implicit in the limitation of the pose. Ingres is not trying to draw more attention to himself than his own reputation deserves (though he has taken the precaution of wearing his *Croix de Légion d'honneur*). He would not dream of putting on a performance. But there are self-portraits in

Self-Portrait, c. 1670

Gerard ter Borch
(1617–81)

which the position, the *disposition*, of the body is as carefully considered as the framing of a film star or the blocking of an actor on stage. It is surely no coincidence that the makers of such images, thinking so much about the relationship between figure and ground, are often the most theatrically inventive of all self-portraitists. Seventeenth-century painters in particular tend to have a very strong sense of self-portraiture precisely as a form of theatre and few more so than the Dutch artist Gerard ter Borch in a tantalizing painting made around 1670, in which the rectangle of the picture is a proscenium frame for the actor who presents himself right at the front of the stage.

The house is shadowy except for a pool of light to the fore. Standing back from this glow, but with one foot forward, is the enigmatic figure of the painter, his face slightly averted, body entirely concealed to the knees in an obliterating black silk cloak. The face, on the far rim of this pool, expresses an intrigued ambivalence that the hands and arms can neither confirm nor deny, being hidden beneath this cloak.

Everything depends upon that foot in its black satin shoe, defining the stage, edging into the limelight. The positioning of this foot is the crux of the performance, where all its drama is focused. A bull's hoof pawing the ground in anticipation, a dancer poised to begin, or waiting for applause, ter Borch's foot is static but it signals imminent or concluding motion. The black ribbons sharply articulated again the pale floor, the position somewhere between ballet's open third and a courtly dance step, the foot acts as a pictorial fuse leading the eye all the way up the noble line of the leg to the riddle of the artist's face. No hands, no arms, no gestures, lips sealed and only this one pointed toe: what a *coup de théâtre*.

Ter Borch is standing back in relation to the picture plane, which might in this case be imagined as the limit of the stage, but he is also taking half a step towards the viewer: approaching, but in retreat. This reticence is a pose, of course, as if he was contemplating some confidential stage whisper; and since the self-portrait is smaller than life the effect is to make the performance even more intimate. The position of the foot, nearly breaching the edge of the picture-stage, suggests that we are all in the same space, separated only by footlights.

Ter Borch is balanced between here and there, one foot in and one foot out of the light. The pose pulls both ways, sustaining an equal tension between the two in an act of perfect brinkmanship. He appears, but his appearance is a teasing mystery; you do not get to know him.

What this pose declares (other than its own suave calculation) is the emphatic presumption of an audience. The artist comes forward to make your acquaintance, but stands deliberately back from you too: your presence is doubly confirmed. In its small way, ter Borch's self-portrait turns on the idea of a spatial continuity between the picture and the world outside it explicitly proposed by Van Eyck's *The Arnolfini Portrait*, which ter Borch surely saw during the years he spent at the court of Philip IV of Spain. At any rate, his recoil is as rhetorical as in most self-portraits that wish to make public overtures without quite appearing to do so.

For self-portraits must admit that some kind of show is involved, must acknowledge their audience; or try to deny it by blocking the viewer. This ought to be easy, but absolute denial is surprisingly hard to pull off. A turned back is too resistant an attitude, resistance once again implying an audience to be resisted, although there is a double-portrait that almost achieves it by that mysterious Danish master, Vilhelm Hammershøi, which shows the artist from the rear looking at his equally secretive wife on the other side of the table. The scene is still but not serene. The conversation has stalled if it ever started. The table is pointedly empty and the artist seems more certain of the pristine folds of the cloth than Ida Hammershøi herself, who is painted in a hazier register. He has moved a little sideways so we may view her too, with her downcast eyes, but his slightly hunched pose implies drawing as much as observation. If one could only see over his shoulder, perhaps her likeness would be lying there on the table — and sure enough, in turn, one understands that she is posing; posing within Hammershøi's averted self-portrait.

In fact, frontality may be the best way of disregarding the viewer, no matter how counterintuitive this sounds, the full-frontal pose having such immediacy of address, such potential for intimacy. There is a clear attraction between a front-facing picture and a front-facing viewer; everything looks even, nothing is tugging our eyes away from the symmetry of picture or face, from their mutual, perceptual centre. Frontality is persuasive; it is a pose that implies candour. And yet it may be the least intimate for the viewer. Think of Dürer's 1500 self-portrait where everything is displayed all at once, a maximum frontage that gives the eye nowhere to relax. Dürer does not invite an exchange; he blocks the viewer.

A maddening number of poses common to portraiture have to be avoided in self-portraiture lest they present the artist as too open or smug, or just too eager to please. Legs comfortably crossed in an armchair facing front; lolling back with a finger raised to one's cheek; easing forward as if in conversation: self-portraits tend to shun them all. But there is one brave seventeenth-century soul who does not care how sociable he seems and he is the Italian painter Sassoferrato, an artist now mainly forgotten except for a self-portrait in which he leans forward with extraordinary candour.

Sassoferrato specialized in religious paintings of great sweetness that were so pure and simple they scarcely looked Baroque even to his peers; so little was known of his life that within decades of his death he was even thought to have been a contemporary of Raphael. But he was once famous enough to have had his own trademark colour, Sassoferrato blue, and it is against this luminous hue that he appears, head and shoulders inclining towards the viewer with such attentiveness he might be listening deferentially to your views before venturing his.

That blue is Sassoferrato's true colour, lucid as the artist himself, his honest face with its burden of cares turned to the world with unqualified frankness. He is at home in his picture, open for viewing, and to modern eyes cannot help looking modern himself, outgoing, engaged, with the immediate appeal of his camera-age pose. This sense of modernity is supported by the expanse of blue that represents nothing but itself, not the usual Old Master backdrop of drapery or wall, but an element of the picture given almost as much weight as the face itself: in effect, an abstract painting. In the long corridors of the Uffizi collection Sassoferrato stands out, communicating with such simple directness. Remove the old-world collar, and he could be one of us.

Sassoferrato achieves with his stance the projection of a social self that others have to spell out with props as well as gestures — Jan Steen raising a glass

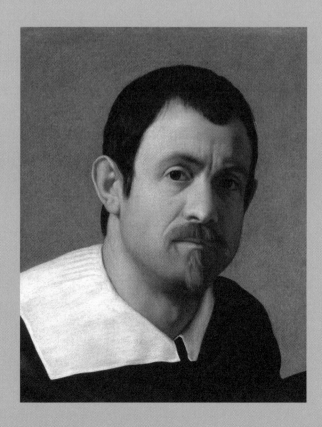

Self-Portrait, c. 1650

Giovanni Battista Salvi
da Sassoferrato
(1609–85)

of Dutch beer to our health; the American artist Charles Willson Peale drawing back a curtain to admit us to his private museum; Giacomo Balla, the Italian Futurist, raising a convivial espresso in his *Autocaffe*.

These painters go for broke. They acknowledge with their full being that self-portraiture is mostly an out-turned art. There may be artists who trouble to represent themselves entirely for their own purposes, or because they are sick or hospitalized or incarcerated, yet even *in extremis* they are probably hoping for at least one other viewer. Dürer drew himself naked specifically for a doctor's diagnosis; the Scottish painter John Bellany, in hospital for heart surgery, wrote messages to the medical staff all over his self-portraits; Courbet and Schiele both painted themselves alone in the cells as political martyrdoms, a public record for the future. But still it is rare to see the most sociable sign of engagement, other than a direct glance, that one person may make to another in life enter the art of self-portraiture.

Self-Portrait wearing a Jabot, c. 1751

Maurice Quentin de la Tour (1704–88)

A smile – a full-beam, gregarious, unqualified smile, a smile that angles for a smile in return – is an event so unexpected that its occurrence is not unlike the very thing portrayed: a real turn-up, sudden as laughter. A smile in a portrait is not such a surprise; less than usual but hardly uncommon. The mystique of the *Mona Lisa* depends entirely on the interpretation of that half-raised hint and between her tepid warmth and the *Laughing Cavalier's* humorous glint lies a considerable spectrum of smiles. But if smiles can have almost as many characters as people in portraits, then why does self-portraiture take such a dim view of smiling? For there is no doubt that some artists look as though they would rather die of lockjaw.

Not among them and perhaps the most exceptional smiler of all is the Frenchman Maurice Quentin de La Tour, a portraitist for whom the life and soul of any human being, and most especially himself, are quite naturally expressed in the smile. La Tour has no qualms about smiling, never worries that it might be thought frivolous or conceited. Where other artists make heavy weather of portraying themselves, he takes the task lightly and seems to have produced more glad-faced self-portraits than any other artist.

The best and brightest is the 1751 *Self-Portrait Wearing a Jabot*. La Tour was forty-seven and overwhelmed by work but presents himself as irrepressibly youthful. His eyes spark directly with yours, his face is as fresh as his lace jabot and his smile as clear as a cloudless morning.

The pose is beautifully balanced between stillness and swagger, a backward tilt that implies forward motion, like a rider at ease on a moving horse or a dancer in mid-sashay; he could have been leaving but instead he is staying, pausing for the pleasure of your company. But the smile is his crowning glory. It is not a sidelong smirk or a simper but delicately done, the mouth just widening a little, the corners turning lightly upwards and the eyes in intelligent accord. It lifts and it is uplifting, a smile to raise the spirits.

What reasons did La Tour have to be quite so cheerful? Perhaps, if nothing else, an unembarrassed delight in having accomplished this nearly life-sized image entirely in pastel. Pastel suits the character of his art, tactile, vivacious and suave, and above all it gives him (and his sitters) immediate and continuing presence. Which is just what he has in this self-portrait, an eighteenth-century man behaving as if there were no barrier of time or place or illusion between us, posing, smiling, presenting himself more than two hundred and fifty years ago as if he lived in the age of the photo.

The smile is the charm that speeds up time, because what he is doing is not yet over. As long as he continues to smile, La Tour is still making overtures. A good smile sends its signal in your direction and is received, back and forth, in unbroken transmission; and even though it is not real but depicted, this smile makes the same connection. Someone is smiling at you, a direct acknowledgement of your presence right now, an action that implies the moment before, when the face was straight, and the moment afterwards when it will once again fall. Looking may carry some of these effects, but not with quite the same sense of . narrative intensity. A smile is the measure of its own brief excursion, a short drama, a little time out of time before everything returns to normal.

————

Anyone wondering why self-portraits look as they do, how or what they seek to communicate, can hardly help starting with expression. It is the first thing we look for in the faces of other people and we do it well and instinctively. We bring the same sensitivity to painted faces too, irresistibly deducing character from expression, but of course they have no power to express anything through movement. They cannot carry on communicating through successive inflections, so to speak, and indeed the fact that they cannot speak means that they lack that most dynamic of facial repertoires, the characteristic expressions that accompany speech.

Facial expressions in narrative art have enhanced privileges; they can correspond with the action and be interpreted or intensified through it. Facial expressions in portraits often tally with pose, dress, props and setting in something like the same way and they generally live by role-playing conventions in any case – the king's regal stare, the pensive gravity of the scholar or cleric, the child's playful glee – of which the most common is dignified formality. Marked facial expressions are rare in portraiture, often because of social etiquette. Imagine the studio session in which a sitter presents the artist with (still less wants to pay for) a leer, a disgusted frown, a bewildered or irritable stare.

Alone in the studio, self-portraitists do not have to prepare a face in response to somebody else and it shows in the many faces that express not much more than working absorption, self-absorption or neutrality. There is nobody else around, no need to adjust or react and even when an artist has a public audience in mind he may go for concealment or denial. None of us wants to expose ourselves completely to strangers, after all, and the border between what we reveal and what we do not is one of the most important attributes of our common humanity. It would be terrible if we could read each other's minds: 'All we communicate to another individual,' wrote the sociologist Georg Simmel, 'by means of words or in another fashion – even the most subjective, impulsive, initimate matters – is a selection from that psychological-real whole whose absolutely exact report would drive everybody into the insane asylum.'[3]

So what can one acceptably reveal from the tropical undergrowth that is one's self? It is surprising just how far artists sometimes appear to go. Take the Expressionists, of whom a lack of inhibition might reasonably be expected. They pull faces, sure enough: Oscar Kokoschka is harrowed, Egon Schiele

tortured and contorted, Max Beckmann bears the world on his well-dressed shoulders. The Expressionists look anguished, persecuted, tense; it is their look; it becomes their convention.

These artists were all serial self-portraitists and yet they display a comparatively narrow range of expression; no question of forcing a smile. One chooses one's mask and one lives with it, whether one is an eighteenth-century conformist or a twentieth-century dissenter.

But is this how we really live? Don't we study the faces of others all the time on the lookout for new expressions, or for the reassurance of seeing old ones resurface in revealing contexts; or in hope of spotting an unfamiliar or transitional look, certainly believing we will see something more profound than a mask. And don't we sense all these different faces in ourselves?

Of course, there is a danger of oversimplification when it comes to expression, as if character can be read in the face, as phrenologists claimed it could be read in the shape of the head. Expression may not be so transparent. For every person who senses sorrow and resignation in Rembrandt's late self-portraits there will be others who insist that he shows nothing but battle-scarred pride, and this ambiguity is the peak of his art. The many shades of nuance in a Rembrandt self-portrait are exactly what deepen one's sense of the artist.

To paint an expression that is not pinned down, not finite, is exceptionally hard. Even Rembrandt, in a little etching of himself smiling, ends with a dead expression. He was working out the physiognomy muscle by muscle, smiling by numbers, to make a crib for himself and his students and it shows that one cannot easily sustain, much less depict, an expression to order.

Joseph Ducreux, La Tour's only pupil, painted 'character' self-portraits in which he puts on a variety show of expressions. Popular in their day, they now seem about as amusing as pie-throwing clowns and induce the same physical discomfort. In one of them, *Self-Portrait as a Mocker*, Ducreux grins and points in your direction as if you were a complete idiot. But the scoffing turns back on the scoffer. The smirk is horrendous, as wooden as the teeth, and though he is meant to look facetious what you really notice is the struggle involved in grinning hard enough to get that lip-curling look while also baring one's teeth. Taken to its extreme, in one of Messerschmidt's bronze heads, a rising guffaw can be completely unbearable. You know this particular expression, a perfectly innocent laugh building up, fit to burst, and recognize its progress through the muscles quite instinctively from your own experience, the lifting, folding, stretching, the pinning back of the cheeks and so on. But a rising laugh is a *changing* face, its essence is mobility. To see it like this, forever immobilized in a terrible metal rictus, is to see the familiar turned alien.

Naturalness is as crucial here in art as in life and the slightest hint of artifice suggests insincerity. It can turn a frown into a stone mask or make a smile look so brittle you feel it could shatter any moment, as in the Disney denouement where Tom runs smack into the frying pan held up by Jerry and his teeth drop out, one after the other, tinkling to the floor like glass.

Early on his career, the Australian sculptor Ron Mueck made a gigantic figure of his own fierce face in silicone. Three feet of glowering frown, from

Mask, 1997

Ron Mueck (1958–)

knotted brow to five o'clock shadow, it is super-real down to the very last bristle. It does not invite your touch – sculptures seldom do, an odd aspect of the genre – and is deliberately made to repel. This head, called *Mask*, looks astoundingly lifelike from its slight sheen of sweat to its receding follicles, but more than that it has intimidating force of personality. Even at point-blank range, where the illusion could so easily waver, and even at this improbable scale, it radiates blazing fury.

Mueck made the work to find out how he came across to others, specifically his two little daughters. He had so often seen shock, but also amusement, in their expressions when he was impotently trying to shout them into bed at night that he wondered how his own large face actually appeared to these smaller people. It is a sculpture in the spirit of Robert Burns's mordant address 'To a Louse on Seeing One on a Lady's Bonnet at Church'. Watching this detested pest crawling on a hapless beauty in the pew in front, Burns realizes that she has no sense of its presence; 'O wad some Power the giftie gie us / To see oursels as ithers see us!' Mueck's *Mask* is a joke against himself, a big lug who should pick on someone his own size.

Sculpted self-portraits, as a rule, have difficulty coming up with anything but the stoniest of expressions. It is even worth asking why sculptors go to the length of making three-dimensional self-portraits when two dimensions would be so much simpler; the eyes can be minutely inflected, the expression endlessly adjusted, whereas with marble, say, one false move and you have to start over. Of course sculptors have unusual advantages. They can make monuments of themselves, sacrificing painting's intimacy and animation to gain eternal authority. In Antonio Canova's self-made museum in Italy a white neo-classical bust of the artist stands by the altar, larger than life, with tousled locks and eyes on the skies; *per ardua ad astra*, code for immortality. Denmark's most famous sculptor, Bertel Thorvaldsen, stands tall in his marble monument, a large man with a face like thunder, chest bare beneath the robe that clings to his biceps as if fondling their strength. He leans on an economy-sized edition of one of his own greatest hits, the *Goddess of Hope*, she looking one way, he looking the other as if in a marital sulk. The self-portrait was a figurehead, a gift for the nation on Thorvaldsen's return from Rome after decades of international success. He agreed to return only on condition that the government build a museum to house several hundred more of his works.

There is a self-portrait by the French sculptor Jean-Baptiste Pigalle that manages to achieve expressive life, modelled in terracotta. The lips are parted as if pausing in speech or drawing breath, the eyes and head swivel slightly to the left, the forehead and cheeks are prematurely furrowed – Pigalle was about sixty – with exhaustion. The face is quick with intelligence, rapidly made with the fingertips, and even the eyeballs have a frisson of motion achieved with darting dabs.

Everything about it opposes the characteristic weight and stasis of sculpture.

Pigalle was an Enlightenment intellectual and his portraits of the Encyclopaedists – especially his friend Diderot – are all about the pursuit of genuine expression. In the case of his startling sculpture of a naked though smiling Voltaire, his emaciated shanks covered by nothing more than a scroll of writing (what else?), Pigalle literally attempted the bare truth. But he found the sculpting of portraits so difficult, Diderot says, 'that he never made one without being tempted to give up'.

———

Artists frown upon smiling for the same reason that they avoid so many other unambiguous expressions in self-portraits. They do not want to appear attention-seeking; they do not want to be limited to one emotion; they do not want to make the same demands upon the viewer that such expressions impose in real life. Perhaps they actually have no explicit designs on other people.

Pose, in this respect, is never as dangerous as expression. To perform as if to an unseen audience is one thing; after all, a self-portrait, like a portrait, is essentially a flat figure in a box which must somehow be brought to life by whatever means. But it is quite another thing for the artist to wink, as it were, at that audience. The self-portraits of Elisabeth Vigée-Le Brun are expressly made for

Self-Portrait, 1790

Élisabeth Vigée-Le Brun (1755–1842)

this purpose, congeniality their unique selling point, intimacy their aim. They are the painted equivalent of advertisements that address the customer, coyly, as 'you'.

A consummate professional who never missed an opportunity to set herself before the world – especially between portrait commissions – Vigée-Le Brun didn't just paint herself smiling over and again, she made duplicates for her admirers. There are many self-portraits and they are all quite obvious attempts to win people's hearts. She appears dressed as the bosomy woman from Rubens's sultry *Chapeau de Paille*, which gets the goat of feminist critics. She smiles as she works on a painting of Marie-Antoinette, as well she might since royalty always helped to attract a better class of clients. She smiles sweetly, modestly, with her mouth open and in artlessly disarrayed muslin, and the idea is that every appearance should look winningly natural. For naturalness is her style – the loose frocks, the unpowdered hair that she liked to arrange herself, the informal hats, the off-duty poses with her charming daughter. Vigée-Le Brun invented a look, a look that Marie-Antoinette herself is said to have taken up, and she promoted it through her self-portraits.

And though hers is a doll's smile, china teeth and pink lips, it looks right for this particular style of painting; for Vigée-Le Brun's natural look is, of course, highly artificial, a blend of rococo sugariness and neo-classical purity. As with all those other professions that specialize in appearances – hairdressing, make-up, fashion, the styling of the photographic shoot – 'natural' is just another contrivance and it is possible that her cheerfulness was put on too. Vigée-Le Brun was a tremendously hard worker whose career in France was twice ended by politics – during the French Revolution she fled abroad; returning later to France, she was forced out of her livelihood by the Prussians in 1814. The epitaph she wrote for her grave is remarkably self-serving but nonetheless very likely true: '*Ici, enfin, je repose.*'

Vigée-Le Brun's smile turned heads. It made the self-portrait a social event. Dropping decorum, abandoning the rules, she did not even try to pretend that her self-portraits had no designs on the viewer. Her smile says you are there and I am here so why not let us have a dalliance. She makes explicit what other artists generally prefer to conceal, if they think of it at all, which is that self-portraits are more often than not made with a public in view. As for her own self-portraits, they are just a means to an end; the medium, not the message. Vigée-Le Brun, one feels, would always have preferred to appear in person.

Chapter Ten

Stage Fright

'No description is as difficult as the description of self.'

Michel de Montaigne

Self-Portrait, c. 1815

Sir Henry Raeburn (1726–1853)

T he man in the picture is trying to hold himself together but he looks closer to falling apart. It wouldn't take much, just a slight lapse of concentration on his part, or an unkind shove, and the elaborate pose he is struggling so hard to maintain would instantly come unstuck. It is not meant to be a pose; the idea is to appear perfectly natural: the artist as a pensive person in a characteristic moment of reflection. Not straining to bring forth a thought, like Rodin's *Thinker*, fist clamped to agonized brow; not brooding on being and nothingness, just looking back at you in quiet contemplation, finger and thumb lightly touching the chin as he gathers himself to a point.

If only that was how Sir Henry Raeburn's self-portrait had turned out. It certainly started that way, with a fine clear image of the intelligent face and a steady flow of light to the forehead. The traces are still there and the light is still upon him but Raeburn changed his mind over time, revising and reworking until the face, and the paint, grew uneasy and hesitant. As for the pose, he kept on trying to get it right day after day until he had muddled it into disaster.

To say that this was not like him is mere understatement. Raeburn was the great portraitist of Enlightenment Scotland. He painted only portraits and more than a thousand of them – lairds in their tartan costumes, lowland gentry with their wives and children, advocates and scientists, philosophers and divines, the Edinburgh intelligentsia who gathered at his New Town studio. He was called the Scottish Velázquez, the Scottish Van Dyck. He was known for the vitality of his faces, his gift for illumination and harmonies of colour, his inventive and graceful poses. So how could a portraitist of such accomplishment be so blocked by the one sitter he presumably knew best, saw every day in his studio?

Perhaps Raeburn was stumped by the arms. It would have been so much easier if he had just let his hands rest in his lap, or restricted himself to the head and shoulders. The raised right arm looks completely artificial, a prosthetic limb or a hand on a stick manipulated by some offstage joker. Propping the chin, but numb to sensation, those false fingers cannot help parodying the seriousness of the gesture; the other hand, supposedly flexed to bear the weight of an elbow, is an empty glove. But the arms are weightless in any case, jointless and deboned, and where they begin is a mystery since Raeburn hasn't managed to give himself shoulders. Nothing fits or fuses and the body is so awkwardly assembled, piece by piece, that the separate parts remain uselessly disconnected.

Yet this is the Henry Raeburn he laboured to portray: an enlightened thinker, at one with the intellectuals he painted, which happens to be exactly how he looked, they said, whenever he stood back from the easel. People often remarked on Raeburn's professional habits – nine to five, three or four sitters a day, four to five sittings for each head, starting with the nose and mouth; no preliminary drawing and no need of a maulstick because his hand was so steady. He talked as he painted, but stopped to step back. This is the Raeburn familiar to the novelist Walter Scott from many sittings: 'I see him, in my mind's eye, with his hand under his chin, contemplating his picture, which position always brought me in mind of a figure of Jupiter.'[1]

If this was just how he stood, so many times a day, a position he naturally adopted, how could it become so awkward and foreign when he tried to describe it on canvas? All sorts of errors and alterations are visible in his portrait. He tried to mask them with brown bitumen, supposed to give a dramatic glow as it dried, but now turned an obliterating black. He tried shifting the image as it sat in the frame, literally rotating the canvas several degrees clockwise so that the figure sagged less to one side, but this only threw greater emphasis on the faults.

Another artist might have given up, but Raeburn was driven by a particular purpose. Famous as he was in Scotland, he still longed for the approval of London and felt so remote from the hub that he begged his compatriot David Wilkie, who had settled there, to write at least once a year with news 'of what is going on among the artists, for I do assure you I have as little communication with any of them as if I was living at the Cape of Good Hope'.

For twenty years Raeburn sent paintings down to the Royal Academy's annual exhibitions and heard next to nothing in return. He wanted to become an Academician without pushing himself forward – 'if they choose to elect me without solicitation it will be the more honourable' – but since no one else seemed to be pressing his case he was forced to wait, and to wait. In 1815, at the age of almost sixty, he was at last considered for membership. An exemplary work was required and the self-portrait was Raeburn's submission: a portrait painter simultaneously representing himself and his gifts. Perhaps he thought it customary down South; perhaps he just thought it an apt conceit. But either way, Raeburn had misunderstood the regulations.

All the protracted misery of painting this self-portrait, trying to sum himself up, trying to find a self of suitable stature to present to London, having to demonstrate his worth yet again after all these years, and possibly with a diffident man's dread of imposing his own image on the public – all of it culminated in instant rejection. Self-portraits were not accepted in the category of portraits. The Royal Academy wrote back requesting 'as early as convenient some other specimen of his talents'.[2] Raeburn need never have painted himself at all, and it seems the challenge was beyond him for it was the worst likeness he ever painted.

––––––––––

Raeburn lived and worked through a revolution in British portraiture, when it was hoisted from the very bottom right up through the hierarchy of genres until painting portraits became almost as respectable as painting Christ or the

Rape of the Sabines. Had he moved to London in his twenties, like Wilkie, instead of visiting once or twice and then retreating home, he would have faced aggressive competition. His contemporaries would have included George Romney, whose portraits were the epitome of Regency style and who worked ten hours a day, seven days a week, to keep up with demand at his studio near Oxford Circus; Thomas Gainsborough, who liberated portraiture from the old 'licked' style of emollient smoothness, and gave it an improvisational flourish that could put a spring in any step and lend allure to the beefiest duchess; and Joshua Reynolds, enthroned in Pall Mall, with his exclusive clientele of Whig grandees and all the famous actors, intellectuals and celebrities of his day; Reynolds, who made it seem absolutely normal to include himself in the social Who's Who, the cast of notable figures to be portrayed and displayed every year for the benefit of the lower orders at the Royal Academy.

Painters who spend their lives studying other people must surely have a head start when it comes to themselves since they already know how to pose a figure, show a face in the best light, combine a subtle essay on the private self with a telling public image. Reynolds seems to make the case for this new age of faces – an artist who slips effortlessly between portraiture and self-portraiture, prolific in both, seeming to see only the affinities and never the troubling distinctions. Yet Reynolds turns out to be the exception; exceptional

in finding so many excuses for painting self-portraits, and in being on such good terms with himself, and the public, in these extrovert paintings.

Sir Thomas Lawrence, Reynolds's follower in so many other respects, resisted all requests from the Uffizi to send a self-portrait and only showed one at the Royal Academy because the king required it. The image is painted with a palpable reluctance as if Lawrence thought the whole practice self-serving, and when not unreasonably accused of making himself look morose, he spat back: 'You would surely not have a man look smirkingly at himself in a glass; and you seem to forget what an irksome task it is to me.'

Gainsborough had such an antagonistic history with the Royal Academy that his self-portrait was only displayed there two decades after his death, following diplomatic discussions with his daughter. It is hard to believe that he wouldn't have been irritated by the supposed honour in any case, because he had left strict instructions 'that after my decease no plaster cast, model or likeness whatever be permitted to be taken'[3] and that if he were to be posthumously represented it should only be by a modest engraving based on a late self-portrait oil sketch. He had long since grown resentful of 'phizmongering' as he derisively called his profession and here he looks shrewdly undeceived. To those who knew him well, to his correspondents, that sly swivel of the eye might have conjured Gainsborough's quick-witted intelligence in an instant; and that was the point of the painting. It wasn't a public performance, but an intimate communication, dashed off like a letter for his friend the composer Carl Friedrich Abel.

George Romney never painted a public self-portrait and could not have viewed himself less smirkingly in the mirror. Depressive, withdrawn, pathologically secretive, with a dread of criticism and 'aspen nerves that every breath could ruffle', Romney recoiled from London society.[4] He may have painted its faces every day, and with a sense of touch not equalled among his contemporaries, but at night he had another life as a visionary Romantic and the drawings he produced, so fluent, free and disturbing – nightmarish figments, figures dragged backwards or leaping forwards in teeming whirlwinds that likely inspired William Blake – seem to have been his true preoccupation.

Some see traces of Romney's own face in these drawings, oblique or densely encrypted. But he did paint self-portraits and one of them is the antithesis of all his other portraits not least because it is deliberately incomplete. The artist slumps back in a chair, arms defensively crossed, face turned to the viewer with a look of piercing, unappeasable honesty. The daylight eye has no illusions; the night eye glares out of the darkness. Only the head is finished, an intense concentration of suspicion and combative intelligence. A kindly patron once wondered why Romney 'whose pencil had delicately flattered so many faces, did not seem to think himself entitled to be commonly civil to his own'. The question contains its own answer; one might lie about everyone else, but one could never lie to oneself. As for the rest of the canvas, except for a few cursory gestures it is shockingly empty. The head was all that mattered. It too was painted for a like-minded friend: Romney didn't have to be polite or presentable.

––––––––

We imagine that the self-portraitist (as opposed to the portraitist) has all kinds of unfair advantages: self-knowledge, a lifetime's experience of arranging one's looks to face the world, a far greater familiarity with them than anyone else. Yet who is to say whether those of us who spend our days with artists couldn't produce a better likeness of them, if only we had the necessary skills? Manet's self-portrait, so out of touch with himself, for instance, is a wavering question mark compared with Henri Fantin-Latour's portrait of a crisp dandy with top hat and cane. We are very clear what other people look like, but which of us has a firm grasp of our own appearance, let alone our inner self?

Self-portraits made for public consumption ought to have some force of conviction if their object is to demonstrate professional standing. The show mustn't falter, there must be no scent of doubt to unsettle the audience. As in life, as in theatre, the confidence of the performance is paramount: if this artist does not appear to believe in himself then why should anybody else?

But reluctance can be precisely the look an artist wishes to achieve and may even be the crux of the image. Titian wishes to be gone. Poussin recoils. The American painter Mary Cassatt, leaning back against a table in a stark diagonal that flouts the usual up-down axis, and giving us nothing more than her profile, appears so indifferent to the viewer and stares so intently to the right that she almost manages to reverse the proposition of a portrait. She is not asking to be seen, but for you to look elsewhere. Everything that really matters, Cassatt implies, is going on in the wings.

These paintings are all making pre-emptive declarations of reluctance, and turning it quite deliberately to visual and even social advantage. But there are less conscious kinds of unease that an artist may try, and fail, to conceal when a definitive self-portrait is required; just the pressure of having to account for oneself to an unknown public and with limited means of address; or a growing disillusion with the idea that whatever one is can ever be represented. This does not need to be an identity crisis, it may simply be an accumulation of inner doubts or distractions. 'For my part,' writes the philosopher David Hume, Raeburn's Edinburgh contemporary, 'when I enter most intimately into what I call myself, I always stumble on some particular perception or other, of heat or cold, love or hatred, pain or pleasure ... I can never catch myself at any time without a perception, and never can observe anything but the perception ... If anyone, upon serious and unprejudiced reflection, thinks he has a different notion of himself, I must confess that I can no longer reason with him. He may, perhaps, perceive something simple and continued which he calls himself; though I am certain that there is no such principle in me.'[5]

We take self-portraits for granted, but we shouldn't. Many artists would never think of portraying themselves and view the prospect with suspicion or horror. Others wouldn't dream of volunteering for such a potentially painful ordeal and only submit to it to oblige a patron, fulfil a commission, keep up professional, or social, appearances.

John Singer Sargent, asked to present his self-portrait to the Uffizi, performed the exercise with glacial detachment. Although he was in Italy at the time, and hung a mirror from a tree so that he could work outdoors in the early summer heat, he might as well have been back home in London, shuttered against an English winter, such is the *froideur* of the portrait. It is just another Sargent, a portrait of himself as one of his own clients, those lawyers and bankers and unapologetically imperious plutocrats who wished to have their power recorded for posterity. Correctness of dress and bearing are all, and the expression is only remarkable for revealing so little.

But even just to say so little takes a certain resolve, a refusal to listen to the whole background noise of one's inner existence; an indifference to the opportunity seized by other artists to address the public, or ingratiate themselves with society. Sargent has all the poise and conviction required of a society 'paughtrait', as he witheringly called them, always threatening to abandon the face-painting racket, but that is exactly what he makes of himself – a man at a gathering, clam-shut, disaffected, bored to death by the company, but fastidiously presentable and polite.

Some artists cannot quite make themselves go through with the whole performance. Jean-Baptiste-Camille Corot, in his Uffizi self-portrait, hovers anxiously on the threshold, every inch of his calico painting smock beautifully turned out but the face hesitant, unfinished, not brought to clear resolution. Shyness, or reticence, or an inability to sum himself up is there in the painting, as if he is being asked to say more than he can. The pressures on a public self-portrait can induce paralysing self-consciousness, a fear of being misunderstood, perhaps, or confused with some other kind of person because one failed to give an accurate representation of oneself; rather like stammering, or gabbling, or falling mute when asked to speak for yourself in unfamiliar or hostile circumstances. John Updike, in 'Getting the Words Out',[8] writes about the speech impediment that trips him up among strangers: 'There seems so much about me to explain ... that when freshly encountering, say, a bored and hurried electrician over the telephone, my voice tends to seize up ... Who I am seems impossibly complicated and unobvious.' The need to represent oneself as fully as possible, as immediately as possible, and without any hope of succeeding, produces an instant stutter. A stutter which disappears at public readings where 'the audience has voluntarily assembled to view and audit the persona within which I am comfortable'.[6]

A stammer, of course, as Updike suggests, may be subconscious honesty, and so it seems in the case of a late self-portrait by the German painter Anton Raphael Mengs. Mengs, exact contemporary of Reynolds, was colossally famous in his own day and is entirely forgotten in ours. In each case the reasons are the same – he painted large neo-classical allegories full of depilated nymphs and upper-class deities that his contemporaries thought unsurpassed in their moral and aesthetic beauty, but which we now regard as deadly academic.

Mengs was one of Goya's predecessors as First Painter to the King of Spain. He had performed the same role for the Elector of Saxony and for a decade held court at his own studio in Rome. Egged on by his great apologist, the art historian Johann Joachim Winckelmann, whose influence was then unchallenged, Mengs stumbled through a long series of overwrought paintings and even issued an almost classically boring handbook, his *Thoughts on Beauty*, at one time published in every major European language. But it seems as though he was burdened by other people's ambitions for him even from the day he was born; Mengs's father named him both Anton, after Correggio, and Raphael, hoping he would somehow continue the line of genius.

Reynolds, in a devastating dismissal published after Mengs's death, accurately prophesied total obscurity within a few years. But during his life Mengs was so popular that he was repeatedly asked to paint portraits of himself. Without exception they are stiff and hopelessly artificial, so weak they hardly seem to cling to the canvas. But there is one, painted for the Earl of Cowper in 1774, that turned out to be unexpectedly moving and expressive.

Mengs is wearing working clothes, a humble jacket and scarf, though their time-faded colours of green and red were laboriously chosen to illustrate various scholarly theories. He gestures backwards at a sketch for one of his mythologies, and you can just see Andromeda daintily lifting her skirt as she takes immoderate care over a very small step. An intellectual with a theory or two, a painter of neo-classical principle: you might think this a well-chosen and comfortable persona for this artist. But the eyes are red with exhaustion, the jaw hangs, the mouth is open and faltering as if trying to form a phrase. The artist stammers; whatever he really is cannot be summoned. Here he is in this false position, turning himself inside out to coincide with some sort of public image. But Mengs seems to doubt not just the imposture but himself as well, as if he knew he could never live up to expectations. Melancholy knowledge, but it gives truth and feeling to the portrait, the best he ever painted.

Self-Portrait, 1774

Anton Raphael Mengs
(1728–79)

Chapter Eleven

Loners

The philosopher Ernst Mach once got on a bus, and saw a
scruffy unkempt bookish-looking person at the far end.
He thought to himself (1) That man is a shabby pedagogue.
In fact, Mach was seeing himself in a large mirror at the far
end of the bus, of the sort conductors used to use to help
keep track of things. He eventually realized this, and thought
to himself: (2) I am that man. (3) I am a shabby pedagogue.

John Perry, *Myself and I*

Self-Portrait, 1794

Jacques-Louis David (1748–1825)

J acques-Louis David is alone, oppressively alone, and he appears puzzled and faintly dismayed. Sitting painfully erect in his chair, taking no comfort from its support, he grips his brush and palette so tightly one imagines he has probably lost all sense of what he is holding as he tries to come to terms with himself in the mirror.

He seems young, and the self-portrait is made with impatient correctness, the lapels of the coat lightly but perfectly described, brevity in the extraneous details and a faint flush still arriving in the cheeks. But David was not young, he was almost forty-seven and there is a hint of silver in the five o'clock shadow. In a self-portrait made three years earlier he looks older, not to say slower and lacking this peculiar intensity of focus. Poised but agitated, he searches the face in the glass without appearing to recognize it completely, or immediately, as if not quite beyond the mirror stage yet. A trace of bewilderment enters the moment, perhaps even tinged with grievance. Speechless, blocked, this most authoritative of painters does not seem in command of the situation, and the odd awkwardness about the mouth only seems to emphasize this lapse.

David was the unrivalled image-maker of the French Revolution, a revolution partly enacted through images. His power to arouse passion and even inspire crowds to action cannot be underestimated. No painting made by him during that decade, from the fervent and agile portraits to the stupendous commemoration of Marat slaughtered in his bath, is untouched by the swift energies of change, and the legend that the citizens of Paris cried out to David to give them their hero Marat back again in a painting is not so incredible when one considers that members of the Convention itself appealed to the painter for such a magical image. Even this self-portrait from 1794, apparently so stalled, has its origins in the Revolution's hour-to-hour tumult.

David was not a just a maker of political images. He was himself a politician. A close follower of Robespierre, elected Deputy for Paris in 1792, he sat with Danton, Marat and the Jacobins against the Girondins in the National Convention and even in such extreme company was nicknamed 'the fiery terrorist'. His political speeches may have lacked flair – Anita Brookner, David's penetrating biographer, calls them 'grindingly obvious and slogan-ridden'[1] – but he was zealous, prolific and so eager to be noticed, as it seems, that he even went so far as to have his speeches collected and published. His is a life lived in public; criss-crossing the centre of Paris from his apartment in the Louvre, at times surely running just to reach the numerous political gatherings and events at which his presence is recorded. His art is explicitly staged as a form of public address, and he staged public events as a form of art. When Marat died, David wanted to re-enact the scene quite literally, posing the naked corpse just as it had been found in full view of the public; it seems that doctors had to dissuade him because the body was so corrupted by skin disease.[2]

The years David spent as a young artist in Rome strongly affected his ideas of what painting might be – he is the great force for neo-classicism in the late eighteenth century – and how it might represent the Roman virtues of stoicism, self-sacrifice and civic duty. Ancient Rome was also the inspiration for his democratic ideals and above all his public ceremonies. The spectacles David designed and organized, from festivals to funeral marches, were more Roman than the Romans and drew the citizens through Paris in their thousands. He had a genius for urgent theatre. When Voltaire's body was denied burial by the church, he arranged for the body to be exhumed from its unmarked grave and laid to rest in the Pantheon in front of 100,000 Parisians. When the Deputy for Yonne was stabbed to death by a Royalist at his dinner table the night before the execution of Louis XVI, David, pausing only to sketch the body in the restaurant, had an elaborate Roman funeral arranged within a day. The corpse of Lepeletier was laid naked, its wounds shockingly exposed, upon the very pedestal that had only days before supported a statue of the king in the Place Vendôme. This devastatingly symbolic bier led the cortège through the city streets, accompanied by the victim's blood-caked clothes displayed high on a pike crowned with cypress and laurel. The funeral had the effect of sanctifying Lepeletier as first martyr of the French Revolution and David went further, commemorating the occasion with *Lepeletier de Saint-Fargeau sur son lit de mort*. Exhibited at the Salon within weeks of the funeral, it was the first official history painting, the first documentary image, of the French Revolution. Nobody knows quite when it mysteriously disappeared.

Whatever this painting looked like, one feels it may only have been a rehearsal for David's shattering masterpiece, *The Death of Marat*, which was begun within hours of the journalist-politician's assassination by Charlotte Corday in July 1793. David had been to visit Marat only the day before the murder and was there almost immediately on hearing the news to make drawings of the still-warm body. The conception of the image seems to have come to him with astonishing speed and clarity. Marat lies stabbed through the heart in the bath where he was forced to work because of the skin disease that needed constant immersion in cold water, a bath that has now become his coffin. In one hand, he still holds the assassin's false letter of introduction, in the other his once-mighty pen is stubbed out for ever on the floor. The simple wooden crate which the indefatigable revolutionary was using only moments ago as a desk now becomes his monument, carrying the date, like a headstone, and David's own epitaph to his hero: 'A Marat'; to – and for – Marat. *The Death of Marat* was carried through the streets of Paris like a heroic corpse in its own right, a body of evidence, and a protest in the form of a martryrdom. The pale corpse, metaphorically taken down from the Cross like Michelangelo's Christ in St Peter's, is presented as a secular pietà.

But in less than a year, the painting was returned to its maker. Robespierre had fallen victim to his own revolution and David, the painter-politician, was damned by association. 'The strength of David's position,' Brookner writes, 'was his ability to translate the General Will of the Revolution into spectacular pageants and ravishing images of extraordinary and deceptive simplicity. Its weakness was a regrettable desire to be seen and heard on every occasion.'[3] To be seen and heard, moreover, calling for anything but freedom of speech or opinion.

In his thirty or so months as a member of the Convention, David is peculiarly harsh towards artists and art. He demands the destruction of all sculptures of Louis XIV and XV in public buildings. He calls for the suppression of the Museums Commission, for the dismantling of the Académie Française and all that it stands for. He produces the appallingly pitiless caricature of Marie-Antoinette as a toothless and dropsical old crone on the way to the scaffold and above all he votes for the execution of the king. David becomes so wildly carried away during sessions of the Convention his own colleagues describe him as '*en délire*'. Yet when Robespierre's power was severed in an instant and his execution announced, David could not distance himself fast enough.

Cock-crow disavowals, in which he was heard to claim that Robespierre was always more interested in David than vice versa, may have saved his neck, but his case was referred to the Committees of Public Safety and General Security where it was sluggishly debated for four months before being quietly dismissed. During this agonizing time, and despite the pleas of his many pupils, David was in prison.

This is where he paints himself in the summer of 1794, not just alone in the sense of closing the workroom door, but in actual solitary confinement. The dismay in his face may be something he cannot hide, or is scarcely even aware of as he stares in the mirror. Certainly he felt he had been grievously abused, even though his first cell was the painting room of the concierge's son at the Hôtel des Fermes where he was being held and even though that son just happened to have been one of David's own students. The mirror, the canvas, brushes and easel he needed to paint the picture were rapidly procured, and he painted several other works including, strangely, landscapes. But his letters are baffled, wounded.

> *Representatives of the people, I repeat with firm assurance that I can be reproached with nothing more serious than an exaltation of ideas which obscured for me the true nature of a man whom many of my colleagues, more enlightened than myself, regarded as the very touchstone of patriotism; but an exaltation of ideas favourable to liberty cannot be a crime to those patriots who know that it is nothing less than the product of an ardent love of one's country, and of that warmth of feeling and vigour of heart without which there would have been no Revolution.*[4]

He should be set free to return to his true vocation. 'I am prevented from returning to my studio, which, alas, I should never have left. I thought, in accepting the honourable but difficult position of legislator, that an upright heart would be sufficient, but I lacked the second quality, I mean insight.' One letter concludes with Hippolyte's beautiful words to Phèdre from the tragedy by Racine: '*Le jour n'est pas plus pur que le fond de mon cœur.*'

Alone, forbidden to communicate with the world, David paints his state without deception or flourish. His isolation is described with innocence. And everything written in the letters is silently repeated in the self-portrait: the end of exaltation – the absence of insight.

––––––––––

Isolation is a central fact of David's self-portrait. The artist is removed from society and does not know who – if anyone – his painting will address. He is not able to come up with any kind of explanation, still less statement, of himself. Yet it is not an introspective portrait; David is in no way self-involved and there is no psychic expression by other means in the controlled brushwork. It is a powerfully poignant image and also a unique kind of self-portrait: not fully neo-classical, in its helplessly injured way, but not quite Romantic either.

How Romantic the painter's plight, though – the wronged artist imprisoned for the ardour of his feelings and his ability to inspire just such feelings in others; the artist misunderstood, cast out from polite society. It is a theme fit for Byron or Shelley, a theme familiar the world over: the artist as neglected genius, outcast rebel, the artist as Romantic martyr. Romanticism puts hearts before heads, lifts feeling above reason, aims for images that express – and excite in others – the strength of one's vision and emotion. It rejects neo-classical harmony, mathematical order, the eternal verities of the Greeks and Romans, believing in freedom of expression. Henceforth art will represent the heaven or hell of being alone in the world. Yearning at the top of a mountain, awe before a sublime sunrise, horror before torrential darkness – Romantic art is overwhelming, transcendent, uplifting. It is the great freedom songs of Delacroix, the inspirational yearnings of Friedrich, the devastating tragedy of Géricault's *Raft of the Medusa*. It is true to the heart – Turner's magnificently improbable skies are not what he saw, but what he felt about what he saw – and it prizes freedom above all. 'I must create a system,' declares Blake, 'or be enslav'd by another man's.'

This is the Romantic cause as its defenders might put it; but the cause is infinitely harder to define than one of its main effects, namely a transformation in the artist's role. Artists no longer strive to please patrons, to educate and entertain according to some notion of public service. They now have a higher calling, a vocation which raises them up to see and understand what the rest of us can only grope towards. They are prophets, shamans, seers. They are born to be special, singled out as if by lightning.

A Romantic artist might not so easily bow to the rulings of a National Convention, or stand for public office in the first place. A Romantic artist might not become a virtual dictator in artistic matters, or end up painting official portraits of Emperor Napoleon as David eventually did, adapting his style to every regime change. The Romantic artist suffers for his art, not for his politics, and if he sometimes seems a cliché he is nonetheless hard to shift from the popular imagination. Artists do not belong, artists do not behave as others do or as daily life requires because they can hear the music of the planets.

This was not some idea invented by the musicians, writers, artists and philosophers whose names are associated with the Romantic Movement. The wider world conspired with it too. Artists became role models for a whole way of living more intensely, being more individual, authentic and free, more reckless and true to one's emotions. Nineteenth-century artists who scarcely produced any art at all pursued this lifestyle and allowances were made for their behaviour, as they still are today. Artistic temperament never ceases to be cited in explanation, or mitigation, of tempestuous or quixotic episodes even though you might expect this cliché to have gone out with the wearing of berets. The old idea of artists as passionate, dynamic, volatile, heedless of day-to-day practicalities remains unshakeable, even though contemporary artists are as likely to live in penthouses as attics and be managed by accountants. An artist is a Romantic. He smokes, drinks, pees in the studio sink, stubs his cigarette out in the coffee cup, works all night and carouses all day, freezes in winter, betrays his wife, is maddened with despair, paints the descent into hell and quite possibly – like Mark Rothko, Arshile Gorky, Nicolas de Staël, Jean-Michel Basquiat and, of course, like Kurt Cobain, for this lifestyle is now lived in its purest form by rock stars – commits suicide before he gets old.

David would not have recognized this idea of the artist as admirable in any way. His deep sense of order, his faith in art as the clear and beautiful elucidation of ideas, his devotion to it as a form of public address all bypass id and ego completely. An artist's inspiration does not come through dreams, passions, laudanum or drink, still less unfettered emotions. David would never have yearned for that advanced state of inner abandon Keats called negative capability, 'when man is capable of being in uncertainties, mysteries, doubts, without any irritable reaching after fact and reason'. He is not a Romantic. And yet his self-portrait is not a staged performance either, despite depicting a moment of political history in its way; rather it seems more like a spontaneous record of the crosscurrents between inner and outer life. The tumorous growth in his right cheek, the result of a duelling accident, which had the effect of slurring his speech, is not glossed over any more than his isolation and incredulity. David is on the brink, on the cusp between two kinds of artist and two kinds of self-portrait: between the Pre-Romantic artist who shows his status in society, and the post-Romantic artist who shows his inner world.

———

David could never have painted a self-portrait, for instance, like that of Sir Joshua Reynolds in the doctoral robes of Oxford University posing with a bust of Michelangelo, which he literally overshadows; one of those instances, not uncommon at this time, of an artist's portrait that could only have been fractionally less embarrassing if it had been painted by somebody else. Nor, jumping forward only a couple of decades, could he have painted anything like the half-naked self-portrait by Victor Emil Janssen in which he shows himself gaunt and ill in his spartan room, the concavity of his chest appallingly pronounced in relation to the straight verticals of picture and easel. Janssen was in life handsome and tall and not yet shrivelled by the bone disease that would kill him twenty years later, nor was he actually starving in what looks like the proverbial garret. Yet he chose to portray himself, without any neo-classical

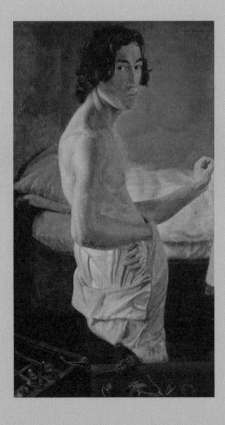

Self-Portrait in front of the Easel, c. 1628

Victor Emil Janssen
(1807–45)

restraint, as a poor bare forked animal, alone and stripped, Christ-like, to the waist. It is not much of a stretch from here to the self-portraits of the Expressionists.

Look at images of artists through the nineteenth century and you see the changes: no more attempts to ingratiate with the public, no more hair-combing or smiling for the cameras. This is the century of free expression: Courbet tearing at his hair, eyes wild, as if trying to break out of the social framework as well as the picture; Géricault with a skull; Tissot lolling back in his chair; Whistler in a cigarette haze. Cézanne, truculently unkempt, with his left-wing newspaper and sketch of Courbet raising a beer glass on the wall behind him: outside civil society altogether. Affiliations are declared. Intemperance is advertised. This is the century of nicotine poisoning and absinthe.

It was also the century in which the art world as we know it came into existence, with the rise of dealers, art magazines, the first solo shows and posthumous retrospectives. Art criticism became a profession for the first time, complete with puffing, damning and championing of new movements: Baudelaire backing Manet and the Impressionists and, significantly, reviving the works of David; Ruskin becoming a one-man megaphone for the Pre-

The Desperate Man,
1843

Jean Désiré
Gustave Courbet
(1819–77)

Raphaelite Movement. The emerging middle classes started to buy art, to the disgust of the avant-garde and of intellectuals such as Madame de Staël, who coined the term vulgarity to describe the kind of art made to appeal to a bourgeoisie eager to decorate its walls.

But none of the pictures so far mentioned, with the exception of Courbet's, is in fact a self-portrait. When one looks at this period, in which the artist supposedly becomes the outrageous hero or marginalized loner, it is a cliché established by other kinds of painting, and other art forms than self-portraiture – novels, short stories, operas and plays, from George du Maurier's *Trilby* and Zola's *Le Chef-d'œuvre inconnu* to Ibsen's *When We Dead Awaken*. The Romantic self-portrait, or rather the self-portrait as a Romantic, is unexpectedly rare. Artists do occasionally kick against the pricks in self-portraits – Courbet did it from first to last, loathing the term Romantic – but the artist as a man of penetrating vision, alone, aloof from society: this is a third-person convention.

You see it in Georg Kersting's famous portrait of the German Romantic painter Caspar David Friedrich at work in his Dresden studio, which takes very literally Friedrich's philosophy as an artist. The studio is a dark wooden chamber, austere as a coffin and completely barren except for palette, easel and the artist's voluminous imagination. Behind Friedrich, the window is half-shuttered to keep out everything but a few needful rays of light. In a thick coat against the cold, the artist stares into the painting as if it held live visions of nature, but, of course, one is to understand that these visions leap entirely from his own mind. Friedrich's mighty oaks, shattered or snowbound; his moons seen from mountains by lone figures silhouetted against screens of light, the immanence of God revealed to awestruck mortals, transcendent images of German Romanticism: these are not landscapes faithfully transcribed in situ. The mind is its own place, and whatever the artist has seen beyond those shutters only becomes a work of art in its chambers. 'Close your bodily eye,' Friedrich wrote, 'so that you may see your picture first with the spiritual eye. Then bring to the light of day that which you have seen in the darkness so that it may react upon others from the outside inwards.' His own self-portrait drawing of 1810, just a head with frighteningly profuse sideburns, makes a great point of the bodily eyes. For more spiritual eyes, you have to consult Kersting.

———

The Romantic artist, if defined in terms of behaviour, is, in fact, timeless. As far back as the Renaissance Vasari was writing about artistic temperaments and the supposed link between madness and genius, citing Michelangelo's anti-social behaviour, fighting in the streets, never changing his trousers; or the queer ways of Pontormo, a recluse who lived on boiled eggs and refused to answer the door. Practically every surviving anecdote about Apelles, first painter of Ancient Greece, has him using his draughtsmanship as a defensive weapon and storming the streets in a massive sulk.

In the seventeenth century, the Italian Baroque painter Pietro Testa, friend of Poussin and former pupil of Annibale Carracci, himself afflicted by depression, seems to have succumbed to melancholy and killed himself. His first biographer wants to describe it as an accidental death brought about by his habit of 'depicting night scenes and changes in the atmosphere of the sky' but it was not night when he drowned himself in the Tiber, and Testa's contemporary Salvator Rosa might be said to have single-handedly invented the Romantic sensibility even before that.

None of these artists was a failure, far from it; none would have seen themselves as in any sense excluded from society (except Rosa and his interludes with bandits). It seems that anyone looking for an archetypal Romantic is as likely to find one long before the early nineteenth century. Take away the Stoic slogan beneath Rosa's image of himself, after all, and you could be looking at that chimera, a Romantic self-portrait.

Wickstead

The perfect instance of an artist plunged into his inner world, in fact, is by that pioneer of Gothic horror, the Swiss artist Henry Fuseli. Fuseli's drawing is all white-knuckle introspection. He shows himself in the standard pose of Melancholy, face sunk in hands, but with fists clamped as if he were suppressing a great outburst of misery.

Fuseli's self-portrait, like everything he ever made, tends towards the camp. It might seem unnecessarily theatrical for a private sketch but it is exactly the kind of face Fuseli's public would have expected from this master of 'gloomth', of moonlit churchyards, malevolent clerics and maidens trapped in dungeons; the creator of *The Nightmare* with its virginal sleeper readied like a sacrificial victim, an excremental troll squatting upon her stomach, the curtains thrust apart by a wild-eyed stallion. His self-portrait is casting to type. But Fuseli, a lifelong friend of the insanely influential physiognomist Lavater, actually believed that character can be read in the face and not just in its changing expressions. Perhaps he was himself tormented by dreams and imaginary horrors; some of his private fantasies are of sadistic degradation. Perhaps, in this enervated self-portrait where even the drawing hand is forced to take part in the fiction, Fuseli might have been more true to himself than one knows.

Before he started to mass-produce the popping eyeballs and weird faeries of the later years, Fuseli was one of those artists whose ideas seem to prefigure Romanticism. But for that note of wildness in the eyes, he could be Wordsworth mourning the death of Shelley, Beethoven isolated by deafness, Coleridge alone in his lime-tree bower at midnight. The curious thing about these proto-Romantic self-portraits is the way they so easily translate into – look so plausibly like – other people. One archetype fits all.

On the face of it, Goya's tense and inquiring self-portrait from the 1790s could hardly be anybody else. The eyes are characteristically sharp and deep-set, the mouth is forming into something like dismay, halfway to the illusion-less scorn that becomes more pronounced in the self-portraits of the later years. Goya faces front, his wild hair a burning bush but also a halo around his furrowed face. He may be an upholder of reason and a judge of human folly, but he is also a man of feeling, disturbed by inner visions. He is Goya, but he might just as well be another great artist of the period. The etching is even known as the Beethoven self-portrait.

Beethoven self-portrait,
c. 1795–7

Francisco José de Goya
y Lucientes
(1746–1828)

There is a necessary solitude in which most self-portraits are made, away from the madding crowd in the silence of the cold studio. Some highly sociable images have come out of such conditions, it is true, for solitude alone does not make one solitary; but the Romantic artist is shown alone because isolation is central to his life and mental state. He has a natural tendency to prolonged introspection, having transcended his professional status to become a kind of hermit or prophet, able to mediate between our terrestrial lives and those powers that are beyond our grasp. Some people think the yearning figures on the mountain tops, backs turned towards us, in Friedrich's visions can only be self-portraits: splendid isolation in climax.

But to depict a generalized state of isolation is easier than to paint one's inner solitude, and sure enough a flourishing strain of nineteenth-century painting is devoted to portraits of the artist as social outcast, Octave Tassaert's *The Artist's Studio* being the tear-jerking classic. It shows a young Parisian artist slumped beside a dying fire with only a few wizened potatoes left to eat which, it is implied, he might conceivably have turned into a still life had he only had enough money for a canvas. His paintbox is empty, the palette and easel are bare and the artist is too weak to sit upright. It is a bleak little painting, sombre, empathetic and not without its truth. One thinks of the Spanish still life painter Luis Meléndez, contemporary of Goya, who painted two self-portraits punctuating the beginning and the end of his career; the first suave, self-assured and handsome, holding up one of his own bravura drawings; the second disillusioned and heavy with woe, the artist by now so hungry he petitioned the king for money. Bread had reached such a price that Meléndez could no longer afford the loaves that used to appear in his dark and powerful paintings and was reduced to working as fast as he could on images of cheap fruit in order to eat them before they putrefied.

Tassaert was also destitute, also forced to appeal for money. The museum director to whom he appealed discovered the painter in a derelict shed. But he seems to have pulled himself out of poverty with *The Artist's Studio*, a hit at the 1850 Paris Salon that won him the swooning nickname 'the Correggio of the Attic'. It was painted the same year that Henri Murger published his *Scenes from Bohemian Life*, later to become the opera *La Bohème*, featuring artists as glamorous bands of brothers, poor but happy and perpetually inspired; but Tassaert's painter is a world away from such spirited comradeship and far closer to the wretchedness described by the Goncourt brothers as 'the Bohemia that embitters'.

Not many Romantic painters were ever hermits, still less Correggios of the Attic as opposed to the well-heated Salon. In a single commanding figure, Eugène Delacroix, the painter most associated with Romanticism, though least according to his wishes, is the antidote to all such platitudes. A recluse only when he wanted to work, Delacroix was not a rebel but a reactionary and, despite longueurs when critics failed to comprehend his work, was continuously successful from an early age. His first exhibited work, painted when he was only twenty-four, was bought by the state for 1,200 francs, roughly the price of a sizeable carriage.

'To look at you, Delacroix, if I didn't know your paintings, I would attribute to you the pictures of Monsieur Ingres.' Thus Baron Gros, fellow Romantic, speaking of the exceptionally fastidious Delacroix of the self-portraits with his neatly clipped moustache, trim outline and immaculate clothes.[5] Gros imagined that the author of *Liberty on the Barricades* could only be dashingly ill-kempt, a torrential force of nature with none of the controlled precision of Ingres. But Delacroix is a lesson to us all, if it were needed, not to imagine we can see the inner man in the outer façade.

Delacroix would not allow any representation of his features to appear in public, 'whether by death-mask or by drawing or by photograph. I forbid it, expressly.' The only likeness he ever permitted to go forth into the world was his own self-portrait, bequeathed to the Louvre on the strict condition that it

Self-Portrait, c. 1837

Ferdinand Victor
Eugène Delacroix
(1798–1863)

would be set before the people only when the Orleans had eventually been restored to the throne. The face he turns to the world is composed, self-contained. What he sees in the mirror is not what he is, but all he is prepared to show. 'The mask is everything' is a phrase and a philosophy that recurs all the way through Delacroix's *Journals*, and it is in these gravely eloquent writings that one discovers the artist's deep introversion, not in his works. 'This convention of refusing to embarrass society with the constant imposition of one's inner life is an essentially classical one; it is the classicism of the highly evolved social animal,' Brookner writes of him, 'more common in the 17th century than in the Romantic period.' For Delacroix the convention is absolute but agonizing, a principle based upon the miserable knowledge that we are all alone. 'It is one of the saddest things in life,' he wrote in his diaries, 'that we can never be completely known and understood by another person.'

A strange truth about Romantic artists, commonly thought to be so self-involved, is that they do not readily turn to self-portraiture and appear quite uncertain when they do, as if unable to own the person they see in the mirror. Gros is a faint figure, almost slipping from the canvas. Géricault's self-portrait as a cheek-in-hand young painter is disputed. Constable cannot keep his eyes upon himself at all. Turner appears out of deep darkness as if he were alone in the universe, all mind and thought, but he looks like a little illustration of a pink-cheeked doll.

What am I? This sudden revelation of oneself as a thing apart, momentarily unrecognizable, out of grasp, as in David's self-portrait, strikes deeply at our sense of self-knowledge. Ernst Mach, noticing the shabby pedagogue in the

bus without realizing that it was his own self in the mirror, began to question all the philosophical proofs by which he had previously claimed to know who he was.

Who are we? The head in close-up emerging out of darkness or void: this is an archetypal self-portrait; it speaks of isolation, inquiry, soul-searching intensity; it is associated with Romanticism. But it is, of course, the way every generation since the invention of the camera has come to present itself before the official lens; in its lowest form, this is the mugshot, the face in the passport, the face we give to the hard world out there when we have no idea who, if anyone, might be looking back.

But it was also the way in which an Italian artist chose to paint himself nearly three centuries before either bohemians or cameras. Look at Tintoretto's self-portrait of 1587: his eyes a steady blaze, coming at us full force out of darkness. The light has gone, the whites of his eyes are no longer visible – 'like two black suns', Sartre wrote in awe. He is living inside his own head.

Tintoretto had painted himself almost the same way forty years before but turning from three-quarter view towards the viewer; the image represented a mutual moment, an incident in which a look was exchanged, something was going on between us. But in the late self-portrait Tintoretto is outside context, society, time, open to view but closed in complexity. He can be seen but not known. Tintoretto appears as artists, and others, chose to present themselves then as now: as beings alone in the world.

Chapter Twelve
Egotists

'L'état, c'est moi.'

Charles de Gaulle

192 | A FACE TO THE WORLD

Detail of *L'Atelier*, 1855

Jean Désiré Gustave Courbet (1819–77)

Gustave Courbet, radical, republican, patriarch of the avant-garde, had himself photographed more than any other painter in nineteenth-century France. A behemoth in braces, he filled the frame every time, challenging the lens with his own shining self-regard. In the early years he squeezes into wasp-waisted jackets, making eyes at the future and displaying his famous pointed beard to sharpest advantage. In mid-life, growing into the part, he becomes a figure of overpowering bulk, seated at the easel with legs splayed and trouser buttons straining to cover his manhood. As the self-declared People's Painter, Courbet sports rustic costumes among ripening fields; as a worker-artist, he rolls up his shirtsleeves for the day's labour – the results of which he is sometimes caught appraising, rapt before his own vast paintings. One photographer incorporates not one but two Courbets in a single trick shot: a society of two, deep in conversation, each manifestly impressed by the other. No photograph more succinctly expresses Courbet's image of himself as a genius without equal – twice the man and double the painter.

Courbet was born at the foot of the Jura Mountains in 1819 and died of drink, just across the Swiss border, fifty-eight years later. All of his traits were cast in an outsize mould – his huge voice and hearty handshake, his massive appetite for meat and beer, his staying power through all-night drinking bouts in Paris. His signature, left-leaning and revolutionary red, was so large it became the butt of cartoonists' jokes. His vanity was so overblown – 'I paint like the Bon Dieu!' – that he actually believed society could be changed by his Realist art. Anathema to the bourgeoisie, an affront to the art establishment, he countered their attacks with gleeful bravado, protected by his own egotism, conviction and rampant vigour, each expressed in the defiant self-portraits he released like a barrage.

Courbet had no sense of himself as a private person. Or at least, he had no interest in keeping himself to himself; biographies of his life are rich and full because there are so many third-party reports of him, out and about, night after night, and so much behaviour to describe. He was known, and mocked, for being extravagantly proud of his looks, which he made available to the public in paintings and the press in photographs. His self-portraits are made at speed and for immediate release like updates off the wires, and he understood the value of a newspaper reputation as no other artist before him, of supplying a familiar face to cartoonists and giving critics and journalists something dependable to rail about.

The first painting he ever exhibited was a self-portrait and it fixed the compass for the future. Where others generally tried to launch their careers with some bold new statement in landscape or history painting, or at least a portrait of somebody famous, Courbet began with himself as a handsome hero sitting by a grotto. His hair is long beneath a wide-brimmed hat and the black jacket, draping over green checked trousers, is thrown back to reveal a flash of pink silk. Courbet is dressed for Paris, where he painted this picture, and not for the sunny landscape against which he is sharply silhouetted. A dandy against a backdrop, with a book as a prop, he appears quite disassociated from nature.

It was a marvellous debut: according to Courbet. Writing home, he claimed that the painting had been honoured with an especially good position on the wall and would have won a medal had it only been larger (not better). This was a begging letter, which may explain the fibs; from the moment he arrived in Paris at twenty, Courbet had run up such gargantuan bar bills – thirty beers a night, his local bar eventually forced to sue – that borrowing became a brazen art. He once persuaded Baudelaire to write him an application to the government's fund for needy artists that was barely honest, right down to the forged signature. *Self-portrait with Black Dog* may be true to Courbet's spirit – hard up but head-in-the-air – but in its image of a dandy in split-new clothes it is pure fiction.

People say that all portraits lie, that there can never be a true likeness among them. They cite Diderot's famous irritation with a painting of himself: 'I warn you that it is not I. I had in one day a hundred different appearances, as determined by whatever was affecting me. I was serene, sad, pensive, tender, violent, passionate, enraptured. But I was never as you see me there.'[1] Self-portraits, moreover, faced with the whole back-to-front illusion of mirrors, may fake the adjustments, falsify the backgrounds and dream up scenarios that couldn't possibly be true to the moment of creation. Perhaps they don't always come up with a true face either, though at least an artist has more choice in the matter than a sitter such as Diderot.

But Courbet's self-portraits are in a different league. They are as close to fiction as it gets in the strictest sense, meaning story, invention, above all pretence. Courbet repeatedly projects himself into fantastical scenarios. He paints himself into the past and even the hypothetical future; he pretends to be somebody else while remaining quite nakedly himself. You are not meant, for instance, to look at the handsome victim in *A Wounded Man*, sprawled beneath a tree with a sword, and think he is some injured dueller from olden times so much as Courbet in period costume, eyes drowsily lidded, mouth half-open and just asking to be kissed.

Courbet painted himself as a cellist, although he couldn't play a note. He painted himself as an elegant Old Master portrait after studying Titian in the Louvre. He stars as a Byronic lover and in *The Sculptor* (he was never a sculptor) even performs a double bluff, appearing as a medieval artist chiselling away at a rock in the garb of a wandering troubadour (troubadours were much in vogue), and, every time he is recognizably Courbet.

The Cellist, 1847

Jean Désiré Gustave
Courbet (1819–77)

These self-portraits exploit passing crazes without the slightest
compunction. Courbet submitted 'The Cellist' to the Salon, for example, with
the more alluring title *Souvenir de Consuelo*, Consuelo being the eponymous
heroine of George Sand's bestselling novel, a beautiful singer whose refined
sensibilities were expressed in an ecstatic passion for music. Courbet could have
painted someone else with a cello and it would still have been a shrewdly
commercial image, but he chose to show himself dreamily fingering the strings.
These self-portraits argue for an almost total lack of self-consciousness, never
mind humility. Had Courbet painted any other man as often, and as adoringly,
as he painted himself, one might have thought him in love.

'You would surely not have a man look smirkingly at himself in a glass,' objects Sir Thomas Lawrence. After deceitfulness, vanity is the charge most commonly levelled at self-portrayers. But if it is vain to stare at oneself for professional purposes, which is arguable, there is surely integrity involved in acknowledging one's shortcomings and flaws and tendency to decay. Not many artists smirk at themselves, or have much to smirk about, though, of course, there are some enthusiastic self-appraisers: Elisabeth Vigée-Le Brun, charmed by her own beauty (can *I* help it if I look like this?); Thomas Hart Benton stripped to the waist, a muscle-bound beach boy with no qualms and, one suspects, little self-knowledge; Robert Mapplethorpe knowingly photographing himself as a handsome young devil. Some tendency towards narcissism perhaps goes with the camera age.

But Narcissus falls in love with his own reflection, and reflection seems to be the source of the problem. Too much time spent in front of the mirror, symbol of vanity, apparently betrays self-love. Everyone knows the exasperation of trying to talk to someone who has just noticed his or her reflection and is sucked in, deaf, dumb and blind to the rest of the world for however long it takes to resist the attraction. People can drown in mirrors. But the self-portraitist needs the mirror as the portraitist needs the sitter; the conceitedness arises from lying about what one finds there. Courbet painted and Courbet photographed are not much in accord; he has, for example, what psychologists call residual self-image: the slim beauty of his youth lingers on in self-portraits made when he was a bloated old drunk. But his narcissism – and here, at last, is an artist truly in love with himself – neither begins nor ends with the mirror.

Take *The Desperate Man* (page 184), in which Courbet thrusts forward, fingers raking at his hair, eyes wild, nostrils flaring, so close to the picture plane that one has the startling sense of standing just on the other side of a two-way mirror. Courbet does not make eye contact with the viewer, in fact his stare is completely sightless, as if he was beyond the mere business of depicting himself. Sensational as a cinema poster, all its melodrama compressed in a single close-up, *The Desperate Man* feels like a break-out: head driving forwards, arm jammed up against the surface, Courbet literally trying to elbow his way out of the picture. If the mirror is a glass that simply knocks back your image, in painting you are free to escape. Courbet, working fast, throws himself into the action of painting to get beyond the constraints of the mirror. This physicality impressed everyone who met him. 'Put him at a table, on horseback, at hunting, at swimming, at canoeing, at skating, or in a good bed and you'll see if he does honour to the situation!'[2] When he was released from prison in 1872, after months of confinement and illness in a tiny cell, the first journalist to interview him reported that Courbet just wanted 'to sprawl on the grass …

seize the earth of the fields in his fists, to hit it, smell it, bite it ... to throw stones in water holes, flounder about in streams, to eat, to devour nature'.[3] There is the same desire in his art – to rush in, rub and smear and finger the paint, handle the surface, impress himself directly upon the canvas.

And the physical truth of reality is always his subject, from the earth of the fields to the fullness of his own rude existence. He paints himself over and again, bodied forth in all his glory, without ever acknowledging – still less reflecting upon – an inner self. These early self-portraits are sometimes interpreted as a prolonged identity crisis, yet they have no real interest in identity. The eyes are averted, obscured, unfocused, half-closed; Courbet never fastens upon the viewer (or indeed himself) in any one of his changing characters. Strongly present in person, but disconnected in mind, at times he appears right out of it. *The Wounded Man*, for all the fake gore, is a vision of gorgeous relaxation; in *Country Siesta*, Courbet has fallen asleep altogether. This is the extreme opposite of the mirror self-portrait, in which the artist at least has to keep his eyes open and appear to be alert. But the face the mirror gave him, no matter how candidly he admired it, was never the subject of Courbet's self-portraits so much as the fascinating adventures of Courbet himself. The artist's real desire is to appear as the protagonist of the story, the principal figure in the painting: to see what he looks like in – and as – one of his own works.

––––––

Courbet was in prison for his participation in the Paris Commune. His politics are remarkably hard to pin down from his blustering letters and statements, but we know he was a committed republican who worked on Baudelaire's leftist journal (although he did not fight alongside him) in the Revolution of 1848; that he was anti-Bonapartist throughout the Second Empire and that one of his mentors was the socialist philosopher Pierre-Joseph Proudhon. But Courbet only surfaces as any kind of activist during the Commune, when he presided over committees charged with ending sleaze and corruption in the official Salon. For this mild subversion he was nonetheless arrested with his fellow Communards and jailed, a punishment considered disgracefully lenient by conservative enemies. If Courbet cannot be executed, suggested the academic painter Jean-Louis-Ernest Meissonier, then perhaps he can be put to artistic death instead. His paintings were banned from public display and he was forced to take exile in Switzerland, bankrupted by a crippling fine of over 300,000 francs – the entire cost of restoring the Vendôme Column, that imperial symbol for whose destruction he was unjustly blamed.

There is no doubt that critical hostility to Courbet's art was fanned by hatred of his politics. One reads it everywhere: distaste for his 'ugly' townsfolk, jeering at his 'messianic' self-portraits, resentment towards his monumental depiction of peasants instead of Napoleonic generals. Courbet was an empiricist. 'I cannot paint an angel,' he declared, 'because I have never seen one.' Reality, it followed, could only be what he himself had observed – the honest folk of Ornans burying their dead, the stonebreakers slogging out their lives by the barren wayside. Courbet himself was leery of the term Realist, announcing in 1855 (in his 'Realist Manifesto') that 'The title of Realist was thrust upon me.' But one thing it patently meant was a rejection of the past as a proper subject for contemporary art and with it all those anachronistic goddesses, nymphs and heroes that infested neo-classical painting.

An audience used to decorum, sentiment and uplifting ideals was bound to be appalled by a queue of distracted and disorderly mourners crammed into a long, low canvas dark as a tomb. *The Burial at Ornans, The Stonebreakers, The Return of the Clergy*: all the famous paintings were scandals at the Salon. Everything he did generated streams of newspaper cartoons: Courbet in wooden clogs or manure-spattered smock; Courbet painting a severed pig's head or using the tip of his trademark beard as a brush. His pictures had a long career of their own in caricature and spoof – but this was nothing compared to his face. People who had never seen a single one of Courbet's paintings could recognize his features, and not just in Paris. Not for another century would an artist's face be so internationally known and Andy Warhol only reached the pinnacle of recognition with the aid of the broadcast media.

The self-portrait that really gave Courbet a public image was *Man with a Pipe*, exhibited – as if to give a face to the increasingly notorious name – alongside *Burial at Ornans* and *The Stonebreakers*. Courbet shoulders up close to the picture plane, hair unkempt, face pale, a pipe hanging from one corner of his mouth. His pupils are completely dilated. He's reamed out with reverie – or maybe something stronger.

Anyone looking for an autobiography in self-portraits – Courbet's own phrase – might find a fragment of it here. Here he is settling on a provocative image to go with his lifestyle at Brasserie Andler, a couple of doors down from his studio. Courbet went there almost every night to smoke, drink and debate with a circle that included Baudelaire and Proudhon; the critic Champfleury, who first planted the term Realism; and Jean Wallon, translator of Hegel and model for one of the characters in *La Bohème*. Bohemians, intellectuals and radicals, they all left written accounts of Courbet – his superb arrogance, his singularity, his wanton independence, all apparent in this self-portrait. One anecdote tells of Courbet studying Baudelaire in an opium trance and maybe he is stoned, though he was a heavy smoker in any case from his earliest schooldays to his last, sombre self-portrait.

Courbet liked to relate that when *Man with a Pipe* toured Germany, the painting became so controversial that notices were pinned up in bars advising customers that no arguments about Monsieur Courbet were allowed. In France, it was known as 'The Christ with a Pipe' because the angle of the head resembled that of the crucified Messiah. It became his emblem, so much so that when asked to portray himself, Courbet would simply draw a pipe on a sheet of paper. Beneath it, he wrote the words '*Courbet: sans idéal et sans religion*.' An image and a manifesto: prototype of his later self-portraits.

The *Man with a Pipe* is a poseur, melodramatic and self-regarding, but he is at least himself and nobody else. Courbet described it several years later as 'the portrait of a fanatic, an ascetic … the portrait of a man disillusioned with the foolishness that made up his education, and who searches for principles of his own to hang on to'.[4] He was always rewriting the legend of his art, burnishing it with newer and better meanings.

This ascetic — or possibly aesthete, Courbet's spelling is unreliable — was bought by a collector in Montpellier named Alfred Bruyas. Rich, eccentric, with hazy theories about art that he published in vanity volumes, he was a capitalist, a Bonapartist and a friend to painters Courbet publicly despised, yet the two became allies for a short but crucial period, and it was for Bruyas that Courbet painted one of the most self-regarding — and mocked — of self-portraits in art.

There are three figures in *The Meeting*: Courbet, Bruyas and his manservant Calas. Courbet has just stepped from a carriage, seen departing in the distance, and is being greeted upon his arrival at the outskirts of Montpellier. He stands in his shirtsleeves on a dusty road, staff in one hand, hat in the other, a heavy box of painting materials strapped to his shoulders. Bruyas has removed his hat and is extending it in a gesture of welcome. Calas bows his head in respect. Beside them a dog, tongue dangling, stares eagerly up at Courbet. The landscape is parched flat beneath a burning blue sky.

There is obviously something self-aggrandizing about the idea of the welcoming party coming all the way out of town to hail the artist, an incident not known to have occurred. But more than that, the abrupt dissonance of the image emphasizes the irregularity of the human relationships. There they stand, a parade of cut-out sentinels in a frieze. Nobody moves, nobody speaks, each planted as stiffly as his staff or walking stick. Bruyas stands to attention, eyes worshipfully lowered before his hero. Calas is so deeply humbled and reverential he might as well be receiving the Eucharist. For all his talk about the dignity of the downtrodden worker, Courbet relegated this one. Only the dog, free spirit and force of nature, is allowed to look directly upon the face of this bearded pilgrim-cum-prophet, not that Courbet notices. His head is tilted back, eyes half-closed — what else? — as he auditions the line-up.

Courbet's contemporaries found the painting hilarious. It was instantly nicknamed 'Fortune Bowing to Genius' or 'Bonjour Monsieur Courbet'. People marvelled that an apparently trivial incident could be inflated into such a vainglorious memorial and they took to greeting each other with the cry 'Bonjour Monsieur Courbet!' Critics noticed that the only person allowed a shadow was Courbet himself — 'he alone can stop the rays of the sun'.[5] Théodore de Banville mocked Courbet's treatment of the desiccated earth with an ode in which the landscape answers back — 'My friend, if I'm sad and ugly to see/It's because Monsieur Courbet has just passed through me.' Caricaturists went to town on the abasement of patron and valet before this messiah with a paintbox. It was the Road to Damascus, the Adoration of the Magi.

In fact, it was a different biblical story altogether. *The Meeting* is based on a popular print of the time in which two gentlemen have turned out to greet

the Wandering Jew on the outskirts of town. He holds a staff, they doff their hats, and so on; reversed, and only slightly adjusted to downgrade poor Calas. Courbet as the Jew condemned to stride the world alone and for ever; as the witness of history and the bearer of truth — the Wandering Jew, after all, was supposed to be the only surviving witness to Christ's life, and a labourer, what's more (a shoemaker to Courbet's 'worker-artist'), who had recently been portrayed as the champion of the proletariat in a sell-out play by the French writer Eugène Sue.

All this before one even begins to look at what Courbet did with the design of the print itself, using its stark simplicity to put across what can properly be described for once as a message. For *The Meeting* makes its point, no matter how familiar the audience, then or now, with the Wandering Jew or the woodcut. Courbet is an artist; he receives ritual homage; this naturally occurs, and continuously, outside the limitations of time or place — the painting delivers its syllogism with unparalleled clarity. The worshippers are totems; the artist has become the irreducible emblem of himself, his famous Assyrian beard a jet-black pennant against the sky.

The Meeting is one of very few paintings that are as bright in reality as they are in reproduction. Its swift transcription of summer light would inspire the Impressionists; its brilliant sky immediately evokes Van Gogh dazzled in Arles some thirty years later, and Van Gogh actually made the trip to Montpellier to see it in the company of Gauguin, whose *Bonjour Monsieur Gauguin* — in which Gauguin meets a Provençal peasant on rather more humble terms, a prophet unrecognized, a *real* outsider — is among the first works to pay homage to this archetype of the avant-garde painter. In the twentieth century, Peter Blake translated *The Meeting* to the sizzling heat of California, playing the role of Bruyas to David Hockney's Courbet. It's an in-joke, of course, the idea of Blake travelling thousands of miles from London to hail his fellow painter (and with famous Howard Hodgkin as the servile Calas). But just as Courbet stood for Realism, so Hockney stands for Pop. Blake replaces the pilgrim staff with a giant Claes Oldenburg paintbrush.

Self-regard is not a neutral term. Courbet's self-portraits are self-regarding in every respect, but he is beyond the narcissism of mere looks. Most artists are too vain to boast about appearances, in any case, when they have so much more to talk about – their gifts, their ideas, their lovers, their sufferings, their place in the pantheon of art, in which respect nobody is as insanely defensive as Giorgio de Chirico. In a long series of self-portraits de Chirico made a statue of himself, thick-set, marmoreal, with a massive head and stone-grey face as if halfway between life and monument. He generally wears a look of pained outrage: I, Giorgio, who have suffered for my art.

Unlike Courbet, who stood up to real critical onslaught, de Chirico had a persecution complex brought on, no doubt, by the vilification of the Surrealists when he ceased to paint the *pittura metafisica* they admired, but sustained by his own egomania in the face of lukewarm reviews for the reheated classicism he turned to next. 'Nulla Sine Tragoedia Gloria' reads the notice he holds in one painting, no glory without tragedy. 'Pictor Classicus' says one to which he peevishly points, while another simply states 'Best Painter'. Needless to say he eventually gives himself a crown of laurels and those resonant words from Ovid: 'Mihi Fama Perennis Quaeritur In Toto Semper ut Orbe Canar': 'I seek eternal fame, to be sung throughout the whole world for ever.' The line is a retort to Envy, and in his paranoid autobiography de Chirico denounces every second enemy with the old and delusional jibe that they are motivated entirely by envy.

Vanity undermines itself, makes a fool of the vain; the more one boasts, the more one forgets to consider how boastful one will look. But Courbet does not care. If nobody else is going to argue his case, then the artist will champion himself. Recognition is the theme of *The Meeting* and recognition is his aim. Nothing must come between Courbet and the public, not dealers or critics or the system itself. When two of the fourteen paintings he submitted to the 1855 Exposition Universelle were rejected, Courbet hired an engineer to design a rival pavilion of brick and iron and build it right there in the gardens opposite.

The 'Pavillon du Réalisme' was an amazing novelty, a one-man show outside the system (or a temple, as some saw it, raised by and for self-worship). Its centrepiece was a massive canvas, twenty feet by twelve, that had been made to be displayed at the Exposition. Displayed, but not sold; unlike his contemporaries, Courbet was capable of expending enormous energy on works he must have known were fated to return to his own studio, in this case because the picture was so profoundly self-centred. Indeed, Courbet's studio is also its setting, as conveyed in the annoyingly paradoxical title: *The Artist's Studio: A Real Allegory Summing up Seven Years of My Artistic Life (L'Atelier)*.

Eugène Delacroix, dropping by the pavilion on 3 August, could hardly believe that the jury had rejected it. 'They have refused one of the most

L'Atelier, 1855

Jean Désiré Gustave
Courbet (1819–77)

singular works of the period,' he wrote without understatement.

The scene takes place in Courbet's cavernous studio, the topmost floor of a converted abbey. The artist is seated in front of an easel raising a brush to the canvas. Behind him stands a model, her clothes shed in a careless heap as if she has just stepped out of them to get a better view of the moment of creation. On the floor, a skittish cat pauses to observe. A few respectful inches away, a small boy gazes reverently up at the master and on either side of this central trio is a huge and disparate cast: a metropolitan group on the right, among them Baudelaire and Proudhon, reading, cogitating, or staring absently into the distance; on the left, a party from out of town, including – in Courbet's own words – 'a Jew I saw in England making his febrile way through the London streets … a priest with a triumphant look and a bloated red face … a hunter, a reaper, a strong-man, a buffoon, a textile peddler, a workman's wife, a worker, an undertaker and an Irishwoman suckling a child'.[6] There is no evidence, incidentally, that Courbet was ever in London.

It is immediately obvious that this is a work of high contrivance. Courbet is so absurdly contorted in his seat, the better to show off his Assyrian profile, that he couldn't possibly make a brushstroke at this angle. There is no accounting for the nude model since the artist is working on a landscape. The urchin is straight out of a production of *Les Misérables* and the intellectuals on the right are not in communication with one another, let alone the artist they have come to visit. As for the figures on the left, whoever they are — and it would be another century before they were conclusively identified — they clearly make the most improbable of gatherings.

Everything about *L'Atelier* is dreamlike, from its strange cast to its hazy somnolence. The studio is full of ambiguous shadows, its perspective warped, its ceiling so high it is out of sight. The paintings hung on the rear wall are as sketchy as theatrical backdrops, although they have also been taken for unfinished views through some putative window. The sense of looking into an open-fronted stage is heightened by Courbet's *mise-en-scène*: the central family so brightly lit; the figures on either side like actors in the wings.

Some of the mystique of *L'Atelier* is accidental. Courbet was a hasty technician, often painting so thinly that his red-brown under-primer shows right through, though his canvases are also frequently blackened by copious use of bitumen. *L'Atelier* suffers from both — a murky darkness in some areas, a ghostly transparence in others — so that the scene seems to hover between gloaming and oblivion.

His method, too, contributes to the oddly disjointed configuration. For the painting is partly a collage of extracts from other works: earlier portraits of Baudelaire, Champfleury, and Bruyas in the coat with the striped collar that he wears in *The Meeting*; a self-portrait Courbet painted in Montpellier, for which he borrowed the same coat — which thus appears twice. The nude model is based on a photograph, the face of Proudhon on a lithograph, and so on; and as for the other characters, Courbet complicated the meaning of the painting even before it was finished with a long and riddling account sent to Champfleury in which he identified the figures on the right as 'shareholders, friends, fellow workers and amateurs from the art world' — so far so good — but the ones on the left as 'the other world of the trivial life, the people, misery, poverty, wealth, the exploited, the exploiters, people who live on death … Those who want to judge [the painting] will have their work cut out for them, they will have to manage as best they can.'

Rarely did Courbet write such accurate words. For over a hundred years, scholars have laboured to produce a coherent interpretation of the painting. It is about town versus country, capital versus labour, art versus nature, or Realism against obsolete tradition. It is an allegory of socialism or artistic freedom; it is Proudhonist, feminist, misogynist. There was so much evidence to consider — social as well as pictorial — that nobody even got round to identifying the figures on the left until the French scholar Hélène Toussaint showed that the back row alone included likenesses of Garibaldi, Bakunin and the Hungarian revolutionary Lajos Kossuth. Asia, Poland and Turkey were also represented, along with various French journalists and cabinet ministers. Most startling of all was the identity of the poacher so prominently seated at the front of the picture: Napoleon III himself.

Entire books had to be rewritten. *L'Atelier*'s real ambition was now coded polemic. Napoleon III had poached France from the people in the 1851 coup d'état. He was being sent a sharp message about international reconciliation at the height of the Crimean war, whose participants included France, Russia and Turkey. Or maybe the seven years of the title referred back to 1848, after all, the year of the revolutions – hence these representatives of so many nationalities and ideologies. Courbet was portraying society as a dynamic progression towards democracy, from the conflicts of the past on the left, to the freethinking future on the right.

None of which is self-evident now, any more than it was in 1855. For it seems that nobody saw the picture's subversions. If anyone recognized the poacher's telltale features – narrowed eyes, pointed beard, waxed whiskers – they kept the revelation to themselves. As for Garibaldi, Bakunin and the rest, it has been suggested that the painting was so large that nobody could actually see the line-up in the back row.[7] Only Courbet was universally remarked upon; his politics remained wilfully opaque. Proudhon, who had declined to sit for his portrait in the first place, was irritated to find his ideas alluded to for the sake of self-glorification. 'Courbet is too ... puffed up with vanity,' he wrote. 'He has painted a purely personal picture.'[8]

And this is nothing but the truth. No matter how complex the political programme, no matter how improbable and confused the allegory, the entire scene revolves around Courbet. He is the mediating figure between emperor and urchin, attempting to unite the disunited. He is the author of this teeming vision, all the way from landscape to portrait to history painting, that recreates art and society. This is a painting, Courbet proudly announced, 'of the world come to be painted at my place'. Once the artist painted himself, over and again, out there in the world. Now he paints the world contained in his studio.

L'Atelier is a monumental image of self-absorption. No matter what revolutionary theories it might float, no matter how many intellectuals Courbet invokes or what wide audiences he seeks, the artist is entirely turned away from us. Self-regard shades into disregard for the actual world of viewers. And though it may be an intensely personal picture – condensing on a grander scale than ever before the central fact of Courbet to Courbet – it is also paradoxically impersonal. Absolutely public, firmly closed, like the artist himself, *L'Atelier* is not so much a scene as a state of mind: the ego entranced by itself.

Chapter Thirteen

Victims

'On a cold blowy February day a woman is boarding the
10am flight to London, followed by an invisible dog.
The woman's name is Virginia Miner ... The dog that is
trailing her, visible only to her imagination, is her familiar
demon or demon familiar, known to her privately as Fido
and representing self-pity.

Alison Lurie, *Foreign Affairs*

Self-Portrait in Hell, 1903

Edvard Munch (1863–1944)

E dvard Munch is in a hell of his own making. He paints himself naked in the furnace, a red blast to one side of him, smouldering fumes to the other, loin-deep in the visible darkness. It looks quite a conventional sort of hell, flame-licked, sulphurous, until you notice that there are no other sinners about; Munch is the only soul in the infernal footlights and he seems to be bearing up with suspicious bravado. The painting is provocatively cropped, ending just shy of the genitals with Munch's dainty little signature, but the artist appears to be holding the pose like a gladiator or a general on horseback. The torture never ends but Munch is taking it like a man, standing up to eternal hellfire.

It has to be some kind of tease, does it not? Or at least a not very serious boast, a trumping of all those paintings of artist as melancholy, anxious, lonely or unjustly treated with a self-portrait right there in the very pit of hell. Others may suffer the slings and arrows but these are as nothing compared to the hell this fallen angel endures; the picture is even called *Self-Portrait in Hell*. Munch surely cannot mean it – the pose is so absurd, the title beyond parody, never mind the scenario – and yet he does. Look closer and you see that no flames, let alone devils, are actually represented, for this is a hell of the mind that has nothing to do with falling from God's grace or being any kind of sinner, heaven forfend. It is, in short, a metaphor made exceptionally literal, and just what you might expect from Edvard Munch, enthusiastic miserabilist: exaggeration in the service of a good story.

A good story, but is it actually *true?* This is not the kind of question usually applied to paintings, the contents of which are more or less openly declared an illusion and fundamentally accepted as such before the audience suspends disbelief, as with cinema or theatre. But the same rules of engagement do not seem to apply to representations of people once living or still alive, which we tend to encounter as real people first before we perceive them as portraits. Here is Edvard Munch – we meet him eye to eye – and then here is Edvard Munch imagining himself as naked and damned in his own living hell. As to the truth of the scenario, is this not what we all feel on a bad day, how we might portray ourselves if only we could cut it with a brush and didn't mind the inevitable accusations of self-pity? Munch has more front than most, but he is only telling it like it is, personifying the human condition. In fact, the very opposite was true; Munch was telling his own personal story.

A story that was true, at least, to the artist's emotions. *Self-Portrait in Hell* was painted in the summer of 1903 and exhibited in an Oslo gallery that autumn. Munch had been having an affair with a woman called Tulla Larsen who had travelled with him – or stalked him, according to one version – all over Europe the previous year. Their relationship had finally exploded because Larsen wanted to get married and Munch, who was almost comically afraid of marriage, refused her. She threatened to kill herself; Munch, not to be outdone, shot himself first. But he only damaged the tip of a middle finger – hardly critical, and not his painting hand in any case.

Munch left a record of this event in which he describes himself crouching desperately on the kitchen floor, brandy bottle in hand, while Larsen stands over him 'with her cold set face, resembling the head of Medusa'.[1] Somehow his gun goes off and he collapses bleeding, but her only response is to fetch a cloth for the blood on the tiles. 'Rage gripped me – you monster – are you going to let me bleed to death – at least go and get a doctor!'

As is so often the way after such cataclysmic crises, Larsen married somebody else within months. The wounded finger was treated and Munch immediately took up with the first of many other lovers. But even five years after the end of the affair he writes of the shattered state of his soul to a friend: 'I have wounds from Norway that have made my life a kind of hell.' Whatever Larsen endured, which we shall never know as she destroyed all her diaries and letters, Munch felt he was uniquely the victim. Friends began to take sides; he felt betrayed; the self-portraits in the Oslo show were made and displayed to set the story straight and as an act of reprisal. Not just *Self-Portrait in Hell*, which in this context amounts to a fit of pictorial pique directed at Larsen – now see what you've done, not that I care – but which still carries universal meaning; Munch also exhibited an even larger painting that commemorates the artist's suffering in more explicit detail, while gesturing grandly at a masterpiece of European painting. *On the Operating Table* reprises Rembrandt's *The Anatomy Lesson of Doctor Nicolaes Tulp*, except that the body on the slab is not technically dead.

Munch is entirely naked (for an injured finger?), wounded hand clenched to breast. Not one but three doctors are attending. A nurse holds a brimming bowl of blood and a vast scarlet patch is seeping through the sheet as dozens of students observe the scene through the theatre window; students or members of some ideal public, they are effectively on the patient's side, a sympathetic audience to his ordeal. Munch believed in painting as all-out theatre. He designed stage sets for Ibsen and in this scenario it is as if he has shot himself like Eilert Lovborg, handed the gun by Hedda Gabler; some have even seen a heart in the spreading gore on the bed: love lies a-bleeding. But what that shape resembles more than anything else is the shrieking worm of a figure in Munch's most famous painting, *The Scream*, icon to adolescent neurotics everywhere and by his own testimony an allegorical self-portrait.

You might think that nobody in their right mind would have exhibited *On the Operating Table* in a city small enough for newspaper journalists to reconstruct the mortifyingly personal backstory in a flash; you might think he should not have posted his martyrdom in full view of acquaintances he now believed to be enemies. But Munch didn't leave it at that; he repeated his claims all over again, this time as an explicit *J'accuse*, in a self-portrait variation on David's *The Death of Marat* with himself as Marat and Tulla Larsen, now also stripped of her clothes, as the murderess Charlotte Corday.

It is an awful painting, 'not one of my primary works, but an experiment' as he himself agreed, but you cannot beat it for victimization: the knifed artist dead on the bed, and once more for emphasis in yet another version where the arm dangles lifelessly over the side exactly like David's hero.

Is this really how Munch experienced his relationship with Larsen? The language of the wronged lover is certainly framed this way – you ruined my life, you broke my heart, you stabbed me in the back, go ahead, you might as well kill me; and, of course, the final impotent jibe: you'll be sorry when I'm dead. Charlotte Corday was not sorry, of course, having killed one man in order to save a hundred thousand as she said at her trial, but some stories become common property. And if poets are allowed to speak of knives to the heart and the killing wounds of love, and playwrights such as Ibsen and Strindberg can put their own unhappiness on stage, and be understood as doing so, and novelists from Chateaubriand to D. H. Lawrence and Philip Roth can air their romantic and marital grievances in fiction without being sued for defamation, then why not their fellow artists? The question is not whether Munch can do it, or even whether he can get away with it (the gossip died down fairly rapidly; these were paintings not publications), so much as how far he fictionalizes the tale.

Compare painting with writing. In the case of an autobiographical novel, for instance, it is just possible for the author's acquaintances not to know the real-life identity of every single character. In *A Far Cry from Kensington*, Muriel Spark managed a devastating character assassination of her former lover, Derek Stanford, who appears as the vicious publisher Hector Bartlett, nickname 'pisseur de copie', without exposing the details of their relationship or attracting public notoriety at the time (although journalists later dug up the revelations). Neither does one assume that Spark is her own protagonist, the buxom Mrs Hawkins, in every degree. But the self-portraitist has the problem of actual faces, specifically his or her own; whether to go in disguise – tricky in an avowed self-portrait – or appear openly as oneself. Munch is relatively indifferent to accuracy of likeness but he and Larsen were both recognizable in their roles as victim and murderer, so one could not fail to understand the crime he was alleging.

But we don't take the allegation literally, of course. The victim is still alive and kicking, his self-portrait a very public proof of survival; for like most victim self-portraits, his were made to provoke sympathy, shock or admiration from the widest possible audience.

Munch painted over seventy self-portraits and it is extraordinary just how many of them present him as the injured party. He is the harrowed figure in *The Flower of Pain*, blood shooting from his wounded breast to keep the blossom of art alive; he is the victim of Judith and Medusa; the head on Salome's platter. He has no fear of appearing ludicrous, self-pitying or weak, from the vain young bohemian in the early self-portraits to the paranoid drunk for whom a breakdown was obviously due and the elderly depressive listening to time as it ticks towards death. He puts himself in the picture for maximum pathos over and again – spurned lover, lone drinker, wounded soul, murdered corpse. He shows himself ravaged by bronchitis, nearly dying of Spanish flu, violently abused by womankind. Munch's sense of his own suffering is not episodic but continuous and his experience is always raw for we are powerless, he believes, against outrageous fate. But the practised calculations in these melodramas, seen one after the other, reveal an artist for whom hyperbole is a way to universal truth. Munch's *Weltanschauung* embraces all mankind, as his titles make clear. *The Scream, Desolation, Anguish, Inner Turmoil, Separation*: the story of his own life is narrated in images and words, but they encompass our common experience.

Munch's despair is dogged, programmatic, but nothing in his life or writings suggests it was anything but sincere. His memory of childhood 'was that disease and insanity were the black angels on guard at my cradle ... I felt always that I was treated unjustly, without a mother, sick and with threatened punishment in Hell hanging over my head.'[2] His mother died of tuberculosis when he was five. His father was a hellfire nutcase who woke him at midnight to witness the death of his closest sister, also from tuberculosis, at the age of fifteen, and many of his paintings are locked in these private agonies. But Munch was surely right to say that in his art he 'tried to find an explanation for life and to discover its meaning ... and also intended to help others understand life'.

But exaggeration turns easily to caricature and even *The Scream* is faintly comic, the little figure with its funny round head, hands to face as if edified by a scandalous bit of gossip, and all against that gorgeous flaming sky. It was a tremendous shape to coin, a great archetype, but it was destined to become a joke-shop mask. *Self-Portrait in Hell* holds no horror for the viewer either, certainly not of the damnation Munch was taught to fear by his father. But it does represent, with all its obviousness and swagger, one of his most profound beliefs about the power of the painted image. 'Photography,' Munch wrote, 'will never compete with painting so long as the camera cannot be used in heaven or in hell.'

———

If a painting is to go where the camera cannot, it must show more than can be seen in the world. Munch could have painted himself bleeding on the floor while Larsen fussed over the tiles, but that wouldn't have given as strong a portrait of his emotions, even, as his own written record. He has to fictionalize his sufferings; victim self-portraits generally do. They have to choose one incident to epitomize all others, to express the sum of one's inner misery. In this respect, artists living in the twentieth century, the century of the ego, were more inventive and prolific than most but history is full of self-portraitists airing their grievances. When Munch depicted himself as the executed head of John the Baptist he was only Salome's latest victim in paint, although with a twist, since he cannot quite bear to show himself dead. This may seem to deny a crucial forensic detail, but it gives him the opportunity to appear as an innocent victim, and Christ's cousin, no less, while also emphatically himself and alive to his fate.

There are other severed heads to choose from – wicked Goliath separated from his body by plucky David, rapacious Holofernes decapitated by Judith with the blade of his own sword – but it would have undermined Munch's case to appear anything other than blameless. Other self-portraitists don't care so much about the finer points of casting. The Florentine painter Cristofano Allori portrayed himself with superb panache as the head of Holofernes held aloft by a handful of hair; and Holofernes is hardly a hero. According to the Apocryphal Book of Judith, the pious Israelite widow Judith infiltrates the enemy camp of this Assyrian general on the pretext of betraying her own people. On the third night, having gained his confidence, she plies him with drink thus thwarting his plan to rape her and once he is sleeping skims his head from his body, carrying it triumphantly back to her people. Allori's face is conceived as waking to his fate at the exact moment of slaughter, no small feat to pull off. And who plays Judith but the artist's treacherous ex-girlfriend. According to his first biographer, Filippo Baldinucci, this is more or less a one-scene account of their entire affair. She has him wrapped around her fingers; the mother gets in the way (she appears as Judith's helpful servant in the background); the girlfriend throws him over, effectively doing him in. Allori is a fool for love; he is the artist who lost his head.

Compare this painting with another by Hendrick ter Brugghen and you see that Allori has composed his picture, and the story, as a triangle: the mother behind her daughter's deeds, the daughter shoving the poor artist down and out into the cold space of our world. His head is not some gory poll dripping with blood but a lyrical portrait, a romantic image of sorrow and loss, and although Judith is beautiful – and was apparently very recognizable to their contemporaries – she is made to look as heartless as Allori no doubt intended by handling his head as if it were some cheap bottle of wine.

Ter Brugghen's self-portrait as the head of Goliath dominates the entire painting: nothing else comes close to the impact of this livid green face, sweaty, open-mouthed, still streaked with blood, popping up in the bottom corner like a puppet master suddenly thrusting his large head into the middle of a performance. Ter Brugghen was a Dutch follower of Caravaggio and the whole scenario — a knot of dark figures with their backs turned to the viewer, raking light, a sudden drama in unexpected outreaches of the painting — tries in vain to follow the master; but the head is all ter Brugghen. A well-fed seventeenth-century Dutchman with Laughing Cavalier moustache trying to imagine how he might look with his eyes closed and, what's more, incorporate the results into a biblical scene he cannot quite manage, he is more hilariously alive than anyone else in the painting.

David with the Head of Goliath, c. 1609–10

Michelangelo Merisi
da Caravaggio
(1574–1610)

If he had been a better painter ter Brugghen might have come across as
the victim rather than just an absurd model. His self-portrait, so big and
clumsily inserted, might have been understood as a vengeful pronouncement or
a plea for mercy or a Munchian *J'accuse*, at the very least as having had some
fascinating private message. For the autobiographical motivations of mediocre
self-portraits can keep them alive, especially when they are pleasingly coded. By
the same token, a great self-portrait can be diminished in the same way.
Caravaggio's harrowing image of a compassionate David regretfully lifting the
bloody head of Goliath has come to be construed as an attempt at plea-
bargaining more than a masterpiece of religious art simply because Caravaggio
cast himself as Goliath.

Coarse, blank, waxy, the eyelids swollen and drooping, the teeth dark stumps in a mouth fixed with a silent cry at the moment of death: it is an awful vision out of darkness. The light that catches David's gracious face and figure as he holds the head at arm's length misses Goliath's hair and strikes only the white mask of encroaching rigor mortis.

It is often said that Caravaggio must have known the face of violent death because he had killed a man himself and witnessed other murders; it is also true that this was one of his last paintings, made when he was on the run from police and assassins. It was among the works he was bringing back with him from Naples, where he had taken refuge, to Rome and which he might have presented to his patron, Cardinal Scipione Borghese, in hope of a papal pardon for the murder charge, had he not missed his boat connection at Porto Ercole, caught malarial fever and died in that mosquito-infested town. Anyone inclined to biographical interpretations may see it as a man faced with execution making a sacrificial offering of his own head.

Caravaggio had been left for dead himself in a dark Neapolitan alley, wounded almost beyond recognition. Perhaps the memory of what he saw in the mirror is there in that damaged face; Caravaggio taking an old tradition – Giorgione painting himself as David meditating on the head of Goliath, Titian as the innocent head of John the Baptist – and giving it a violent reality, with the added admission of his own guilt. But it is above all a Christian story and all of Caravaggio's late painting is profoundly religious, dwelling upon the meaning of penitence and salvation more deeply than almost any other works of art.

After the blaze of the early dramas the stage grows bare, the light more sacramental, the gestures become so singularly empathetic they make you think of Caravaggio's contemporary, Shakespeare. David and Goliath are linked together for ever, the beautiful boy and the fallen brute: the one a hero sorrowful in victory, the other a monster redeemed as his victim.

———

Never too distraught to paint: that is the paradoxical precondition of self-portraits in which artists parade the wounds inflicted on their bodies, souls or self-esteem. A cooling off has to take place for the act of creation to occur, one cannot just fire off in anger. Yet the result may approximate to those injured letters we compose in our heads in the middle of the night, rewriting the lines until they become unimpeachably righteous, but very rarely send in the morning. Almost every self-portrait by the German artist Max Beckmann has this overwrought tone, unrelieved by irony. When he painted himself in 1919 with wing-collar, cigar and fizzing champagne, he was not parodying the lounge lizard who keeps on smiling as the ship goes down at the end of the war; this was not

some social disguise (Beckmann really wore tuxedos) and his red-rimmed eyes
and hollow cheeks speak of traumatized exhaustion. The self-portrait is no less
sincere than the one he painted two years later as a miserable clown still holding
his slapstick but with his laughing mask fallen and one bare forearm
outstretched, showing his stigmata, but as if begging for a veinful of morphine.

Beckmann witnessed the devastating annihilations of the First World
War firsthand. In the *Self-Portrait with Red Scarf*, made during the war, he wedges
himself into the picture like a climber jammed in a crevasse, using hands and
elbows to keep from falling. His veins stand out, livid and green, and the
stricken face is emaciated. Through the window, the sky admits not light but
further pressure, as if there were no escape from this hell, which there never
would be again in Beckmann's prison-house of art, where people are crammed
into canvases too narrow to contain them, space is as hard and solid as shards
and the eye has nowhere to go for comfort. None of this had anything to do
with Modernist space; Beckmann couldn't stand Matisse, despised the Cubism
of 'chequerboard' Picasso and had no interest in flatness per se. His art is as
blunt and brutal and direct as the subjects it portrays, including himself.

Not many martyrs have actually gone at the canvas with their own
precious fluids (though Munch notoriously painted with his own semen) but the

metaphor is there for the self-dramatist. 'I paint,' declared Beckmann's compatriot
and fellow Expressionist Ernst Ludwig Kirchner, 'with my nerves and my blood.'
Nothing else would do. The combination produced some atrocious hacking and
stabbing and doing his damnedest to get over the sheer horror of modern
existence, but it also produced one of Kirchner's best paintings, *Self-Portrait as a
Soldier,* in which he appears in German army uniform with his right hand lopped
off at the wrist, mutilated in a war he never quite fought.

Kirchner was a reluctant conscript in the Great War. In the spring of
1915, when he was almost thirty-five, he applied to become an artillery driver,
what was known as 'an involuntary volunteer'. Within months he suffered a
nervous breakdown and was sent home on temporary leave, where he began to
drink heavily and soon became addicted to sleeping tablets and morphine. By
November he was ill enough to be pronounced unfit for military service.

The self-portrait was painted – somehow – that autumn. All dressed up
in the uniform of Field Artillery Regiment No. 75, its number embroidered on
the epaulettes, Prussian and German cockades on the cap, Kirchner could not
be clearer about the disgust he feels for everything these symbols represent. A
cigarette dangles mockingly from one corner of his mouth. The black eye slits
are sightless with disaffection and turned away from the model who poses so

pointlessly in the studio behind him. For Kirchner cannot paint any more. He holds his arms up as if in bitter parody of surrender – please don't shoot. Not only are there no paints or brushes but his painting hand has gone too, leaving only a gangrenous cross-section.

It is a trope, this image of the artist mutilated by a war in which he sustained no physical injuries; the point is obviously that his soul has been crippled. Once there was art, as represented by the model (Kirchner was passionate about the nude as 'the foundation of all visual art'), now there is only the wounding memory of war and all it has done to destroy him. Though here is the paradox rephrased, for it is hard to say exactly what war has destroyed if it produced what he himself regarded as one of his strongest paintings.

Kirchner thought he was *the* German artist, born to revive the tradition of Dürer. To begin with this meant jagged woodcuts and pastiche Lucas Cranach, but it also meant a commitment to one's deepest inner being. French art, Kirchner thought, was all about appearances whereas 'the Teuton seeks out what lies beneath', hence the severed hands and blinded vision. But the influence of French painting, most particularly Matisse, is there in every second canvas, along with hints of Van Gogh. Kirchner greatly admired Van Gogh's *Self-Portrait with a Bandaged Ear*, a literal wound displayed, by contrast, without a trace of self-pity.

But Kirchner stops borrowing and comes into his own in *Self-Portrait as a Soldier* with its jammed-up space, terse brushwork, strident angles and diagonals, stiff figures with sickly yellow skin and chopped bodies. He hasn't lost his touch; on the contrary he has overcome misery to paint this very picture. Sardonic rather than triumphant – Kirchner wouldn't want you to think the wounds had actually *healed* – this image does not slither into the self-pity of future self-portraits where the painter is a bleary drunk alone with his best friend, alcohol. Munch painted exactly this same scenario, the bottle and I, together for ever, with far more pictorial ingenuity: the bottle seated next to him as an upright and commanding figure who cannot be refused, two black-clad waiters at the back of the room appearing like a double-headed demon above the artist's head, presiding over his faltering will.

Kirchner and Munch both overcame their addictions after psychiatric treatment; Munch at a clinic in Copenhagen, Kirchner in a sanatorium before retreating to the mountains of Switzerland. Despite, or because of, the fact that Kirchner's art had lost most of its edge by the end of the war, he enjoyed huge success back home until his work was included in Hitler's 'Degenerate Art' show in the 1930s. Where other artists considered this a bitter honour – Oscar Kokoschka's *Self-Portrait as a Degenerate Artist* is all arms-folded defiance – Kirchner went out into the Swiss woods and shot himself. Munch, who by poetic justice ought to have died young, lived to be over eighty. 'The second half of my life is a struggle just to remain upright,' he remarked of the illness, despair and fear of death that filled his days, but the pressure of all three eventually produced his greatest self-portrait.

———

Pictures of martyrs parading their wounds as marks of heroism and sanctity: such images are designed to have *agency*, the power to harrow, inspire, arouse compassion and even convert the viewer. They ask you to take sides, to decide between victim and tormentor while being positively one-sided in themselves. Even the most exalted levels of Western art from the Sistine Ceiling to Titian's *Flaying of Marsyas*, from Piero della Francesca's *Flagellation of Christ* to *The Death of Marat*, are in this sense political.

But the self-portrait as martyr is exceptionally partisan. There are no sides to be taken because there are no other versions of the story. In so far as they tell a story, and this is a distinctive trait, it is presented as a closing argument, a public protest, a performance conspicuously meant to persuade and recruit. When Egon Schiele portrayed himself as Saint Sebastian in a hail of arrows it was not some private act of self-pity for the relief of injured feelings, embarrassing had it been found by a stranger, but the most direct form of public appeal – a self-portrait for the poster to his first show.

Detail of *Self-Portrait as Saint Sebastian*, 1914–15

Egon Schiele
(1890–1918)

It is a scarifying piece of graphic art: the arrows like hurtling vectors meeting Schiele's bony fingers tip to tip, pinioning his arms as if he were being crucified on an invisible cross. The ink lines shoot electric shocks through his flailing scarecrow of a body. Look upon me, Egon Schiele, suffering for my art even unto death. The allusion to Sebastian is flagrant and emphatic. If the drawing were not so superb, you would need a heart of stone not to laugh.

Schiele is wearing a long orange overcoat. It is the same coat you see in a painting he made of himself two years earlier in jail, awaiting trial on charges of kidnap and indecency. There he showed himself with a beard and cropped hair lying on a prison pallet wrapped in this greatcoat against the cold, shocked and gaunt and wounded. But the picture has been upended so that the figure now seems to turn in white space, like so many of Schiele's emaciated men and women, and beneath it he has set forth his case: 'To restrict the artist is a crime. It is to murder budding life.'

The charges of abducting and sexually abusing an underage girl were finally dropped, but Schiele was found guilty of displaying a drawing of a girl, naked from the waist down, on his studio wall, where it would be visible to the children who came to model. His offence lay not in making but showing such pictures.

Schiele was sentenced to three days in prison. A very qualified martyrdom, and it takes a lively narcissism if not a persecution complex to translate such punishment into the arrows of Saint Sebastian. But there is no reason why artists should be denied the freedom of poets to communicate in metaphor, and Schiele was only following pictorial tradition anyway. What raises issues of proportion and taste, however, what complicates credibility here, is the very fact that this is a self-portrait.

Artists who protest too much either way – self-pity, self-satisfaction – raise suspicions of exaggeration on the one hand and egregious self-love on the other. Suspicion breeds doubt. One no longer believes the self-portrait.

Disbelief is not a common response to art. Nobody stands in front of *The Death of Marat* with mistrust feeling cheated of the truth, even though, to take two different classes of fiction, the painting shows a man who has clearly never suffered from skin disease, unlike Marat; and a makeshift desk that already bears, within moments of the death, the wording of David's tribute. Neither does anyone doubt a flight of angels, whatever Courbet may say, in the context of a Tiepolo sky.

Portraits sometimes raise suspicion, it is true, especially that most implausible of genres the royal portrait; think of Reynolds's ten-foot George III in a tide of ermine that washes out of the picture in waves; we understand the commission as a poisoned chalice and perhaps even look for unconscious signs of strain on the artist's part. Likewise when a portrait is poorly made, like

*The Wounded Deer,
Self-Portrait*, 1946

Frida Kahlo
(1907–54)

a bad novel, we might wonder why this writer, that artist, is trying to make us believe all these lies. But the suspicions induced by images of the artist as victim or martyr are of another kind altogether, more like those that attach to real people.

Take Frida Kahlo's painting of herself stuck with arrows. This self-portrait goes further in the victim stakes than anything by Schiele, for Kahlo is not just wounded in nine different places, she has given herself the body of a hunted deer. There is other symbolism too – a broken branch beneath the dainty hooves, dark trees, lightning striking in the background – but nothing to compare with this cute and fragile victim, a Bambi with Kahlo's head.

The cult of Kahlo, or the war for her soul, has now reached such a pitch that interpretations of this stiff, faux-naïf picture go in quite opposing directions. One insists that the painting represents Kahlo's immense and much documented sufferings. These begin with the horrifying bus accident at eighteen that broke her spine in three places, causing lifelong pain, as depicted in *The Broken Column*, which shows her nude body split in two to expose the classical column of her spine, the halves held together by straps and martyrs' nails. They continue with her marriage and divorce and remarriage to the philandering Diego Rivera; her miscarriage; his affair with her sister; the amputation of her right leg; her relentless hospitalizations and premature death, at forty-seven, from complications following pneumonia. Kahlo, this tiny woman with her wild and mysterious beauty, her free spirit and delicate body, chooses the emblem of a little deer with good reason; though she was never so fragile that she couldn't muster the strength (or courage, depending on your empathy) to tell her terrible story to the world.

But a counter-campaign wants to make a serious political artist out of the feminist icon, to detach the damaged life from the paintings. The deer is an Aztec symbol and Frida is a Mexican nationalist. The inclusion of the word Carma at the bottom of the painting, alluding to Oriental beliefs in reincarnation, reflects 'her espousal of a hybrid multi-cultural world view'.[3] This way comes trouble. Although Kahlo did paint some political satires in the 1930s they are slight and tendentious and in later life, when she became dependent on painkillers, her politics could be generously described as naïve. She idolized Mao and Stalin, whose 'portrait' she painted, and she even seems to have had a slight weakness for Hitler, whose face appears among the pantheon of heroes in her late (1945, of all dates) and very regrettable allegory, *Moses*.

But before all this comes the painting itself and the way it first strikes as an image: weird, crude, maybe even borderline mad in the manner of the Outsider Art so admired and plundered by the Surrealists. Kahlo was well versed in Surrealism (André Breton tried to co-opt her) and there is a touch of Max Ernst to those trees; and fetishes, from animals to eyes and masks, Mexican gods and pre-Columbian fertility symbols, infest her art. That the deer is evidently male complicates the symbolism somewhat, but it hardly diminishes the intended pathos of *The Wounded Deer*.

'I've done my paintings well and they have a message of pain,' said Kahlo with frank understatement.[4] For what else do her self-portraits convey — a sword to the heart, neck noosed with bloody thorns, alone with her monkeys and dogs in despair, riven in two, trussed back together, her head emblazoned with a chakra containing a skull and crossbones, her mouth emitting a cornucopia of dead fish, weeping and showing her wounds. Even her birth, the baby recognizably bearing Kahlo's distinctive monobrow, is a dreadful psychodrama: the mother's legs wrenched apart to show the exit of the bleeding head, the rest of her body covered from the waist in a shroud. In our beginning is our end.

Kahlo's admirers are generally as au fait with her life as her art, though it is hard for any viewer to remain ignorant since the paintings *are* the story. Kahlo is not interested in paint per se, has no strong gifts as a painter as opposed to an inventor of motifs that have immense public reach, rather like Munch, whose graphic art carries his meanings just as well as and often more

Self-Portrait with Cropped Hair, 1940

Frida Kahlo (1907–54)

Mira que si te quise, fué por el pelo,
Ahora que estás pelona, ya no te quiero.

1940 Frida Kahlo.

strongly than his paintings. Her main motif is her own face and she fixed its depiction early on – stern, unsmiling, beautiful, in a three-quarter view with a hint of a moustache, you must take her as you find her – and it never changes because Kahlo has to be the recognizable protagonist from one frame to the next. The scene may shift from Mexican landscape to American hospital, the costume from Western bride to Mexican peasant, but she never alters or ages. She turned herself into an icon.

But there are paintings in which Kahlo goes beyond her customary self-portrait, the victim as heroine relating her tale of anguish, and which drop the simple opposition between martyrdom and resistance. In *Self-Portrait with Cropped Hair*, which you feel she might almost be performing before an audience, Kahlo is wearing a man's suit. She sits on a chair on a bare stage, scissors in one hand, one of her own braids lopped off in the other and the floor strewn with severed tresses. The face and body are cartoon-rudimentary but this hair – single strands, hanks, the other braid – has active life, falling and tangling and draping over her knee and the chair; painted every time with feeling. And what a retort to the words and music above, voicing a man's cruel rejection of a woman: 'Look, if I loved you it was for your hair, now that you have no hair I don't love you any more.' Call it self-martyrdom, bitter fulfilment, vengeance or lament, the painting has exceptional nuance. It does not illustrate an episode (the incident never happened, though she painted it when Rivera divorced her), it invents a new pictorial metaphor with a sardonic twist, written in Kahlo's own hair.

To portray oneself as a martyr is to be unembarrassed at the very least, to see oneself as immune to accusations of narcissism, egotism, self-pity. In a way, Kahlo's very failings as an artist are possibly what protect her from being seen as self-sorry; put crudely, the pictures are as raw as they have to be. Any more eloquence and they would not howl; any more expressiveness of touch and the ex-voto style would become kitsch. She is a presentiment of the future, the way in which artists have come to be seen as personalities and their works expressions of a personal legend, from Joseph Beuys crashing his plane in Russia and being kept alive, wrapped in fat and felt, by Tartars on horseback to Tracey Emin's tormented early life. Emin's miseries reach even further than Kahlo's in a sense; we can relate more easily to a broken heart than a broken back.

———

John Berryman once bitterly observed that the best thing that can happen to a young poet is a disaster that does not actually kill him. Kahlo's first self-portrait was made in hospital after the crash; Emin's entire early life qualifies as her disaster.

Tracey Emin needs no introduction. That is her defining characteristic as an artist. The subject of her work is being Emin; the object is to make herself known. This has been achieved as much through her work — the spindly self-portraits, the photographs and embroideries, the famous tent embroidered with the names of everyone she has ever slept with from her twin in the womb to her aborted fetuses, the notorious unmade bed — as through the incessant newspaper interviews and columns, the appearances on television, the advertisements for vodka.

One result of this sustained exposure to Emin's story is that more people know about her youth in Margate and her abortions, drinking, despair and the alleged rape than have ever seen the bed or the drawings. Her torrentially outspoken behaviour on television and her emotional appeal as some sort of wronged Medea equal her popularity as an artist. This is why some prefer to think of the woman as a total artwork in herself, and why it is so hard to separate the life from the works.

When Emin shows a hospital gown on its peg you cannot help wondering if she herself once wore it. You cannot look at the two tiny chairs she exhibited some years ago without wondering if they stand for the children she lost, whose names were embroidered in the tent. They aren't asking to be viewed as works of imagination so much as relics of her experience, the more so when they are presented as literally that: Emin's menstrual knickers, torn tights, empty fag packets, bottles and multiple forms of contraceptive (why so many?) strewn around that lost weekend of a bed. This is why it can be dismaying to learn that her more recent embroideries with their signature wonky lettering — 'It's fucking agony, and I'm alone', 'I do not expect to be a mother but I do expect to die alone', 'I'm going to get you, you bastard, and when I do the world will know that you destroyed my childhood' — are made by teams of professional seamstresses.

Emin is a good old-fashioned Expressionist. Her favourite artist is Munch. Her rachitic little drawings of herself — wretched and drunk, slumped beneath the shower, bleeding, post-coital, desperate — have overtones of Schiele though none of his fierce graphic register. If their fragility is at odds with her barnstorming public persona that only seems to enhance the air of truth to experience: the secret sadness, the private confessions brought very plaintively, if also very fully, into the open. Look at the photographic self-portrait called *The Last Thing I Said to You Was Don't Leave Me Here* where she huddles with her back to us in a corner of the room, naked, thin, forlorn, the image of a Schiele nude.

Expressing shameless self-pity as the rest of us could not, or would not, Emin has acquired a public persona in Britain by now about as cherished as John Betjeman's. The paradox does not escape her. She once titled a whole show *You Forgot to Kiss My Soul*, the pathetic words written up in Barbie-pin neon, and included a video in which she played two roles, a good-girl Tracey in dressing gown and slippers cowering as her bad-girl counterpart hammered drunk and maudlin on the door in the middle of the night. The battle between marauding ego and abject id has always been her best performance – dramatizing, but also sending herself up as the double-act of victim art.

Emin eventually produced the autobiography she was clearly destined to write. The words of her art were always like fragments of a diary or confessional memoir in any case, and with its public announcements of outrage and grief the book extended the art. But some of its worst stories were disputed by those involved, rather like those survivor memoirs in which the victim tells it – *somewhat* – as it was. 'It is not the true reality, but it's my reality,' wrote Monique de Wael in defence of her memoir *Surviving with Wolves*, in which she depicted herself as a Jewish girl who survived the Shoah through the kindness of wolves. No matter how far-fetched that sounds, millions of people actually believed de Wael's story and even when she was exposed, opinion divided between those who felt robbed of this sensational suffering and the indulgent relativists who still believe the book offers some kind of universal truth.

You could make the same comparison with Munch, in one sense; he really did have a nervous breakdown, really did survive Spanish flu, but Larsen never tried to kill him. The difference is that Emin's tales revolve around her, whereas Munch's greatest self-portraits rise above the level of My Private Hell, become true to the whole human condition.

The second half of Munch's life was a long struggle against the dread of extinction that taints our days, threatening to make our ambitions appear impotent and aimless. But the very fear that might have paralysed another artist produced that deathless masterpiece, *Between the Clock and the Bed*, one of the last pictures Munch painted in the solitary house in Norway where he spent the last twenty-eight years of his life in almost total seclusion.

The artist is seen in his characteristic late stance, legs planted, arms dangling by his sides, feet splayed as if to give himself just a little more ballast. He stands there like a butler waiting for instructions, walled in between time and sleep, between the high clock and the narrow bed, both by now silent heralds of death. Munch is infirm, and so is the painting itself to some degree, with its weak brushstrokes, washy reflections and vaguely summoned furnishings. But there is self-deprecation in the parallel between himself and the grandfather clock that rises beside him, another rickety old man with a blank face, lacking numbers and time. The clock stands still like this sightless man who will eventually pass away in the bed. But not yet...As a depiction of old age straining to remain upright in the shadow of mortality, the image is incomparably poignant and heroic. You feel the courage in Munch's forlorn will-power, and his self-portrait inspires you to take courage yourself.

Self-Portrait between the Clock and the Bed, c. 1942

Edvard Munch (1863–1944)

Chapter Fourteen
Pioneers

'I am my style'

Paul Klee

Self-Portrait with a Bandaged Ear, 1889

Vincent van Gogh (1853–90)

V incent Van Gogh paints himself free of self-pity. It does not occur to him to complain. No matter what he endures, no matter what anguish and penury and isolation he suffers, he does not feel sorry for himself in his self-portraits.

This seems counterintuitive. Vincent, as we intimately call him, is surely the most wronged and downtrodden painter in art, a lone soul struggling to sing like a bird while the brutes shoot him down, a misunderstood genius excluded and eventually suicided – as Antonin Artaud said – by society. The passion of his painting equates, somewhat, in our minds with the missionary passion of his life: he is ill but he cares for others; he is poor and yet takes the indigent into his home; he preaches a message of hope through the whole of his life without ever being given a reason to hope. He fails as a preacher, his zeal unheeded; he fails in the art trade, just as we feel a spirit so high above commerce should. Unrequited in love, unrecognized as an artist – not a single painting sold in his lifetime, as legend has it – he was locked up by public petition as not fit for the liberty of the streets. At his lowest point, desperate for brotherhood, abandoned by the treacherous Gauguin, he finally shoots himself in a field where the black crows caw, unable to walk any more through the shadows of depression. Of all painters Van Gogh is the nearest to martyrdom and the furthest from ego, the one we would most like to protect and the one we would most readily embrace if he chose to lament his lot.

But he never does. Van Gogh is not wretched in his art and he is not a martyr. There may be melancholy and a look of aftershock in the self-portraits from time to time, but he keeps the agonies to himself in the endeavour to make strong paintings. This strength is visible and palpably uplifting yet it has not prevented generations of viewers from believing that they experience his sufferings when they look at his works, that they can hear the fine high notes of Vincent's grief. In that sense, these are among the most unexamined – and misunderstood – of all self-portraits; as if people could not see them clearly because blinded by their own fellow feeling.

Consider *Self-Portrait with a Bandaged Ear*, generally thought to show Van Gogh at his most harrowed. The very title speaks of injury, and of Vincent's notoriously self-inflicted injury – the severing of his ear lobe during the fateful visit of Gauguin to the Yellow House in Arles. In that title the whole of Vincent's tragedy is compressed. But the title is not his. He did not give the self-portraits titles (they came later) and on the very rare occasions when he writes of them to his brother, Theo, the descriptions are terse: 'three-quarter length on a light background', 'dark violet-blue and the head whitish with yellow hair, so it has a colour effect'. A colour effect: what an understatement!

Self-Portrait with a Bandaged Ear certainly has a colour effect. It pits the arsenical green of the overcoat, buttoned against the cold, and the aqueous green of the eyes, brilliant as the sea surrounding an iceberg, against the yellow walls of the house in Arles. 'Yellow,' wrote Van Gogh, 'is the colour of hope' and so it always seems in his art. He may be bandaged, but to see him in his familiar bedroom, opposite the window and the bed and the rush-seated chair, with the walls glowing encouragingly behind him, is to know that whatever else he is feeling, Van Gogh is at the very least at home. He has all his possessions around him: the easel in the background bearing a work in its early stages; the Japanese print pinned to the wall, its pale Mount Fuji a tiny circumflex echoing the dark triangle of Van Gogh's body and the lighter triangle of his face; the fur-trimmed hat with its curious prow of brushy furze protecting his head against the cold. It is a congested scene, all hemmed in except for the opening on the right which, like stage wings, implies another place to go and gives, moreover, onto daylight.

Van Gogh must have painted the picture in January 1889. His final row with Gauguin, apparently triggered by a disagreement over Rembrandt whose work they had admired in Montpellier on the same trip where they saw *Bonjour Monsieur Courbet*, took place on Christmas Eve 1888. As is well known, Van Gogh had severed a part of his ear in a wild fever and taken it as a gift to a girl he had seen in a bar. He was in hospital for some time and then lovingly cared for at home by the redoubtable postman Roulin. At the time of painting, before the dressings were finally removed in late January, he is writing almost daily to Theo, not just about Rembrandt and his own aspirations for art but about the serenity he aims to achieve. Everything ran against this. His landlord was trying to have him thrown out of the Yellow House, the local police were keeping a close watch, there was no money and Gauguin, who had long since departed, kept pestering him for the return of certain possessions and for a painting of sunflowers he insisted he had been promised. Van Gogh was frail, undernourished, chronically insomniac and tormented by nightmares whenever he did manage to sleep. But still — *and* still — he continues to paint.

To those who see him as a holy man of art, the Van Gogh of this self-portrait is displaying stigmata. Brutally shaven, with his martyr's wound, he freezes in the January cold, every brushmark raw with horror. He had come to Arles to follow the light, find the way and the life, hoping to gather around him a band of like-minded brothers, but the only one who had come had already deserted him. Yet he must go on, on towards the truth, painting even when hungry and ill, even when flayed. Doctor Gachet, the physician who looked after Van Gogh so tenderly in his final days, was the first to use the term. 'The words "love of art",' Gachet wrote, 'are scarcely applicable to him, one ought to say: belief unto martyrdom.'[1]

But paintings are their own evidence. In *Self-Portrait with Bandaged Ear* the brushmarks are slower than usual, carefully laid, as if trying to keep the picture steady. There are no whorls and striations, no speeding vectors, and the bandage is not sacramental, no matter how we might cherish the legend of the Holy Ear. It is just there as part of the scene, a matter of fact like the coat or the hat, not something that magically transforms the meaning of the picture. A picture that is extraordinarily still, moreover, the storm having passed, the wreckage having been repaired. The incident is not forgotten – Van Gogh could have chosen not to paint himself with a bandage, just as he could have painted himself *unbandaged*, hacked and bleeding like the Expressionists who venerated his work – but Van Gogh has achieved a degree of pictorial composure. Perhaps it was hard-won (the eyes betray a long and weary relationship with the mirror) but the face is not so much harrowed as stoic and strange to itself in convalescence. This is a dignified and austere self-portrait, its mood swings confined to form and colour. It is not a martyrdom.

————

It is not true that Van Gogh never sold a work. A young Scotsman he met in Paris bought a picture directly from him – a basket of apples, surging like a plucky raft on a sea of brushstrokes so exuberant the canvas is practically overflowing: joy in all things. Van Gogh received nothing more than the price of the fruit, but some bitter consolation can be found in the fact that the buyer's horrified father stupidly disposed of the picture for £5 not many months later. Early collectors often lost their nerve. In 1893, three years after Van Gogh's suicide, the British consul in Amsterdam bought what must be the wildest painting of crustaceans in all art, a bizarre portrait – no other word will do – of two raging-red crabs thrashing against a tight green ground as if protesting their freedom. Stranger than Salvador Dali's lobster telephone, it still looks staggeringly avant-garde today and it is just as well the consul died soon after selling it for a mere £8, escaping inevitable remorse, for it soon changed hands for a small fortune and entered the National Gallery in London.

Unlucky in life, Van Gogh was blessed in death to have his reputation cherished by an extraordinary woman, his sister-in-law Jo Bonger, who inherited his estate upon Theo's premature death only six months after his brother. Bonger seems to have had a keen sense of the future and of the way Van Gogh's fortunes would turn. She sent his paintings to exhibitions all over Europe instead of simply handing them, in her grief, to a dealer. She also refused to allow the publication of his incomparably eloquent letters to Theo before the paintings were well established, realizing that the tragedy of his life might overshadow the art. 'It would have been unfair towards the deceased artist,' she wrote in the preface to the first edition in 1914, 'to awaken an interest in his person before his work, to which he dedicated his life, was recognized and adequately appreciated.'

French collectors bought sunflowers and starry skies. The Dutch bought the Southern sun of Provence. A London stockbroker had the wit to collect the dark and knotted drawings of peasants made when Van Gogh was teaching himself to draw with do-it-yourself manuals in his father's house; these exceptional images, with their bent and humbled figures, their delicate wintry branches so much like Hiroshige's cherry trees, show how early and swiftly Van Gogh absorbed the lessons of Japanese art. It's a mere few years to the blazing glory of the irises and sunflowers, for Van Gogh's is one of the shortest careers in art, not more than a decade from beginning to end. But the self-portraits only arrive in the last five years and were not the first of his pictures to find fame. Jo Bonger's instincts about the letters protected the self-portraits, at least in the early twentieth century, from being valued less as art than as relics.

In 1885, returning to his father's parsonage after several failed careers, Van Gogh paints himself with eyes red and swollen but piercingly vital. In Paris two years later, he shows more of himself, dressed like an urban dandy. He holds a pipe, smokes a pipe, shows himself with pipe and beer glass in the unconvincing manner of Courbet. He clasps his palette like Rembrandt, whose work he is studying in the Louvre; you can see the influences he absorbs by the season in the self-portraits – from Rembrandt to Courbet, Millais and Monet; in Arles, during Gauguin's nine-week stay, he even painted himself flattened and rugged as a Gauguin. Yet no matter how much he venerated the work of other artists, his mannerisms are indelibly his own – the vectoring hyphens, the unfurling spirals and whorls, the auraed suns and starlit haloes, the crisp flakes of sunlight seen through dark leaves, the pigment almost unmixed from the tube, the pressure of the brush firm on the resistant canvas, the unmistakable mark. Van Gogh's signature is in every stroke. He never needed to sign a painting.

And the self-portraits keep pace with each new phase of his art. Van Gogh is a pale ghost against a dark ground, very nearly Art Deco; or his head is as explosive as a sunflower. In one self-portrait, the face is almost entirely green – 'the green of summer sky' – apart from a bright glint on the forehead, and then the sudden flaming of hair. In another the eyes are cobalt against a salmon-pink ground, an inversion of cherry blossom against a bright spring sky. His face is like a wind-flurried wheat field, or a curlicued pattern of tendrils. There is a self-portrait where an ear has the intricate origami-folds of an iris, and another where the dark eyes are fringed with bright lashes like a sunflower.

'What impassions me most, much, much more than all the rest of my work is the portrait, the modern portrait.' Van Gogh is writing during the Paris years, and unable to pay for models, resorts to his own face. His aim is to be more truthful than the academic conventions of portraiture have ever been and he will get there with his colour effects: 'Instead of trying to reproduce exactly what I have before my eyes I use colour arbitrarily to express myself forcibly.' Around this time he made the *Self-Portrait with Felt Hat*, a painting composed of short sharp lines like exclamation marks without the dots, each laid quite visibly one to the next. One imagines him tilting sideways to work his way up the collar, round the hat, into the eye sockets, the marks a continuous radiation that reaches its culmination in the vibrant halo around his head.

Van Gogh was coming to the end of his time in the city and his spirits were failing. 'When I left Paris seriously sick at heart and in body, nearly an alcoholic because of my rising fury at my strength failing me – then I shut myself up within myself.' Yet the painting communicates neither weakness nor failure, as one might expect, let's say, from a more conventional *fin de siècle* self-portrait. You cannot look at it without being intensely aware of its singular idiom, of the way the hand must have held the brush and pressed its freight of paint over and again on the springy canvas, of the rose madder and ultramarine and burnt umber and violet that build up the figure against its ground. Standing before it in the Van Gogh Museum in Amsterdam, you feel held in a force field the source of which is not in the facial expression, or the palpable intensity of the eyes, but in the working of the surface itself.

It does not seem an exaggeration to speak of the *aura* of Van Gogh's paintings. In the self-portraits that follow, the marks are like hyphenations, Morse code, war paint or tribal markings. The whorls in the background resemble the dizzying morphology of migraines. Moist brushmarks elongate around the neck or arms and turn dry and staccato among the close alleys of the face. How hard it must have been to navigate the human countenance with this evolving system of notations, striations, spirals and minims, so much more easily applied to furrowed fields or the wallpaper behind the postman's wife, and yet Van Gogh strives on, never letting himself off, making no exception for his own face. And though the rhythms flow relatively easily through cloth and hair and even nostrils, the whole structure of the eye defies him. In *Self-Portrait with Felt Hat* the pupils are eventually described simply as dark circles, as if the pioneering of this new way of painting reached its limits at this deepest of points.

'It is difficult to know yourself,' he wrote to Theo during the last months at the asylum of St-Rémy, 'but it isn't easy to paint yourself either.'

Those who want to find, and perhaps protect, the harrowed soul in Van Gogh's self-portraits are generally those who find madness there too. But the conviction that his marks are indices of neurosis, if not full-blown insanity, is slowly beginning to weaken. Van Gogh did not paint, could not paint, in the grip of the paranoia and depression that sporadically assailed him. Lucidity and calm – he writes constantly of the *calmness* of his art – were absolutely necessary and, without them, he would have been a quite ordinary painter.

Self-Portrait with Felt Hat,
c. 1887–8

Vincent van Gogh
(1853–90)

Between these bouts of paranoia and depression, he tells Theo, he must take advantage of every moment. 'I am not strictly speaking mad, for my mind is absolutely normal in the intervals … but during the attacks it is terrible – and then I lose consciousness of everything. But that spurs me on to work and to seriousness, as a miner who is always in danger makes haste in what he does.'

There is no disorder in the letters. They are lucid to the end. The one found in his jacket when he shot himself is as ever concerned for Theo, encouraging him not to downgrade himself as a 'simple dealer in Corot' but to consider the part he has played in the actual paintings of others, and observing with devastating clarity that he is in a considerable crisis, his own reason 'half-foundered' in the making of art. But the handwriting holds steady, somehow, in the service of communicating reassurance and news to Theo, unlike the nearly illegible scratching in the last letters of his contemporary Nietzsche, which, in their every word and mark, express a mind vanishing into the tunnel of insanity.

There is a self-portrait in which Van Gogh is visibly losing his grasp – his grasp of the lexicon of marks. It was made at St-Rémy in late August 1889 and one has a sense of some kind of neurological failure, of the mind trying and failing to transmit its stream of commands to the hand. Or of the hand being the wrong hand, struggling to do just as its brother has always done so well; indeed the hand holding the palette in this slowed and stalled painting is itself an oddly shrunken invalid. But if there is less physical dexterity, there is no loss of intellectual strength – the man is still here in the art – and it makes the fortitude exceptionally poignant.

This is not the last self-portrait, no matter how funereal the black background or emaciated the pale face, any more than *Crows over the Wheatfield* is Van Gogh's last painting. We take it to be so because its apocalyptic energy and beauty seem to be a fitting herald of death as much as the dark harbingers hovering over the field. But scholars have shown that the marvellously controlled *Daubigny's Garden*, beginning with its plot of vivid irises and rising to its distant church steeple, is more likely to be the final work. And just as the last letter is not a suicide note so what seems to be the final self-portrait does not speak of last things, though it does stand as a tremendous summation of all he hoped to achieve with the modern portrait.

Dazzling and yet solemn, it is the painting of a man resolute in infirmity, sure in dilemma, upright in the sea of brilliant blue whorls. He stands within a *Starry Night* in daytime as if there were no world except that of his painting. The song of the colour is strong, the movement of lines radically idiomatic yet nonetheless perfectly descriptive of the crag of the cheekbones, the eyebrows sinking within the folds of the frown, the red beard stark as ever. Van Gogh talks of himself as he talks of sunlight and fir trees: in exactly the

Self-Portrait, 1889

Vincent van Gogh
(1853–90)

same language. He is of a piece with his painting. It has been said that in some pictures it hardly matters whether the subject is a bedroom or a pair of old boots, Van Gogh's style is so powerful, so overwhelmingly uppermost, that he might as well be painting one of his own paintings. But the counterargument is here in this very late self-portrait, so sane and unself-pitying, so triumphant over life's miseries, where the style represents the man who is both its channel and source. Van Gogh never explained exactly how he hoped his colour effects would act upon others, but the strange outcome of so much radiance here is a kind of uplifting quietude in the music of marks. Calmness was what he sought in his art and achieved in this tremendous self-portrait.

———

How should an artist represent him or herself – in or out of idiom? It is a question Van Gogh repeatedly ponders and answers very differently. There is the late Van Gogh who has become one with his style, but there are also self-portraits that look quite solidly realistic. He could make himself look like a nineteenth-century Salon portrait, very ordinary, even academic, but an exact match with the existing photograph; or he could make himself look like a Van Gogh.

In or out of style is the great issue that comes with Modernism, or at least with the end of naturalistic figuration. It is true that self-portraitists in earlier centuries had to make decisions about style – whether to paint themselves in miniature, like the Dutch Frans van Meiris, who has his back to the viewer and turns laughingly with a tiny mandolin in his hand (a neat conflation of all the amusing conceits he could offer potential patrons from his box of tricks); whether to paint themselves as a swagger portrait, like Van Dyck; whether to depict oneself in tondo or full-length, in profile or grisaille; whether to go to the furthest extreme, like Poussin, and embody all the principles of one's art in a self-portrait. But the question of style presents itself more clearly, and more unusually, than ever before once art moves into Modernism.

It might seem a question that answers itself: why should modern artists drop their idiom, their defining characteristics, jump out of character, as it were, in order to speak of themselves? It would be like taking off a mask, stripping away the pretence, regressing from blank verse to prose; it would be to imply that a realistic likeness is all that matters. Which artist would ever do that, depict themselves in anything but the style of their own work? Modigliani, long, lean and linear with his tilted head and moué mouth, looks just like an unusually feeble Modigliani. Soutine, with his poor bockled face and ragged body, is a typical Soutine. Picasso, in 1906, has already been looking at the African sculptures in the Paris Trocadero and will soon be moving swiftly, one senses, to *Les Demoiselles d'Avignon*.

But there is no Cubist Picasso. There is no Ab-Ex Jackson Pollock, and the issue is evidently not so simple for makers of abstract art who nonetheless want to bequeath a recognizable self-portrait to posterity. For them there is the camera, of course, and a photograph together with a specimen work may suffice; in Brancusi's ruggedly handsome photo of himself, the Endless Column rises totemically like an alter ego. But for many abstract painters there is an urge to self-portraiture that cannot be fulfilled either by photography or abstraction. Willem de Kooning, Mark Rothko, Ad Reinhardt, Ellsworth Kelly (in more than forty self-portraits) – they all resort or retreat, depending on your prejudice, to cave art figuration. Even painters who have the option of figuration built in, because image and subject remain representationally linked to some degree – the Fauves, for instance, or some of the Futurists – revert to something less distractingly advanced in their self-portraits. It seems that one does not sacrifice one's *own* face to the cause of modern art quite so readily.

There is a self-portrait by Piet Mondrian that is so unexpected as to seem quite implausible. He looks like a Fayum portrait, one of those beautiful oval faces with their liquid eyes painted on Egyptian coffins from the Roman period. That Mondrian was capable of painting something so romantic and even antique comes as a revelation; persuasively realistic, it feels like a sudden aside, an intimate monologue. It disturbs one's sense of the painter.

In fact, the picture was painted before Mondrian became a single-minded master of abstraction and was still innocent enough for simple depiction. But as it turns out, there were other surprisingly naturalistic self-portraits.

Five years after he had signed his last figurative painting, Mondrian produced a self-portrait that could only be described in exactly those terms, showing the artist dapperly dressed in front of one of his own abstract canvases. He is staring out from the painting (and the painting within the painting, which puts another rectangle round his head) in a neat collar and what looks remarkably like a bowtie. From Manet to T. S. Eliot onwards it is, of course, well known that Modernists do not always dress like artists, though in this case there is a telling correspondence here between the tailored painter and the fastidious paintings. But it feels a furtive and even irascible self-portrait, not simply because the atmosphere is shadowy, the palette subfusc and the painter perceptibly annoyed. There is an exasperated tension here and it may be instructive to know that Mondrian once took a pistol to a self-portrait and drilled it full of holes.

A perfectionist? Indubitably so, but the famous anecdote about Mondrian's hatred of the colour green may give more of a clue to the peculiarities of this self-portrait. In the hall of his flat, this monastic Dutch bachelor displayed a tulip that was symbolic, he said, of the presence (though also the absence) of a woman. But Mondrian cancelled nature by painting it white.

This self-portrait has been falsified too. Mondrian hasn't signed it Mondrian, the name he used for his abstract art, but Mondriaan, the spelling he used before; not so much faking the date as predating the artist. A stylistic compromise is also attempted between the two ages of his art.

Rejecting nature, Mondrian had reduced his work to linear grids of black on white plus the three primary colours; exactly the palette of this self-portrait, mixed to a dingy monochrome. The rectangle of one painting within the other is an echo of his system of grids. The face is a series of light and dark areas and you are made to feel that the same brush, the same paint and palette have been used to describe the dark features of the face and the dark lines on the canvas behind him. Mondrian has fretted away at the idea of some visual, if not emotional, connection between himself and his painting but the subtlety of the conceit is undermined by the obvious effort involved and the almost comical severity of the face.

In the fake masterpiece factory at Shepherd's Bush, Stamp sat at his workstool easily, with limber grace: erect in the saddle. A frowning eye was fixed upon his image in the glass. He was disguised in the fur cap of a Canadian trapper. A heavy white bandage, descending under his chin, covered his right ear. He was supposed to be Van Gogh. He was engaged in the manufacture of a Van Gogh 'self-portrait'.

Stamp is the faker in *The Revenge for Love*, a novel by the writer, painter and pioneer of English Modernism, Wyndham Lewis. He is clearly faking the *Self-Portrait with a Bandaged Ear*, or rather inventing a new one, an undiscovered self-portrait to add to the stock. What a shocking idea – a fake self-portrait of Vincent at his most wounded, what's more, cynically worked up for cash; this was Lewis's blasphemy against art's martyr.

Lewis's black joke is funny because it sends up the cult – sanctity through sincerity – rather than the artist himself. Van Gogh's special touch with the brush, the living trace of his presence on earth: it's the idea of faking these that offends religious sensibilities, and yet these are precisely what cannot so easily be faked. People have tried and failed for decades and though it is true that the market is amazingly more gullible than one might like to believe – bug-eyed Vermeers and acrylic Rembrandts have made good money in their time – fake Van Goghs are not nearly so common. Stamp might be able to mock himself up as a crop-eared Dutchman in a trapper's hat but he cannot mock himself up as a Vincent van Gogh, still less a Van Gogh self-portrait.

But what does Van Gogh's style give the self-portraits other than proof of authenticity? One answer is absolutely everything. His style is not just what carries, describes or characterizes a subject, it amounts to an equivalent subject. If visitors to the Van Gogh Museum in Amsterdam report reactions of inarticulate emotion, which they do, often to the point of tears, it is not just because they are looking at the artist in a straw hat. The content of his late self-portraits, for instance, may not be exactly impersonal (most particularly *Self-Portrait with a Bandaged Ear*, which could be construed as autobiographical) but the movement of hand and brush is blazingly, ineffably personal.

It is not a feat achieved by many modern or contemporary artists, for whom faces don't often fit the bill in any case. Naturally the Expressionists are hell-bent on self-expression through the roiled and harrowed, slashed and flurried surfaces of their canvases and by the stabbing and scoring of their brushwork; and the perfectly uninflected surface of Warhol's screen-print self-portraits is commonly, but mistakenly, held to be evidence of a total lack of personality. But style per se, or a highly evolved one, can be a way of keeping oneself to oneself: a dependable mask. The Australian artist Sidney Nolan took this idea to the *ne plus ultra*, painting himself as a tribal mask streaked with war paint in his characteristic colours, eyes staring through a helmet of bone resembling the hat he always painted for Australia's beloved outlaw Ned Kelly. Nolan's brushes are like arrows, his palette a warrior's shield; fighting for his art, but concealed behind it.

Chuck Close, the American painter, has made so many self-portraits that whole shows have been composed over the years of these gigantic images of his face in close-up. Working from photographs, Close recreates his own craterous countenance with an almost absurdly heroic patience in millions of tiny pixels, or blasts from an airbrush, or thumbprints – literally, the painterly touch – to get the continuous tone of the original image, an enterprise once described by the late Kirk Varnedoe as roughly equivalent to hewing Mount Rushmore with a dentist's drill. And Mount Rushmore is an apt analogy, for the paintings size up before you: still, awesome and grand.

Close applies exactly the same technique to others. He makes no distinction between himself and the friends he has been painting again and again for decades. Some faces are recognizable – Philip Glass, Richard Serra and, by now, the artist himself – but his art is not about capturing a likeness so much as evolving all sorts of pattern styles that the mind can still read as a face even when that face is so big that you feel like a billsticker up a ladder, eye to eye with an iris the size of a rock. Each face has its own impact, of course. His self-portrait at twenty-eight, made in 1968, is a knockout in black and white: head back, jaw thrusting, he stares out through heavy-framed specs, a shirtless, straggle-haired rebel, fag clenched in tenacious mouth. As an expression of the counterculture, it's up there with draft dodging and Woodstock. But it's also a disquieting inventory of grain and pore, bristle and crease, in widescreen

photo-real format. Close refers to the man in these self-portraits as Him and that is how they strike the viewer; no matter how immoderately intimate they might sound, they are not remotely personal. You have the Brobdingnagian experience of crawling across Close's face like an ant, but his self-portraits never bring — never wish to bring — his character or person into focus.

To fuse oneself wholly with one's style may be to lose oneself in the end. Van Gogh is an extraordinary exception, but most artists who want to be completely one with their art and make an extreme point of it tend to vanish into the painting, like Tamara de Lempicka in her Art Deco Bugatti, not much more than a gleaming body part polished and painted with lipstick and brilliant eyeshadow; or the Spanish artist Antoni Tàpies, who portrayed himself as just two more of his own symbols, A and T fingered in a slab of claggy oil paint.

In fact, Wyndham Lewis himself is one of the few high Modernists of the twentieth century whose style is perfectly conceived to represent him, and as almost no other sitter in his portraits. In *Mr Wyndham Lewis as a Tyro*, the artist appears as a cut-and-thrust assembly of jagged blades, flint axes, fishhooks and Stanley knives, hard as metal against a fierce mustard ground, the smile a bright sneering grille, parody of the 'keep right on to the end of the road' cheer that kept the British Tommy going through the First World War. Lewis's Vorticist movement, more or less Britain's only home-grown contribution to the European avant-garde, was forged in the horror of that war. The paintings of his early life can stand comparison with the European art of the period in their dynamic, accordion-pleated, syncopated images of modern times. In his satirical self-portrait — a Tyro is a creature invented by the artist around 1920, 'a new type of human animal raw and undeveloped, his vitality is immense but purposeless, and hence sometimes malignant' — Lewis is one of his own violent anti-heroes, mocking himself but mocking England too, seeing just how much it could take of this new kind of cutting-edge artist, jeering and vicious and clever; to which the answer, of course, was not very much. Lewis decamped to the British Library to work up an enormous critique of European society and did not exhibit again for more for more than a decade. But all his energy and ambition are there in that goading, spearing style: the artist represented but also personified.

Every painter paints himself: so runs Michelangelo's famous adage, anticipating the modern view that all works of art are in some sense self-portraits by other means, permeated with the character and soul of their maker. Many high constructions have been put upon the phrase but at the low end of interpretation it need not mean much more than that the painter really put himself into the work, or that style equates with persona. It is an idea one might expect advanced art to endorse in all sorts of self-portraits, though this

very rarely happens. But the point is deftly made in Henri Matisse's *The Painter and His Model*. Here the artist is seen from behind, seated before a canvas on which the model is represented. She is faceless on the canvas, and faceless in the room, just as Matisse's face is not visible, though it has to be Matisse by pictorial logic. Here is a painting by Matisse, his signature in every passage; and here is another inside it, representing the identical model in the identical idiom. It follows that the man at the easel must be the self-same painter.

Windows, interiors, paintings within paintings, lapses in conversation, models sunk in daydreams, mirrors, curlicues, even the exquisitely sonorous hue of black: everything speaks of Matisse, his touch, his view, his world, his presence. Here is a self-portrait that defies the idea that such works must offer a likeness, a self-portrait which does not so much depict as identify the painter.

Chapter Fifteen
Falling Apart

'A first point that must be noted, in attempting to
depict the self unrelated to others, is that it exists
only intermittently, and, when all is said,
comparatively seldom.'

Michel Tournier, *Friday*

Untitled Film Still (#7), 1978

Cindy Sherman (1954–)

A tearful blonde sits alone with her woes, eyes bleeding mascara. She is dressed for the Fifties and trying to hold herself together with a cocktail, though this may only be making things worse for she seems unaware of the prying camera.

Another girl from another era, a brunette in a mini skirt, kneels to pick spilt groceries from the floor. She is looking up at someone unseen who is evidently staring angrily back down at her, and words linger in the air. A man's jacket is draped around her shoulders.

The character and scenario are so familiar you feel you've seen each movie before, and sure enough these black and white shots are actually from a series called *Untitled Film Stills*. There are many others, for this show runs and runs, some of B-movie starlets in characteristic scenarios, waiting bravely by the window for the date that never comes, or gazing wistfully into a mirror as the camera creeps up behind them. The raven-haired vamp, the Sixties student, the blonde goddess in her negligee: you recognize the type every time and the game is to spot the allusions – Hitchcock or Hawks, Fellini or Godard, Italian Realism or New Wave French cinema? So authentic is each still, atmosphere, lighting, casting and all, that people have claimed to remember the actual movie. But the films are not real and the stills are all fictions. Every role (and, it follows, every star playing that role), young or old, glamorous or raddled, slender or stout, is played by the same woman, the American artist Cindy Sherman.

When the *Untitled Film Stills* started appearing in galleries in the 1970s it was not immediately clear what they were. The actresses were unknown, the films could not be identified, no matter what viewers insisted, and it seemed bizarre that every picture was credited to the same photographer, C. Sherman. That they were *of* Sherman as well as by her seemed hard to believe – and still is, although it's been common knowledge for decades; for how can the sullen adolescent, Manhattan dowager and busty cover girl all be Cindy Sherman, as well as the mall chick and the corpse? The more you see of her work, amounting to several hundred photographs by now, the more remarkable the shape-shifting illusion. Either Sherman is more than one woman or she does not have a single persona.

The illusion itself is a complex achievement that goes far beyond dressing up. Andy Warhol once said Sherman was good enough to be an actress and so she is, and must be, if any of her characters are to come alive. But she is not just a female Alec Guinness playing all the parts, young blood to dowager aunt, in *Kind Hearts and Coronets*; her gift is for inventing whole lives, then devising apt representations of these fictional people – not just stills but snapshots, studio portraits, official photographs and so on – that act upon you with the full force of reality: pictures of people who really exist somewhere out there in the world.

Except that they cannot because they are all Cindy Sherman. Sherman's art hinges upon this blatant contradiction. On the one hand you have to know that she is playing all the parts – that these people are neither real nor actresses following directions, but a single artist inventing a succession of selves – otherwise you might mistake them for reality not art, and the conceit would be lost. On the other hand if you could identify the artist herself then the illusion would obviously falter. She has to be unrecognizable, not to say unknowable: you mustn't think that any of these images represent Cindy Sherman and yet they all do in the most literal sense for she is the subject of each shot.

Of Sherman and *by* Sherman: the artist by herself. But the usual definition of a self-portrait does not cover this case because Sherman is not just the model, she is also the medium. Knowing this, one cannot help searching for the artist herself as a constant among all these faces, which completely throws the emphasis of the work. Instead of seeing them as portraits (albeit of people who have never existed) you regard these pictures as self-transformations, as evidence of the extent to which one person may look and act and seem to *become* exactly like another even through the most surprisingly minimal adjustments of expression, wardrobe and make-up.

And who hasn't tried it? Dressed differently for social or professional reasons, maybe in self-defence, to seem more powerful or attractive or just less like one's usual self, to blend in or stand out. The belief that clothes maketh the man is taken so literally in law courts, for example, that male defendants are advised to wear suits and women to look as prim as Mary Poppins. Every time Madonna fixes on a new look we are told she has reinvented her self. But can you get another self off the peg, as it were, assume another self like a garment? That was what Sherman's *Untitled Film Stills* implied with its one-woman permutations of character.

But the *Stills* took professional performers as its subject, people actually paid to impersonate others. It thrived on our ability to recognize all sorts of cinematic clichés, scenarios, roles and styles of performance in which character is literally an act, and Sherman went on to play others who are also performing a role – fashion models, celebrities posing for publicity shoots, the sitters in Rembrandt's 'portrait histories'; these images seemed to play upon the twentieth-century dogma that identity is only a construct. But in Sherman's more recent work, the ultimate value of appearances is strongly in doubt. Perhaps true identity cannot actually be depicted at all, she wonders, perhaps the self is not a versatile mask but a world we must live inside.

Conventional self-portraits might be a mug's game, offering only the most limited description of oneself; obvious, you may say, and a fact that all great self-portraits, and portraits, acknowledge and strive to overcome. But still we are stuck with appearances, we all have to go out into the world and look like ourselves, or whatever version of ourselves we are struggling to devise. We all have to put ourselves together to some extent, produce our own daily self-portrait no matter how reluctant, or botched, or wide of the mark. And it is this distance between the inner and outer being that Sherman examines in her latest series, women whose performances of themselves – the selves they are stuck with, would like to be or imagine they are – are really falling apart.

These women are not so young any more. They may be considering plastic surgery. Nameless, as always, they are very familiar kinds of American. The woman who thinks she looks a bit like Hillary Clinton and has taken Annie Leibovitz's famous *Vogue* portraits to some makeover artist who hasn't quite pulled it off. The trailer-trash mother with her halter-neck top and ironed hair, showing off the tattoo she's had done with her teenage daughter; the Republican matron in her Stars-and-Stripes blouse brightly smiling as if she were still her husband's cheerleading sweetheart.

Untitled (#400), 2000

Cindy Sherman
(1954–)

Some of them used to model, you feel, but now they groom dogs or host charity dinners. Past and future narratives spool through each image. Their husbands have left or are leaving. Perhaps there's been a facelift or two, and certainly the cracks are beginning to show: foundation melts in the flashlight, lipstick leaves a ridiculous tidemark, concealer, caught in the glare, underlines the eyes with clownish white crescents. These women are keeping up appearances, putting a brave face on it; heroic, hopeful, that's what their clothes and body language express as they sit in the studio of some local photographer with his corny backdrops. But the truth breaks through. Make-up artists (and artists too) can make a fool or a stranger out of any of us.

————

Cindy Sherman began her career as a painter but quickly gave up when she discovered what she could make of herself with a camera. Her images have to be photographs and not paintings, because painting declares its own status as fiction. The condition of a photograph, however artful, is that it represents its subject as a one-to-one record of reality presenting unmodified truth. Seeing is believing, and the belief, however brief, that you are looking at a real person – and not at Sherman, in the first instance – is crucial to the illusion she aims for.

She was not the first artist to use herself as medium as well as model, having an ancestor in the nineteenth-century narcissist and make-up artiste, the Countess de Castiglione. For thirty years the countess called the shots in a Paris studio for nearly four hundred photographs of herself. She turned in some classic performances – Lady Macbeth, Anne Boleyn, Goya's voluptuous Maja on her couch – but more generally she appeared as personifications of her self.

These compositions are never conventional: sometimes just eyes reflected in a mirror, or apparently disembodied legs. Castiglione would stand on a stool, concealed beneath elongated skirts, to appear improbably tall; or wear a policeman's hat holding up Exhibit A – one of her own ageing arms – as if it were criminal evidence. When her much-cuckolded husband tried to take custody of their child, she posed with a murderous expression and a bloody knife and sent him the image, captioned 'Vengeance'. Towards the end of her life she even had herself photographed in a coffin, the camera bending pruriently over the corpse, as if she wanted to know how she would look when dead. Yet even these staged images are not quite as weird as those of her compatriot, the French writer, artist and Resistance heroine Claude Cahun, whose self-portraits were rediscovered at the end of the twentieth century.

Cahun, it seems fair to say, could not have cared less how other people saw her and was prepared to appear entirely shaven-headed before the public as well as the camera. Her bald head and beak-sharp nose are the subject, or subjects, of a frightening self-portrait from 1928. Two heads, conjoined like Siamese twins by double-exposure, marry together for ever at the neck. One Cahun is watching, waiting, mouth half open, anxiously attentive to the other; the other is in-turned and pathologically disengaged, the hooded eye as wild as an animal. These shaven heads speak of lunacy and incarceration; of being locked inside a double self, unable to escape one's mind. The facial expressions could be illustrations for Normal and Abnormal from some

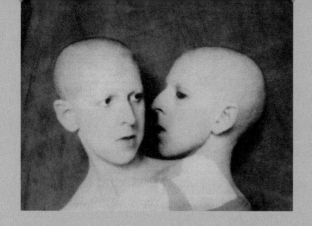

What Do You Want from Me?, 1928

Claude Cahun
(1894–1954)

textbook on early psychiatry and this is poignant given that Cahun was androgynous, a lesbian and the lover of her own stepsister, Suzanne Malherbe, and must therefore have had some sense of how it felt to be outside polite society. The title is a stricken question addressed either to herself or the whole world, ambiguous as it is: *What Do You Want from Me?*

Cahun was born Lucy Schwob in Nantes in 1894. She was for a time associated with the Paris Surrealists but is very obviously an artist apart. All of her several dozen self-portraits, and they are the body of her work, stand outside time and the traditions of art.

Head shaved, she sits silent like a monk on the floor or poses in profile as her own father (like father: like son). Plaits coiled into earmuffs, awkward in a long frock, she looks like a faltering, out-of-kilter Coppelia. Hair now grown and slicked, she stands deadpan in a dinner jacket with one hand on her hip, a female Noel Coward.

There is no hint of parody or escapism here. Cahun is never trying out characters she couldn't get away with in life. On Jersey, where she lived with her stepsister from 1937, carrying out an underground propaganda campaign against the Nazi occupation, she was accepted everywhere as an eccentric who wore the most outlandish of guises. The Nazis eventually caught up with her during a raid on her house when she failed to register as Jewish. She and Malherbe were sentenced to death for 'undermining the morale' of the German forces, but released during the last months of the war. A fellow prisoner gave her the souvenir she flaunts in a self-portrait made as soon as she was released. Cahun appears as a respectable matron in raincoat and headscarf against the bracing sea air, but she has a Nazi badge clamped savagely between her teeth.

Far from a sustained meditation on the slipperiness of the self, Cahun's self-portraits are perfectly direct. They admit the miseries of a double life and they rejoice in it too; they acknowledge, above all, that one can seem strange even to oneself.

Photography, of course, offers self-portraitists a chance to see themselves as others see them without the inevitable self-consciousness of looking in a mirror. But even from its earliest days it has been used to challenge this supposed objectivity. Degas's self-portraits, made at night using an elementary Eastman Kodak, are full of doubt and unease, redoubled by photographing himself in a mirror, as if he already foresaw, even in the nineteenth century, that the camera could be used to twist reality, doctor the record, suggest complexities untold, even just through multiple images.

Many artists have produced double self-portraits using camera and mirror, deliberately showing their workings. Claude Cahun used one to imply a play-off between darkness and light – black-haired in the mirror, blonde as she turns away from the glass; the Scottish artist Douglas Gordon went further, drawing upon James Hogg's great novel of brooding Calvinism, *The Private Memoirs and Confessions of a Justified Sinner*, and using a mirror to video himself viewing his own doppelgänger – a premonitory lookalike, or evil twin – emerging out of theatrical mists.

Photographs are easily manipulated to suggest split personalities or twin selves, but the double-take has to be immaculate to persuade. The Italian maverick Alighiero e Boetti so convincingly holds hands with himself in his self-portrait you might almost think you were looking at identical twins in identical suits. Which is Alighiero and which is Boetti? A roving autodidact of mysterious origins who emerged from nowhere as the youngest star of Arte Povera in the Sixties, nobody could pin this artist down. When he disappeared just as swiftly into the wilds of Afghanistan to classify the world's longest rivers, it was said, or to study mathematics, or to run a hotel in Kabul, he sent back such an unusual variety of work and from so many different places that he was rumoured to be not one man but two, as his name and self-portrait imply: Alighiero *and* Boetti.

The Canadian artist Jeff Wall made a double self-portrait when still quite young that might stand as an account not so much of himself as the modus operandi of his whole career. Wall creates images which look like photographs and obviously make use of a camera, but which baffle one's belief in photography as a record of fact. In his *Self-Portrait*, using digital manipulation, he turns himself into a pair of identical twin brothers wearing different clothes, one casual, one slightly more formal, but neither particularly congenial; the Jeff Wall on the left has his arms defensively crossed, while keeping a beady eye on the viewer, and the Wall on the right indicates a chair with one peremptory hand as if trying to force you to choose between them.

Which is the real Jeff Wall? It's image versus image, twin versus twin. The presumption of photography's truth to reality is turned on its head (since there can never be more than one Wall at once) along with the never-lying status of the camera. And the picture implies that it does not matter how many times the artist shows him or herself, self-portrait photographs cannot necessarily tell you more about an artist than any other kind. They cannot offer you the naked truth, despite their appearance as unvarnished fact, a pessimistic contention that the critic-turned-photographer John Coplans, whose only subject was himself, tested to the limits.

For the last twenty years of his life Coplans photographed his own body – naked, hirsute and stocky – in the most cheerfully undignified of poses. He appeared bent double, widely splayed, basking like an odalisque, flat-out like a dog by the fire. Each of his photographs magnifies a section of his anatomy to wall-sized proportions – two middle fingers making a pair of legs, a heel sizing up to resemble the scale and shape of a plumped-down bottom. The more Coplans scrutinized his own body, inch by inch, the more it started to look like something else. This must count as the least narcissistic of all self-centred art.

Coplans once joked that his work wasn't what collectors liked to hang behind their couches: too much hair and thigh, too much grizzled genitalia. In fact, his images were collected all over the world, palpably (and valuably) photographs of the artist even though they never show the one obvious clue to what Coplans called 'my passing identity' – his actual face.

And what he captures in these black and white frames seems to be anything but a self-portrait at first, for you don't see his features, cannot read his character or life from his countenance. His skin yields no life story beyond the occasional graze and although the hands talk, they would hardly stand out in an identity parade. Coplans shows what we have in common with each other instead, with our ancestors and even the landscape. His back becomes a slab of granite; his feet, braced on tiptoe, look like a pair of gloomy crags separated by a seam of daylight.

The latter photograph includes a little pun on the vertical zips of Barnett Newman; Coplans was once a painter and liked to play with art history, posing as Raeburn's skating vicar or Velázquez's Rokeby Venus. At a distance, a huge shot of his torso will look like an Abstract Expressionist painting; closer up, it might be more like one of Rembrandt's flayed carcasses. Then you notice that the navel forms a comically downturned mouth, or that, in another shot, a torso becomes a scowling expression with nipples for eyes. Coplans is pulling faces.

This is where the self-portraiture lies, in the mirthful, inventive character of each composition and comic substitution. In the way he cracks jokes with his body – a physique that was still astonishingly burly into his eighties, so that the late photographs acquire a death-defying humour. The more there were, the more you knew it was Coplans; that the face is never shown seems to cap it all off, a final joke: even headless you'd recognize the old guy anywhere.

———

Cindy Sherman once told an interviewer that she was horrified to find herself being snapped by paparazzi at a party, spotted *as* herself, and realized it was time to create some new guises. Her exceptional plasticity of face – the press photos revealed an ageless and anonymous blonde, pretty like the girl next door – had not prevented her from being recognized even though she frequently appeared in disguise outside her studio.

This fear of being taken for oneself seems almost pathological and it goes with a compulsion to dress up. Sherman has been doing it since she was tiny and admitted to *The New Yorker* many years ago that it was in some way therapeutic: 'I guess whenever I would get moody or depressed, I would spend a couple of hours turning myself into somebody else with makeup or clothes. It was a cathartic thing that I needed to do.'

Getting out of it – out of one's self – has to be appealing for anyone with a modicum of imagination, let alone a need for catharsis. But surely dressing up is only a game, cannot make you into somebody else. Sherman's art seems to be in two minds about this. You make yourself up, gull people into believing you're a model, an actress, a bag-lady or a man, and there you have it: the self is just today's most convincing disguise. It may happen to coincide with some essential sense of one's own identity, but even so it is a fiction and perhaps we are all just fakes in any case (a conviction sullenly held by teenagers the world over).

A woman's ability, in particular, to devise a whole new appearance is an evergreen subject for satire. In *The Rape of the Lock*, Alexander Pope presents a mock-heroic pageant of all the items – powders, puffs and patches – that allow Belinda to have a radiant beauty that is not her own. In the cruel striptease of 'A Beautiful Young Nymph Going to Bed', Jonathan Swift imagines the eponymous nymph first removing her crystal eyes, then her mouse-skin eyebrows, then her false breasts and turning back into a haggard London prostitute. But Swift is more sympathetic than Pope in recognizing the ordeal involved in keeping up appearances: 'The Nymph, though in this Mangled Plight/Must ev'ry Morn her Limbs unite.'

That is the spirit of Sherman's recent portraits of women past their prime, hanging on by their false nails and archly pencilled eyebrows. In a photograph she took of herself around the same time as this series, in the guise of a particularly wretched clown, her own mouth and eyebrows are just for once exposed beneath the layers of greasepaint. This clown wears a black satin bomber jacket with the name Cindy embroidered on it in pink. But it's one of those jackets from a rock tour, the sort of thing roadies wear and groupies buy – just a souvenir of the Cindy Sherman show.

If you want to undermine the idea of self-portraiture as representing any kind of truth then photography, perversely, ought to be your medium. You make yourself up and authenticate the illusion with a camera; take so many different portraits of yourself as to come across as an unreliable narrator; pit one image of yourself against another to the point of contradiction. Or perhaps you portray yourself, like the pioneering photographer Walker Evans, as nothing more than a series of shadows: all that the camera can be said to record. Yet you have to be substantial enough to cast a shadow in the first place. Sherman's contemporary, the portrait painter Chuck Close, once described a photo session with her at his Manhattan studio. 'Someone showed up who said she was Cindy Sherman. I tried to photograph her but there was no one there.'

But photography does give one tremendous advantage to the self-portraitist who aims for truth: it allows for as many images as he or she wishes to make. When Claude Cahun said she would never be done stripping the face from beneath the face from beneath the face, she wasn't describing herself as a series of masks covering a blank. She was acknowledging an idea that held fast through the twentieth century: that we are never fixed, a work in progress, just the sum of our day-to-day selves.

———

At a mass gathering of Andy Warhol's self-portraits some years ago, the ambience was unsurprisingly glassy and chill. Warhol was always as boring as he wanted to be, and as repetitive even with his own face. But there was a mounting sense from self-portrait to self-portrait, eighty or more (only a fraction of the output from the aptly named Factory), that the viewer was just about to find the real Warhol, grasp him out of the shadows.

Of course, Warhol was a shape-shifter and the self-portraits are characteristically diverse: he portrays himself as child, gangster, film star, the victim of a strangling, a woman in a lavish dark wig. He appears as a mugshot, in profile, or quite literally as a series of shadows. He does himself like a Marilyn or a Liz, that is to say as a screen-print diptych or quartet. But there are some heavily hand-worked paintings too, and towards the end of his life images that go beyond the obsessive concern with surfaces. So straightaway it seems as if Warhol is offering an insight, that he is no more fixed than anyone else but a great multiplicity of selves, a man of many faces who cannot be confined to just one (though he is the artist, above all others, whose face is as recognizable as his paintings). But if that seems too profound, harking back to Montaigne, there is a less philosophical interpretation of the self-portraits, that as in so many other ways Warhol is just shattering the genre.

Take the old imperative of self-portraiture: to leave a likeness of oneself. Warhol's early self-portraits avoid it like the plague: Andy as an illegible outline; Andy as a butterfly; Andy with his face hidden behind his hands. In a

sketch from 1948 he is picking his nose, and he even worked this up as an oil painting for the annual Pittsburg artists' show: the very thing they couldn't possibly display, an affront to his home-town society. With the exception of Egon Schiele's raw-red masturbation self-portraits, it would be hard to think of a more explicit act of self-exposure – except that you couldn't recognize Andy in the first place.

Most self-portraitists have some slight faith in the idea of a substantial self, or even just a substantial body, that might be susceptible to depiction. For Dürer body and soul are represented in one; for Rembrandt, sensing a distance between the two, the aim is to find a visual embodiment of consciousness. But Warhol sees the self, or the depiction of this self, as not more substantial than the paper on which it is printed. A 1963 work consists of four headshots taken in a booth in Times Square enlarged and silk-screened on to canvas. Warhol is messing about – hand rising to throat, head tilted and neck arched like a hanged man, posing like a police mugshot – and the images feel as thin and remote as these mechanically impersonal shots always do, no less so for being emblazoned on an outsize canvas. What's more, Warhol is wearing a large pair of dark glasses. What man goes into a photo-booth in sunspecs, apart from a poseur, but the man who is not eager to show himself? 'The best American invention,' Warhol once murmured, in full view of the cameras, of course, is 'to be able to disappear.'

How could such a world-famous man possibly vanish? In a sense, one Warhol already had. The artist lost his pigmentation at an early age, hence the colourless face and wispy hair that he concealed beneath those wigs, though he didn't regret this because it turned him into a monochrome figure from a black and white movie, perfect for Sixties television. Loathing his pocked complexion and ruddy nose, he took himself off for primitive dermabrasion, which in those days involved the use of actual sandpaper. He dyed his eyebrows to get the Bette Davis look, and kept his blotches unseen beneath thick concealer. The sunglasses were worn even by night and through the darkest of winter days; ever ready, Warhol was able to present a perfected image of himself at any moment to a stranger's camera. If there was a backstage Warhol, unmasked, unwigged, it was never glimpsed in public. We may be shocked to think of Tony Blair paying hundreds of pounds for a can of spray-paint to even his skin tone when he was Britain's Prime Minister, but Warhol established maquillage as a necessary vice for the public figure long before in the Sixties.

If he was a beautician to others in their portraits, he was just as kind to himself. 'When I did my self-portraits, I left all the pimples out because you always should.' Acne is a temporary condition; one must look for the quintessential self beneath the transient pox. One of his most peaceful self-portraits, a diptych from 1981, was based on a couple of unforgiving Polaroids in which the fiftysomething Warhol is thin, mottled and weary. In the painting, care and age are smoothed away and he is ready for his close-up. Warhol is the patron saint of Photoshop.

The silk-screen self-portraits only came about in the first place as a commission from that shrewd collector, Ethel Scull, who saw as early as 1963 how completely Warhol's two-tone image would fuse with his art and how his face might be his (and her) fortune. And it is a face fit for mass-reproduction: posters, advertisements, album covers, stamps, all of which Warhol understood and manufactured. He even turned himself into wallpaper, one Warhol after another, until the face is not so much a face as a pattern. Serial self-portraiture, a vigorous strain in twentieth-century art, has its *reductio ad absurdum* in him: to portray oneself over and again was not to expand so much as deplete one's precious self. Standardization, uniformity, comforting repetition – he liked

America, he said, because everyone was the same, and individuality could be an awful burden. The famous claim of Walter Benjamin that in the age of mechanical reproduction the 'aura' of art objects, their very uniqueness, disappears would have presented no worries for Warhol; though even before he died his mechanically made and repetitious works had already acquired a golden aura that has never faded as among the most expensive modern art on the market.

Yet no matter how much Warhol appears to hide, as people claim, he can never escape the trap of self-portraiture: which is that every self-portrait is a conscious decision, a revealing and deliberate choice that presents its own form of evidence. It is not nothing, in the end, to show oneself persistently in dark glasses, or beneath layers of army camouflage, or erased by one's own pen, or three-faced, as in a very late sketch, like Janus with yet another mask. It is not nothing to present oneself as a chirpy cove with a skull perched like a pet monkey on one's shoulder, or as a surrogate skull, eyes sunken into their sockets; or posing as unimpeachably cool, yet with an expression perfectly calibrated to betray its own trumped-up theatricality.

To look at even a few of Warhol's self-portraits one after the other is to become caught in a loop of feedback – assertion and denial in endless repetition. He looks like this; but then again he does not. This is Warhol, but how can you tell behind those glasses? It may come as a surprise to find that some of the paintings are not as prophylactically sealed as they appear in reproduction, that their surfaces are hard-worked by hand, the pigment palpably manipulated; a very personal kind of involvement. And for all the mass-production of each self-portrait – a trio of Warhols, a quartet, even half a

Self-Portrait with Skull,
1977

Andy Warhol
(1928–87)

dozen – there is singularity at the very end of Warhol's life. Just before he died of a botched operation, he made a solo self-portrait in which he printed the head reversed out in inky negative on silver. It is a frightening but beautiful image – the black mask, the luminous irises, the hair standing on end; a supernatural death's head and a premonition of what it is to go from flesh to spirit, to pass through the looking glass from life into death.

————

What is a self? Is it the rings of experience that grow within the tree? Is it the soul begotten and not made in the womb, or the being nurtured in the world outside? Is it the narrator in one's head, the teeming consciousness that keeps one sleepless at night or distracted during the day, brave in danger or paralysed in a crisis? Is it the source of that anger that flames spontaneously at slights to one's honour, or the source of this honour in the first place? Is it in one's capacity to love, forgive or endure, or in one's desire to lead a moral life? Is it the will that governs everything one ever says or does, or something far bigger than that?

The self – one's self – has a history at least. You come across it in old letters and pencilled notes in long forgotten books, in the handwriting of your schooldays and the expressions of adolescence glimpsed in photos, in the dreams and the nightmares of adulthood that are still set in the first houses of childhood. When the English artist Helen Chadwick turned thirty, she made a self-portrait composed of ten wooden solids arranged in an expanding spiral, each representing a totemic childhood object – a church font, a pram, a school vaulting horse – growing larger and larger and concluding with an upright oblong representing her first grown-up front door. Her past was depicted as a simple ABC lexicon of shapes but she showed herself trying to re-enter that past in sepia photographs imprinted on the implacable surface of each solid – a tiny figure trying to reach into a piano, or climb back into a cot; this return to the past that is only ever partially achieved in memories or dreams was poignantly expressed in images of the adult Chadwick scaled to her respective age. With its classical geometry and its matching of form to image and emotion – two dimensional images trying to penetrate three dimensional objects – *Ego Sum Geometria* was a new kind of concrete poetry, a lament for the last little Chadwick who searches in vain for the first little Chadwick, for the experience of being her earliest self.

If we are the sum of our former selves, as poets tell us, then what are these selves, are they intervals of time like the Seven Ages of Man, are they intellectual or emotional phases? How long do these former selves last? Can one deselect the self who behaved shamefully or the self who was terribly injured as representatives of our present selves, is there a limbo for these ex-selves of ours? Does one start with a new and improved self every day, or drag the whole lot behind us like the links of an increasingly cumbersome chain? One could argue, with unimpeachable logic, that a true self-portrait would have to be a record of every lived minute in real time; and Warhol went some way to achieving that state, spending so much of his adult life before one kind of lens or another. But who has time for even a portion of the total self-portrait? Even when Warhol made a series of portraits in which the element of time was introduced, where friends and celebrities were required to pose before a film camera – just be themselves – he stopped the clock at a nearly intolerable eight minutes. Some people took the so-called *Screen Tests* literally as old-fashioned portraits and stood dutifully still for the duration, others broke out into nervous tics, or laughter, or impatient grimaces within a few moments. But without wishing to overburden a relatively modest conceit, there seems to be some mortal truth in these unstill portraits. Those who knew the sitters involved said that their behaviour, their reaction to Warhol's lens, was always strikingly characteristic.

And is it in our continuous behaviour that our selves emerge (or others perceive these selves)? We cannot stop being ourselves from minute to minute until those minutes finally end because we cannot stop *behaving*. Is our future self somehow inherent in our present self, or is one always and continuously oneself?

In the twentieth century – a century supposedly devoted to discovering the secrets of the self as if it were a distant planet, or a sub-atomic particle or something mummified and entombed – a certain interest in the quiddity of the self might have been expected in artists as much as philosophers, psychologists or writers. Just as much or even more, since some of these artists were actually bent on *representing* themselves, in which case having some idea of what this self might be could seem a fundamental requisite.

But look at Frida Kahlo: she paints herself in a lifelong drama, yet one feels she was never troubled about the nature of the self because she was so busy being it. Look at the American artist Lucas Samaras, one of the most prolific self-portraitists of all time, who discovered in the early Seventies that the wet dyes of Polaroids could be easily dragged about and transformed and who has been transforming these shots of himself ever since – what does he have to say about the self, his own self? Almost nothing at all, except that a Polaroid can transform anyone from Jekyll into Hyde.

The twentieth century was the century of the naked self-portrait. We don't talk of them as nude, just as we don't talk of the nude truth, because nude implies something carefree or even seductive. Naked means stripped bare, exposed: a truth revealed. Egon Schiele strips to show himself as an emaciated martyr, Edvard Munch as a soul in hell, Robert Mapplethorpe as a saucy devil. A long line of woman from the American photographer Hannah Wilke onwards

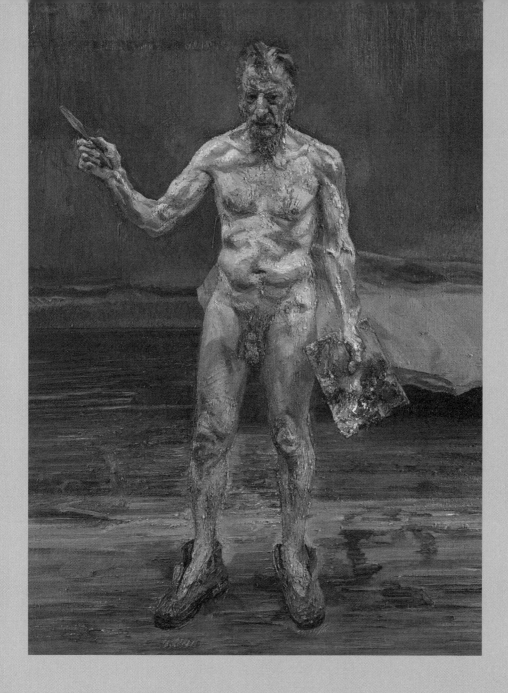

Painter Working,
Reflection, 1993
—————————
Lucian Freud
(1922–)

have done it for social reasons, to expose the truth of the female body or describe
its frailty during illness; to make the viewer uncomfortable by giving him an
eyeful in return, like Jemima Stehli performing her photographic striptease; or to
flaunt old age, as in Alice Neel's marvellously insouciant self-portrait in
spectacles, wicker chair and nothing else but her own defiant intelligence.

The naked self-portrait is Pierre Bonnard stripped in the mirror and
Picasso stripped for strength, it is Stanley Spencer popping up naked beside his
bare voluptuous wife – a nude – his meagre self a featherless bird by contrast.

Naked artists, whatever the object of their nakedness, have chosen not to rely upon the usual combination of pose, clothes and expression to put themselves over, but they inevitably end up making themselves known by other means; by resisting the fact of their nakedness like Alice Neel; by gloating over their naughty rudeness like Gilbert and George. Lucian Freud, for whom the nakedness of sitters may become a central condition, casts a similarly cold eye over his own body. Standing naked, knife and palette in his hands, his heavy workmen's boots unlaced and flapping like the fetlocks of some hooved animal, he is a maestro with a baton, a bare King Lear of the studio, a satyr or something more devilish. Identity emerges even without clothes, and, of course, it emerges even without faces. Whatever we are as human beings, we are infinitely more than our bodies.

But what exactly? The Self and oneself – worlds apart; one is academic, an issue, a theory, a philosophical knot; the other is alive and brimful of being. Artists who take it upon themselves to consider the former in self-portraits almost always kill off the latter. Marc Quinn's vial of his own DNA, called *Self-Portrait* and momentarily pleasing in its concept of the self as an invisible essence, is nonetheless the dead end of scientific materialism. Robert Morris's *I-Box*, in which the American minimalist sculptor created a life-size lidded box in the shape of the letter 'I' which, when opened, was found to contain a photograph of the naked artist himself – ta-da! – is a punchy play upon the relationship between mind and body, but in no sense could it possibly be a personification of the artist by the artist except as a philosophical *jeu d'esprit*. Morris also made a work called *Self-Portrait (EEG)* in which an electroencephalogram recorded the movements of his brain while he thought about himself, until the graph had grown as long as he is tall. Both works stand in the category of art that never has to be viewed for its import to be known, and in the class of self-portraiture that is bent on discovering the very furthest limits, or definition, of the genre. One would say Morris had hit the boundary wall with *Self-Portrait (EEG)*, literally hiding behind his thoughts, were it not that Quinn has since taken the Self as an invisible and irreducible puzzle even further.

Twentieth-century doubts about self-portraiture spill into this century too, doubts about the possibility of ever depicting oneself. The assertion 'This Is Me' does not work any more for many artists, and since we like to think of ourselves as complex and fragmented, not susceptible to concise description, unable to be pinned down, it is hardly surprising that is the way modern self-portraitists show themselves too, from Francis Bacon's swerving body parts to Chuck Close's walls of pixels and Maurizio Cattelan's thousands of little sperm each with the artist's own, but always fractionally different, visage. Mass self-portraiture, serial self-portraiture, partial self-portraiture – it is safer that way, for there never has to be any limiting finality. There can be no last word because one never gets to the end of one's self.

Chapter Sixteen

Farewells

'I am sending you my portrait in order that we may always be with you, even when death shall have annihilated us.'

Erasmus to Thomas More

Self-Portrait on an Easel in a Workshop, c. 1604

Annibale Carracci (1560–1609)

It is twilight in the studio, perhaps even night. The eye of a little dog glints in the shadows. On the easel stands a picture of the artist but he has hung up his palette and disappeared, leaving only this piece of tacked canvas behind him.

The dog and a spectral cat skulk at the foot of the easel as if trying to keep close to some remnant of their master. The eerie shape at the window looks like a ghost. That the room is empty of human life is the painting's melancholy testimony: whoever was working with that palette, its patch of white still catching the half-light, has departed — if he was ever really here in the first place.

Yet the here of this painting is not quite a place, more of a no-man's land than a studio. The space is dark and ill-defined and the window floats like a veil on the surface. The easel is unsteadily propped, its third leg barely there at all, and the strongest presence here is the picture on its ledge, or rather the man in the picture, for the portrait is presented as nothing more than an object.

The man's picture: in the simplest sense, the narrative sense, the self-portrait shows how the artist looked and what he was making before the light died, but this little self-portrait is not so straightforward. The picture is propped at a slant, the face is partly in shadow, the expression poignantly withdrawn and above all it is seen to be only a painted thing, an image at one step removed. Yet by comparison with everything else in this hesitant scene, the face feels about as strong as the artist could manage.

Self-Portrait on an Easel in a Workshop is by the Bolognese painter Annibale Carracci, who was widely considered one of the most powerful minds in Italian painting of his time, equal only to his contemporary Caravaggio. This was not just the opinion of the aristocrats who lured him away from Bologna to paint Rome's palaces and churches; it seems that Caravaggio thought so too. Taken by some friends to see an altarpiece by Carracci in a church that had bypassed him for the commission, Caravaggio is reported to have given it more than his usual grudging once-over. Perhaps, he conceded, there was after all *one* other painter deserving of that title in the city.[1]

Carracci had come to Rome primarily to paint the immense ceilings of the cavernous Farnese Palace with illustrations from the poems of Ovid. Conceiving of these ceilings as open to the sky, he pictured each mythological scene as an easel painting framed against a vast blue heaven. With their eye-deceiving statues and tapestries, their *trompe l'œil* medallions and operatic figures, their frissons of passion and blasts of bright air, these were easily the grandest ceilings in Rome since the Sistine Chapel and for the next two centuries would remain the unrivalled masterpieces of secular fresco.

Pictures on easels; one recognizes the connection but it is lost in the shocking disparity. How could this master of soaring grandeur make such a lowly little image of himself? For the picture within the picture, the self-portrait on its rickety easel, is not even as big as a playing card. Fragile and forlorn, it is shown to be no more than a work of paint, and an unfinished work at that. It speaks of the artist in a most uncommon way, not a definitive statement so much as a tentative rehearsal, hoping to say something out of the darkness, and yet barely raising a voice. If this oblique little thing stands for Carracci at all, it is the artist *in absentia*.

————

What will we leave behind of ourselves after death? A memory, or at least the strands of some ever-changing cobweb of memories strung between other people's minds. A face in photographs and moving images. A voice on tape, in letters or in words that might resurface in others' conversations. A few relics that nobody can quite bear to dispatch: spectacles, wedding ring, paintbrush, pen, objects that were always with us. A bottle trapping perfumed air; a slipper retaining a footprint. The great works – the principles, paintings, symphonies, novels, the discovered gene, the miraculous cure: these are the lasting public monuments, not the intimate expressions of these transient selves that haunt us. And it is often said that the closest connection we can ever have with artists after they have gone is the quick sketch that we can hold in our hands, the image on the back of the envelope, the rapid drawing in the margin that comes over live and direct, transmitted straight from the brain to the hand.

Artists who want to represent themselves have, at the very least, to decide between now and for ever, between the provisional drawing and the permanent presentation in which one is no longer talking only to oneself. Perhaps what defines the latter is precisely that there has been no decision, no choice between conscious and unconscious effect. Small self-portraits, made on paper or board or the pages of a sketchbook, speak of a mind completely absorbed in the moment, or turned in on itself by affliction. Pierre-Auguste Renoir, crippled with rheumatism and suffering agonies standing for hours at the easel, turned to making small self-portraits instead, tragically at variance with the rosy Renoir of legend but infinitely more affecting. His ward, Julie Manet, mentions a self-portrait in her diary for 1899. 'It is so painful to see him in the morning not having the strength to turn a door knob. But he is managing a self-portrait. At first he made himself a little stern and too wrinkled; we absolutely insisted that he remove a few wrinkles and now it is more like him. "It seems to me that those calf's eyes are enough," he shrugs.'[2]

His contemporary Edgar Degas lived into his eighties, long after his eyes were failing and his light was gone. A friend, Paul Valery, writes of the long diminuendo, 'little by little, work became impossible and all that he lived for had gone, while life still remained'. But still he made images and one was a pastel drawing of his own face, which he had not depicted for decades. It shows him with a white beard, bloodhound eyes and the peaked cap artists often wear against light and cold in the studio but which can suggest second childhood. Degas seems to have been bemused by what the picture showed him of himself: he would show it to his guests, remarking that he looked like a dog.

It is no stretch to imagine Carracci doing the same thing, handing his self-portrait to visitors, observing this sad little relic of himself. But Carracci's painting is more than a sketch, and less than a monument; it is the shadow between the idea and the act. The artist is presented as one of his own works – what a pleasing summation of self-portraiture, perfectly communicating the way that his own works come into being, what is more; except that this one has not been fully born. Although there is a preliminary sketch for the painting (and even, remarkably, a second version) the finished work of *Self-Portrait on an Easel in a Workshop* remains touchingly provisional and uncertain.

Carracci is an indistinct figure in life as well. We know what he looked like for he left several self-portraits; we know his place in art between the Renaissance and the Baroque, between the mighty art of Michelangelo – who also painted the walls of the Farnese Palace – and the new realism of Caravaggio. But if his work is less well known it is because his magnum opus is generally perceived to be exclusively these immobile frescos. In Rome, Carracci worked for the richest princes of the Catholic Church, yet he lived in the attic of Count Eduardo Farnese's palace for several years and recoiled from the role of courtier. His first biographer, Giovanni Pietro Bellori, says he used to live 'shut up in his rooms … spending hours at his painting, which he was wont to call his lady … He despised ostentation in people as well as painting, seeking the company of plain, ambitionless men … and he fled the haughtiness of courtiers.' Taciturn and introspective, with an unpretentious man's dislike of patronage, Carracci would duck into alleys rather than meet Farnese face to face. He once allowed himself to be taken to prison rather than offer the simple admission that he was a legitimate employee at the palace.[3]

The other reason he appears elusive, particularly to art historians, is that he often worked with his brother Agostino and his cousin Ludovico and it seems that the three Carracci, in terms of finished works, did not want anyone to tell them apart. When a patron asked which Carracci had frescoed the walls of the Palazzo Magnani-Salem, they refused to divulge. 'All of us made it. It is by the Carracci.' Opening an art school in Bologna – The Academy of the Incamminati, or Progressives – they taught above all the value of draughtsmanship, and it is here that Annibale first surfaces as a strong identity, for his drawings are peerless: quick and sensitive and amazingly versatile. He could turn his pen to the street, the restaurant and the court, to the infant trying to pull on a sock and the breeze stirring autumn leaves, from Venus settling on a couch to a butcher weighing meat in a shop. He goes from high to low with no loss of power or originality and is even credited with inventing the caricature. One of his innovations, along with the Ideal Landscape, is a kind of pictorial riddle still popular in playgrounds four centuries later. A horizon line topped with a crescent and next to it a triangle. Guess what? A builder with his trowel peeping over a wall.

As the weeks turned to years and the frescos in the Farnese Palace built up, room after room, Agostino gradually filtered away to other work, leaving Annibale to paint the main ceiling on his own. An immensely difficult and protracted labour, so physically and intellectually exhausting, so absolutely the apex of his entire career, the grand salon was the work of half a decade. When the scaffolding was taken down tourists were writing letters home about the astounding spectacle within weeks. Yet the one person who might have offered the highest praise, and who owed the greatest gratitude, was the one person who gave nothing. Or worse than nothing; the miserable bag of cash Farnese sent his painter on a saucer seems to have brought on a nervous breakdown that blighted the rest of his life. He began to falter, to doubt his own worth.

The doctor who treated Carracci wrote of 'a deep depression, accompanied by emptiness of mind and lapses of memory. He neither spoke nor remembered, and was in danger of sudden death.'

To some eyes, *Self-Portrait on an Easel in a Workshop* can *only* be the portrait of a breakdown, no matter whether made just before or just after this shock. Everything about its peculiar space and vague forms, its uncertain brushwork and fading easel, above all its portrait of the artist as a lonely object in a dusk of brown shadows, speaks to them of a broken psyche. What is more, he seems to be painting himself as he once was, younger than he could have looked in his forties, younger than the Carracci in another self-portrait painted when he was actually forty. Painting himself as he used to be, trying to preserve or remember his former self.

The preliminary drawing shows an alteration too: there is the curious statue-like form at the window, the easel with its painting, but with one big and telling difference. The Carracci in the sketch is much larger and stronger, ostentatiously dressed and altogether more formal. At some point between drawing and painting Carracci must have wondered what he really was and decided on a stranger and humbler truth.

In 1600, Carracci had some kind of breach with his beloved brother and Agostino returned to Bologna. They never saw each other again. Agostino died very suddenly, Carracci returned to arrange the funeral and the self-portrait is thought to have been painted some time after that. It may be that the death also contributed to his paralyzing depression, for by 1603 no paintings are recorded and Carracci could no longer work. His pupils began to complete pictures for him. A note survives showing that they tried to encourage him back to art with a mutual pact to do two hours a day together at least (the second version of the self-portrait seems likely to have been made for one of them).

Carracci left the palace and moved to temporary lodgings behind the Capitoline Hill, and then to another address and another. The years passed without work or payment. The same doctor, by now a friend, described visiting him one morning in 1609 and finding him tranquil of mind. When the doctor returned in the evening Carracci was dying. 'He went to Bologna to find death but did not discover it there. He returned to Rome and now he has found it.' All that remained of whatever he earned during a life of stupendous achievement were a few pieces of silver and an elderly mattress, on loan from the Farnese Palace.

Carracci shows himself as an illusion, displaying the paradox of art: the living presence of a man summoned in two dimensions out of lifeless paint and canvas. To that extent, the self-portrait is a conceit.

The artist is known to have been impatient with Michelangelo's grand maxim that 'we paint with our brains not our hands' – and to have impressed upon his devoted pupils the immense skill and practice required to make a work of art. But this is not just an oblique manifesto. The shy man is shown to be a thing of cloth, a person and yet an object, it is true. But he is also incomplete, like all men a work in progress.

Incomplete and uncertain: that is the character of both the face and the painting. With this tiny image Carracci measures the limits of self-portraiture. For all a self-portrait can ever be is the illusion of the artist's self. It can never be a substitute, an embodiment, the last word or the whole summation, and yet the artist paints, even as he doubts, uncertain whether anything of himself will ever get through. This is the brave pathos of Carracci's farewell self-portrait: now I am here – and yet I am not.

————

Acknowledgements

The first pictures I ever saw were by my father, the Scottish painter James Cumming, whose work took the form of lyrical and sometimes geometric abstraction. But like most children I preferred to see the world transformed into figurative images, materializing on the page through the magic of his hand. A camel, two acrobats, a carousel with my brother riding one of the horses: they are there by special request in his sketchbooks, as distinct and beautiful as his pictorial variations on the Golden Mean and the newly revealed wonders of sub-atomic particles. They are there, but he is not. My father did not depict himself.

I longed for a self-portrait, for some knowledge of him that would be independent of my own perceptions and entirely drawn from his – to see my father through his own eyes. Years after his death, we finally found a thumbnail image in a sketchbook. It is there on a page with cell structures, pine-cones and planets; he saw himself as just another tiny element in the universe.

This book is for him, my first guide and mentor in art, and for my mother, without whom it could not have been written. Her love of images and words and her passionate curiosity have helped me to see more than I could have otherwise and her response to some of the self-portraits in this book has been as inspiring as her constant encouragement.

Births, deaths and marriages occurred during its writing and Dennis Sewell has been with me through all of them, beloved friend, supporter and husband. I thank him for his ideas and his constant love.

Three friends deserve special thanks. David Edgar, who saw the theatre in self-portraits and sent me postcards from all over the world; Jonathan Coe, who saw the novel in *Las Meninas*, and read the book so carefully with a view to narrative; and Tom Lubbock, who has made me think more about art than anyone, and whose marvellously original way of looking at

paintings excites and inspires me every time we talk.

Arabella Pike has been a patient and enthusiastic editor. My agent David Miller has been both and more. Annabel Wright, whose subtlety, ingenuity and all-round care have contributed so much to the final version of the book, has been a pleasure to work with. Mel Haselden is queen of picture researchers.

I have been lucky to have a correspondence with Professor Joseph Leo Koerner at Harvard University, whose work on Dürer is to my mind unrivalled, and with Professors James Rubin and Klaus Herder on the paintings of Courbet. I would like to thank Dr John Leighton of the National Galleries of Scotland, Dr Deborah Swallow of the Courtauld Institute, Elizabeth Fuller of the Rosenbach Museum, and the staff at the Alte Pinakotech in Munich who let me see the archives in which I came across the story about the injury to Dürer's eye, in particular Dr Martin Schawe. I am very grateful to my celebratory friend Kate Kellaway and her father William Kellaway, who gave me a first edition of *500 Self-Portraits*, published in 1929, with its sombre and dramatic reproductions; also to Carol Anderson, Professor Michael Dobson, Sarah Donaldson, Tena Kozic, Luke Jennings, Irena Vincek and Jane Ferguson, who first invited me to write about art.

Finally, I had close conversations about Rembrandt with the Scottish poet George Bruce. He went off and wrote a poem. Here it is. In Memoriam, George.

He kent as thae een lookt at his
Oot'e the dark he made in yon picter
He lookt on a man, himself, as on
A stane dish, or leaf fa' in winter.
That calm was his strang sough.
But in that dark twa wee lichts,
Een that is hope like lit windaes
An in that hoose muckle business.

Notes

Preface

1. 'I dread the vision of a statue ... shiver and tremble at the thought of another graven image', Charles Dickens, Letter to William Hepworth Dixon, EL3.D548 MS3, Rosenbach Museum, Philadelphia.
2. Jorge Luis Borges, *Everything and Nothing*, trans. Donald A. Yates *et al.* (New York: New Directions Publishing, 1999).
3. Anna Gruetzner Robins, ed., *Walter Sickert: The Complete Writings on Art* (Oxford: Oxford University Press, 2002), p. 418.

Chapter 1 Secrets

1. 12 March 1435; Document 24 in W. H. James Weale, *Hubert and John Van Eyck* (London: Lane, 1908).
2. Edwin Hall, *The Arnolfini Betrothal: Medieval Marriage and the Enigma of Van Eyck's Double Portrait* (Berkeley, CA, and London: University of California Press, 1994), p. 123.
3. Linda Seidel, in *Jan Van Eyck's Arnolfini Portrait: Stories of an Icon* (Cambridge: Cambridge University Press, 1993), declares that it is only circular logic, or rather illogic, that leads people to believe that these little men in turbans are self-portraits at all, each claim piggybacking on the idea that the man in a red turban in *Portrait of a Man* (National Gallery) is a self-portrait, in turn perpetuated by the existence of all the other men in turbans, and so on.
4. X-rays have shown that the infant was not always blessing the chancellor, and the chancellor once had a money bag lashed to his waist, but somebody took exception to that telltale item, which was later and hastily overpainted. Anita Albus, *The Art of Arts: Rediscovering Painting*, trans. Michael Robertson (Berkeley, CA, and London: University of California Press, 2001), p. 14.
5. Erwin Panofsky, *Early Netherlandish Painting, its Origins and Character* (Cambridge, MA: Harvard University Press, 1953), p. 181.
6. See note 3, Seidel among others.
7. Lorne Campbell *et al.*, *Renaissance Faces: Van Eyck to Titian* (London: National Gallery, 2008), p. 178.

Chapter 2 Eyes

1. Lorne Campbell, *Renaissance Portraits* (New Haven, CT: Yale University Press, 1990), p. 81.
2. Francis Darwin, ed., *Life and Letters of Charles Darwin* (London: John Murray, 1888), vol. 2, p. 296.
3. Filippo Baldinucci, *Notizie dei professori de' disegno da Cimabue in qua* (Florence: Batelli e Compagni, 1847), *Vita de Lippi*.
4. Lorenzo Lippi, *Il Malmantile racquistato*, published posthumously in Florence, 1688.

Chapter 3 Dürer

1. Bettina Von Arnim, *Goethe's Correspondence with a Child* (London: Longman, Orme, Brown, Green and Longmans, 1937; originally published in German in 1835), e-edition prepared by Bruce Charlton, 2004.
2. *Reportorium für Kunstwissenschaft*, ed. Henry Thode and Hugo von Tschudi (Berlin: Druck und Verlag von Georg Reimer, 1914), p. 424.
3. Email correspondence with the author.
4. Julius Bard, ed., *Albrecht Dürer schriftlicher Nachlass* (Berlin: 1910), I.59.
5. Michael Levey, *Essays on Dürer*, ed. C. R. Dodwell (Manchester: University of Manchester Press, 1973), p.14.
6. Joseph Leo Koerner, *The Moment of Self-Portraiture in German Renaissance Art* (Chicago and London: University of Chicago Press, 1993) p. 185.
7. Email correspondence with the author.

Chapter 4 Motive, Means and Opportunity

1. *The Complete Poems of Michelangelo*, trans. John Frederick Nims (Chicago: University of Chicago Press, 1998).
2. Thomas Hess and John Ashbery, *The Grand Eccentrics* (Collier Books, 1971), p. 69.
3. 'I've done a lot of self-portraits really because people have been dying off around me like flies and I've had nobody else left to paint but myself … I loathe my own face.' David Sylvester, *The Brutality of Fact: Interviews with Francis Bacon* (London: Thames and Hudson, 3rd edn 1987), pp. 129–33.
4. John Rewald, *Seurat: A Biography* (New York: H. N. Abrams, 1990), p. 190.
5. This was the view of the authors of the catalogue to Georges Seurat, 1851–1891 (Museum of Modern Art, 1991).

Chapter 5 Rembrandt

1. Christopher White and Quentin Buvelot, eds., *Rembrandt by Himself* (London: National Gallery, 1999), p 17.
2. *Ibid.*, p 17.
3. *Ibid.*, p 19.
4. The idea of making such comparisons is raised by Tom Lubbock in 'Supreme Dramatist of the Face', *Independent*, 8 June 1999.
5. Gary Schwartz, *Rembrandt: His Life and Paintings* (London: Penguin, 1991) p. 328.
6. *Ibid.*, p. 362.

Chapter 6 Behind the Scenes

1. Svetlana Alpers, *The Vexations of Art: Velázquez and Others* (New Haven, CT: Yale University Press, 2005), p. 34.

Chapter 7 Velázquez

1. Kenneth Clark, *Looking at Pictures* (London: John Murray, 1960), pp. 38–9.

Chapter 8 Mirrors

1. Mark Pendergrast, *Mirror Mirror* (New York: Basic Books, 2003).
2. www.truemirror.com
3. Tom Rockwell, ed., *The Best of Norman Rockwell* (Philadelphia: Courage Books, 1988), Preface.

Chapter 9 Performance

1. Tom Lubbock, 'Great Works', *Independent*, 18 Nov. 2005.
2. Michael Prodger, 'In the Grip of a Terrible Beauty', *Sunday Telegraph*, 14 Aug. 2005.
3. Thomas Nagel, 'Concealment and Exposure', *Philosophy and Public Affairs*, 27 (1) (1998), pp. 3–30.

Chapter 10 Stage Fright

1. Sidney Lee, ed., *Dictionary of National Biography: Supplement* (Oxford: Oxford University Press, 1901), p. 157.
2. Duncan Thomson, *Sir Henry Raeburn 1756–1823* (Edinburgh: National Galleries of Scotland, 1994), p. 174.
3. John Hayes, ed., *The Letters of Thomas Gainsborough* (New Haven, CT: Yale University Press, 2001), p. 175.
4. Richard Cumberland, *Memoirs of Richard Cumberland, Written by Himself*, 2 vols. (London: Lackington, Allen & Co., 1806–7), p. 464.
5. David Hume, *The Philosophical Works of David Hume* (New York: Little Brown, 1854), p. 312.

6. John Updike, *Self-Consciousness* (London: Penguin 1990), pp. 75–106.

Chapter 11 Loners

1. Anita Brookner, *Jacques-Louis David* (London: Chatto & Windus, 1980), p. 50.
2. T. J. Clark, *Farewell to an Idea: Episodes from a History of Modernism* (New Haven, CT, and London: Yale University Press, 1999), p. 32.
3. Brookner, p. 102.
4 *Ibid.*, p. 124.
5. Yvonne Deslandres, *Delacroix: A Pictorial Biography* (London: Thames and Hudson, 1963), p. 93.

Chapter 12 Egotists

1. Denis Diderot, *Diderot on Art*, vol. 2, *The Salon of 1767*, ed. and trans. John Goodman (New Haven, CT, and London: Yale University Press, 1995), pp. xvi, 81–2.
2. Sarah Faunce and Linda Nochlin, *Courbet Reconsidered* (New Haven, CT, and London: Yale University Press, 1988), pp. 193–4.
3. Michael Fried, *Courbet's Realism* (Chicago: Chicago University Press, 1990), p. 278.
4. Jack Lindsay, *Gustave Courbet: His Life and Art* (Bath: Adams and Dart, 1973), p. 115.
5. *Ibid.*, p. 117.
6. Gerstle Mack, *Gustave Courbet* (London: Rupert Hart-Davis, 1951), pp. 127–30.
7. Email correspondence with Professor James Rubin, author of *Courbet* (London: Phaidon, 1997).
8. Pierre-Joseph Proudhon, *Du principe de l'art et de sa destination sociale* (Paris: 1865), p. 283.

Chapter 13 Victims

1. Iris Müller-Westermann, *Munch by Himself* (London: Royal Academy of Arts, 2005), p. 108.
2. *Edvard Munch: Lithographs, Etchings, Woodcuts* (Los Angeles: Los Angeles County Museum, 1969), p. 9.
3. Frida Kahlo, *Frida Kahlo*, ed. Emma Dexter and Tanya Barson (London: Tate Publishing, 2005), p. 42.
4. *Ibid.*, p. 11.

Chapter 14 Pioneers

1. Wilhelm Udhe, *Van Gogh* (London: Phaidon, 1972), p.7.

Chapter 16 Farewells

1. Giovanni Pietro Bellori, *The Lives of the Modern Painters, Sculptors and Architects*, trans. Alice Sedgwick Wohl (New York: Cambridge University Press, 2005), p. 77.
2. Paul Valéry, *Degas, Manet, Morisot*, trans. David Paul (Princeton: Princeton University Press, 1960), p. 99.
3. Cesare Malvasia, *Malvasia's Life of the Carracci*, trans. Anne Summerscale (University Park, PA: Pennsylvania State University Press), p. 227.

List of
Illustrations

Preface

Van Rijn, Rembrandt (1606–69), *Self-Portrait*, c. 1663, oil on canvas, 114.3 x 94 cm
The Iveagh Bequest, Kenwood House, London / Bridgeman Art Library

Chapter 1 Secrets

Van Eyck, Jan (c. 1390–1441), *Portrait of a Man (Self Portrait?)*, 1433, oil on wood, 33.3 x 25.8 cm
National Gallery, London / Bridgeman Art Library

Van Eyck, *Madonna and Child with Canon Georg van der Paele*, 1436 (and detail), oil on panel, 122 x 157 cm
Groeninge Museum, Bruges / Bridgeman Art Library

Van Eyck, *The Madonna of Chancellor Rolin*, c. 1435 (detail), oil on panel, 66 x 62 cm
Louvre, Paris / Bridgeman Art Library

Van Eyck, *The Arnolfini Portrait*, 1434 (detail), oil on panel, 83.7 x 57 cm
National Gallery, London / Bridgeman Art Library

Chapter 2 Eyes

Botticelli, Sandro (c. 1445–1510), *The Adoration of the Magi*, 1475 (detail), tempera on wood, 111 x 134 cm
Uffizi, Florence / Bridgeman Art Library

Tintoretto, Jacopo Comin (1518–94), *Self-Portrait*, c. 1546–1548, oil on canvas, 45.7 x 38 cm
Reproduced by kind permission of the Philadelphia Museum of Art

Graff, Anton (1736–1813), *Self-Portrait*, 1813
bpk / Nationalgalerie, Staatliche Museen zu Berlin. Photo: Andres Kilger

Chardin, Jean-Baptiste-Siméon (1699–1779), *Self-Portrait with Spectacles*, 1771, pastel on paper, 46 x 37.5 cm
Louvre, Paris / Bridgeman Art Library

Rembrandt, *Self-Portrait, Wide-eyed*, 1630, etching and burin, 5.1 x 4.6 cm
Kupferstichkabinett, Staatliche Museen zu Berlin. Photo: Joerg P. Anders Scala, Florence / bpk

Lippi, Lorenzo (1606–65), *Self-Portrait*, c. 1655, oil on canvas, 49.5 x 36 cm
Uffizi, Florence / Scala. Courtesy of the Ministero Beni e Att. Culturali

Titian (c. 1488–1576), *Self-Portrait*, c. 1560, oil on canvas, 96.4 x 74.8 cm
Gemäldegalerie, Staatliche Museen zu Berlin. Photo: Joerg P. Anders. Scala, Florence / bpk

Reynolds, Sir Joshua (1723–92), *Self-Portrait*, c. 1747–49, oil on canvas, 63 x 74 cm
National Portrait Gallery, London

Klee, Paul (1879–1940), Versunkenheit, 1919, 75, *Absorption*, pencil on paper on cardboard, 27 x 19.7 cm
Norton Simon Museum of Art, Pasadena, California. The Blue Four Galka Scheyer Collection. © DACS 2009

Goya, y Lucientes, Francisco José de (1746–1828), *Self-Portrait*, plate I, *Los Caprichos*, pub 1799, etching and aquatint, 21.9 x 15.2 cm
Private Collection / Bridgeman Art Library

Chapter 3 Dürer

Dürer, Albrecht (1471–1528), *Self-Portrait*, 1500, oil on wood, 67 x 49 cm
Alte Pinakothek, Munich / Bridgeman Art Library

Dürer, *Self-Portrait at 13*, 1484, silverpoint on paper, 27.5 x 19.6 cm
Graphische Sammlung Albertina, Vienna / Bridgeman Art Library

Dürer, *Self-Portrait in the Nude*, c. 1503, black ink heightened with white on green paper, 29.2 x 15.4 cm
Schlossmuseum, Weimar / Bridgeman Art Library

Dürer, *Self-Portrait with Eryngium*, 1493, oil on parchment on canvas, 56 x 44 cm
Louvre, Paris / Bridgeman Art Library

Dürer, *Self-Portrait with Gloves*, 1498, oil on wood, 52 x 41 cm
Prado, Madrid / Bridgeman Art Library

Chapter 4 Motive, Means and Opportunity

Michelangelo, Buonarroti (1475–1564), *The Last Judgement* (Sistine Chapel Ceiling), c. 1538–41, fresco (details)
Vatican Museums and Galleries, Vatican City, Alinari / Bridgeman Art Library

Bazzi, Giovanni ('Il Sodoma') (1477–1549), *St Benedict's First Miracle*, 1502 (detail)
Monte Oliveto Maggiore, Tuscany

Caravaggio, Michelangelo Merisi da (1574–1610), *The Taking of Christ*, c. 1602, oil on canvas, 133.5 x 169.5 cm

Photo © National Gallery of Ireland. From the Jesuit Community, Leeson Street, Dublin, who acknowledge the kind generosity of the late Dr Marie Lea-Wilson

Van Dyck, Sir Anthony (1599–1641), *Self-Portrait with Sunflower*, c. 1633, oil on canvas, 60 x 73 cm
Private Collection / Bridgeman Art Library

Leyster, Judith (1609–60), *Self-Portrait*, c. 1630, oil on canvas, 74.3 x 65 cm
Photograph courtesy of the Board of Trustees, National Gallery of Art, Washington. Gift of Mr and Mrs Robert Woods Bliss

Poussin, Nicolas (1594–1665), *Self-Portrait*, c. 1650, oil on canvas, 98 x 74 cm
Louvre, Paris / Giraudon / Bridgeman Art Library

Murillo, Bartolomé Esteban (c. 1617–82), *Self-Portrait*, c. 1670–73, oil on canvas, 122 x 107 cm
National Gallery, London / Bridgeman Art Library

Nussbaum, Felix (1904–44), *Self-Portrait with Jewish Identity Card*, 1943, oil on canvas, 56 x 49 cm
Kulturegeschichtliches Museum, Osnabrück. Scala, Florence / bpk
© DACS 2009

Seurat, Georges Pierre (1859–91), *La Poudreuse*, c. 1888–90, oil on canvas, 95.5 x 79.5 cm
The Samuel Courtauld Trust, Courtauld Institute of Art Gallery, London

Chapter 5 Rembrandt

Rembrandt (1606–69), *Self-Portrait*, c. 1663, oil on canvas, 114.3 x 94 cm
The Iveagh Bequest, Kenwood House, London / Bridgeman Art Library

Rembrandt, *Self-Portrait*, 1640, oil on canvas, 93 x 80 cm
National Gallery, London / akg-images

Rembrandt, *Self-Portrait as a Young Man*, c. 1628, oil on wood, 22.5 x 18.6 cm
Rijksmuseum, Amsterdam / Bridgeman Art Library

Rembrandt, *Self-Portrait aged 51*, c. 1657, oil on canvas, 53 x 54 cm
National Gallery of Scotland, Edinburgh (Bridgewater Loan, 1945)

Rembrandt, *Self-Portrait as Zeuxis*, 1662, oil on canvas, 82.5 x 65 cm
Wallraf-Richartz Museum, Cologne. Photo: Jochen Remmer Scala, Florence / bpk

Rembrandt, *Portrait of Jacop Trip*, c. 1661, oil on canvas, 130.5 x 97 cm
National Gallery, London

Rembrandt, *Self-Portrait*, 1658, oil on canvas, 131 x 102 cm
© *The Frick Collection, New York*

Chapter 6 Behind the Scenes

Gentileschi, Artemisia (1593–c. 1652), *Self-Portrait as La Pittura*, 1638, oil on canvas, 98.6 x 75.2 cm
The Royal Collection © *2009. Her Majesty Queen Elizabeth II*

Borgianni, Orazio (c. 1575–1616), *Self-Portrait*, c. 1615, oil on canvas, 95 x 71 cm
Museo del Prado, Madrid

Anguissola, Sofonisba (c. 1532–1625), *Bernardino Campi painting Sofonisba Anguissola,*
c. 1559, oil on canvas, 111 x 109.5 cm
Pinacoteca Nazionale, Siena / akg-images

Resani, Arcangelo (1670–1740), *Self-Portrait*, c. 1713, oil on canvas, 105 x 87.3 cm
Uffizi, Florence / Bridgeman Art Library

Labille-Guiard, Adélaïde (1749–1803), *Self-Portrait with Two Pupils*, 1785, oil on canvas, 210.8 x 151.1 cm
Metropolitan Museum of Art, New York. Gift of Julia A. Berwind, 1953. Photograph © *Metropolitan Museum of Art / Art Resource / Scala, Florence*

Goya, *Self-Portrait in the Studio*, 1790–95, oil on canvas, 42 x 28 cm
Real Academia de Bellas Artes de San Fernando, Madrid / Bridgeman Art Library

Guston, Philip (1913–80), *The Studio*, 1969
Copyright © *Estate of Philip Guston*
Reproduced by kind permission of The McKee Gallery, New York

Chapter 7 Velázquez

Velázquez, Diego Rodriguez de Silva y (1599–1660), *Las Meninas*, c. 1656 (and details), oil on canvas, 318 x 276 cm
Prado, Madrid. Giraudon / Bridgeman Art Library

Velázquez, *Infante Carlos Baltasar in the Riding School*, c. 1640–45, oil on canvas, 130 x 102 cm
Wallace Collection, London / Bridgeman Art Library

Vermeer, Jan (1632–75), *The Art of Painting*, c. 1665–6, oil on canvas, 120 x 100 cm
Kunsthistorisches Museum, Vienna / Bridgeman Art Library

Chapter 8 Mirrors

Parmigianino (1503–40), *Self-Portrait in a Convex Mirror*, 1524, oil on wood, diameter 24.4 cm
Kunsthistorisches Museum, Vienna. Ali Meyer / Bridgeman Art Library

Marcia in her Studio (St Marcia, d. 632), from *De Claris Mulieribus* by Giovanni Boccaccio (1313–75)
French School, 15th Century. Ms Fr 124220 fol. 101v. Bibliothèque Nationale, Paris / Giraudon / Bridgeman Art Library

Vuillard, Jean-Édouard (1868–1940), *Self-Portrait in a Mirror with a Bamboo Frame*, 1890
Private Collection. © ADAGP, Paris and DACS, London 2009

Corinth, Lovis (1858–1925), *Self-Portrait*, 1925
Reproduced by kind permission of the Kunsthaus Zürich

Gumpp, Johannes (1626–1728), *Self-Portrait*, 1646, oil on canvas, diameter 89 cm
Uffizi, Florence / Bridgeman Art Library

Rockwell, Norman (1894–1978), *Triple Self-Portrait*, 1960, oil on canvas, 114.2 x 88.8 cm
Printed by permission of the Norman Rockwell Family Agency.
Copyright © 1960 Norman Rockwell Family Entities. Collection of the Norman Rockwell Museum, Stockbridge, Massachusetts

Freud, Lucian (1922–), *Self-Portrait, Man's Head, Portrait III*, 1963, oil on canvas, 30.5 x 25.1 cm
Copyright © Lucian Freud / National Portrait Gallery, London

Bonnard, Pierre (1867–1947), *Self-Portrait*, c. 1940, 104.5 x 88.3 cm

Art Gallery of New South Wales, Sydney / Bridgeman Art Library
© ADAGP, Paris and DACS, London 2009

Chapter 9 Performance

Rosa, Salvator (1615–73), *Self-Portrait*, c. 1645, oil on canvas, 116.3 x 94 cm
National Gallery, London / Bridgeman Art Library

Ter Borch, Gerard (1617–81), *Self-Portrait*, c. 1670, oil on canvas, 61 x 42.5 cm
The Hague, Mauritshuis / Scala, Florence

Sassoferrato, Giovanni Battista Salvi da (1609–85), *Self-Portrait*, c. 1650, oil on canvas, 38 x 32.5 cm
Uffizi, Florence / akg-images / Rabatti-Domingie

La Tour, Maurice Quentin de (1704–88), *Self-Portrait wearing a Jabot*, c. 1751, pastel on paper, 64 x 53 cm
Musée de Picardie, Amiens / Giraudon / Bridgeman Art Library

Ducreux, Joseph (1735–1802), *Self-Portrait as a Mocker*, 1793, oil on canvas, 55 x 46 cm
Louvre, Paris. Photo © Réunion des Musées Nationaux (RMN) / Jean-Gilles Berizzi

Mueck, Ron (1958–), *Mask*, 1997, mixed media, 158 x 153 x 124cm
Copyright © Ron Mueck. Reproduced by kind permission of Anthony D'Offay, London

Vigée-Le Brun, Élisabeth (1755–1842), *Self-Portrait*, 1790, oil on canvas, 100 x 81 cm
Uffizi, Florence / Scala, courtesy of the Ministero Beni e Att. Culturali

Chapter 10 Stage Fright

Raeburn, Sir Henry (1726–1853), *Self-Portrait*, c. 1815, oil on canvas, 89.5 x 69.9 cm
National Gallery of Scotland, Edinburgh / Bridgeman Art Library

Gainsborough, Thomas (1727–88), *Self-Portrait*, c. 1787
Royal Academy of Arts, London / Bridgeman Art Library

Romney, George (1734–1802), *Self-Portrait*, 1784, oil on canvas, 125.7 x 99.1 cm
National Portrait Gallery, London

Mengs, Anton Raphael (1728–79), *Self-Portrait*, 1774, oil on canvas, 73.5 x 56.5 cm
Walker Art Gallery, National Museums, Liverpool / Bridgeman Art Library

Fuseli, Henry (1741–1825), *Self-Portrait*, date unknown
Copyright © V&A Images / Victoria and Albert Museum, London

Goya, *Self-Portrait*, c. 1795–7, brush and grey wash on laid paper 15.3 x 9.1 cm
Metropolitan Museum of Art, New York / Art Resource / Scala, Florence

Delacroix, Ferdinand Victor Eugène (1798–1863), *Self-Portrait*, c. 1837, oil on canvas, 65 x 54 cm
Louvre, Paris / Lauros / Giraudon / Bridgeman Art Library

Tintoretto, *Self-Portrait*, 1587, oil on canvas, 62.5 x 52 cm
Louvre, Paris / Lauros / Giraudon / Bridgeman Art Library

Chapter 11 Loners

David, Jacques-Louis (1748–1825), *Self-Portrait*, 1794, oil on canvas, 81 x 64 cm
Louvre, Paris. Photo © Réunion des Musées Nationaux (RMN) / Gérard Blot

Janssen, Victor Emil (1807–45), *Self-Portrait in front of the Easel*, c. 1628, oil on paper on canvas, 56.6 x 32.7 cm
Hamburger Kunsthalle, Hamburg / Bridgeman Art Library

Courbet, Jean Désiré Gustave (1819–77), *The Desperate Man*, 1843, oil on canvas, 45 x 54 cm
Nasjonalgalleriet, Oslo / akg-images / Archives CDA

Kersting, Georg Friedrich (1785–1847), *Caspar David Friedrich in his Studio*, 1812, oil on canvas, 51 x 40 cm
Nationalgalerie, Staatliche Museen zu Berlin. Photo: Joerg P. Anders / Scala, Florence / bpk

Chapter 12 Egotists

Courbet, *L'Atelier*, 1855 (and detail), oil on canvas, 361 x 598 cm
Musée d'Orsay, Paris / Giraudon / Bridgeman Art Library

Courbet, *The Cellist*, 1847
Reproduced by kind permission of the Nationalmuseum med Prins Eugens Waldemarsudde, Stockholm

Courbet, *Man with a Pipe*, c. 1846, oil on canvas, 45 x 37 cm
Musée Fabre, Montpellier / Giraudon / Bridgeman Art Library

Courbet, *The Meeting 'Bonjour Monsieur Courbet'* (Alfred Bruyas and Gustave Courbet), 1854, oil on canvas, 129 x 149 cm
Musée Fabre, Montpellier © Réunion des Musées Nationaux (RMN), Paris / Droits réservés

Chapter 13 Victims

Munch, Edvard (1863–1944), *Self-Portrait in Hell*, 1903
Munch Museum, Oslo / Scala, Florence. © Munch Museum/Munch – Ellingsen Group, BONO, Oslo/DACS, London 2009

Allori, Cristofano (1577–1621), *Judith with the Head of Holofernes*, c. 1613, oil on canvas, 139 x 116 cm
Palazzo Pitti, Florence / Bridgeman Art Library

Caravaggio, *David with the Head of Goliath*, c. 1609–10, oil on canvas, 125 x 100 cm
Galleria Borghese, Rome / Bridgeman Art Library

Beckmann, Max (1884–1950), *Self-Portrait with a Red Scarf*, 1917, oil on canvas, 80 x 60 cm
Staatsgalerie, Stuttgart. Scala, Florence / bpk. Photo: Lutz Braun © DACS 2009

Kirchner, Ernst Ludwig (1880–1938), *Self-Portrait as a Soldier*, 1915, oil on canvas, 69 x 61 cm
Allen Memorial Art Museum, Oberlin College, Ohio / Charles F. Olney Fund / Bridgeman Art Library

Schiele, Egon (1890–1918), *Self-Portrait as Saint Sebastian*, 1914–15 (detail), gouache, black crayon and ink on cardboard, 67 x 50 cm
Historisches Museum der Stadt Wien, Vienna / akg-images

Kahlo, Frida (1907–54), *The Wounded Deer, Self-Portrait*, 1946, oil on hardboard, 22.4 x 30 cm
Private Collection / akg-images © 2009, Banco de Mexico Diego Rivera & Frida Kahlo Museums Trust, Mexico D.F. / DACS

Kahlo, *Self-Portrait with Cropped Hair*, 1940, oil on canvas, 40 x 28 cm
Museum of Modern Art (MoMA), New York. Gift of

Edgar Kaufmann, Jr. / Scala, Florence. © 2009, Banco de Mexico Diego Rivera & Frida Kahlo Museums Trust, Mexico D.F. / DACS

Munch, *Self-Portrait between the Clock and the Bed*, c. 1942
Munch Museum, Oslo / Scala, Florence. © Munch Museum/Munch – Ellingsen Group, BONO, Oslo/DACS, London 2009

Chapter 14 Pioneers

Van Gogh, Vincent (1853–90), *Self-Portrait with a Bandaged Ear*, 1889, oil on canvas, 60 x 49 cm
The Samuel Courtauld Trust, Courtauld Institute of Art Gallery, London / Bridgeman Art Library

Van Gogh, *Self-Portrait with a Felt Hat*, c. 1887–8, oil on canvas, 44 x 37.5 cm
Van Gogh Museum, Amsterdam / Bridgeman Art Library

Van Gogh, *Self-Portrait*, 1889, oil on canvas, 65 x 54 cm
Musée d'Orsay, Paris / Giraudon / Bridgeman Art Library

Close, Chuck (1940–), *Self-Portrait*, 1991, oil on canvas, 254 x 213.4 cm
Photograph by Ellen Page Wilson, courtesy PaceWildenstein, New York © Chuck Close, courtesy PaceWildenstein, New York

Lewis, Wyndham (1882–1957), *Mr Wyndham Lewis as a Tyro*, c. 1920–21, oil on canvas, 75.9 x 45.4 cm
Ferens Art Gallery, Hull City Museums and Art Galleries / Bridgeman Art Library © by kind permission of the Wyndham Lewis Memorial Trust (a registered charity)

Matisse, Henri (1869–1954), *The Painter and His Model*, 1917, oil on canvas, 146.5 x 97 cm
Musée National d'Art Moderne, Centre Pompidou, Paris / Lauros / Giraudon / Bridgeman Art Library. © Succession H Matisse/DACS 2009

Chapter 15 Falling Apart

Sherman, Cindy (1954–), *Untitled Film Still (#7)*, 1978, black and white photograph, 25.4 x 20.3 cm
Courtesy of the Artist and Metro Pictures

Sherman, *Untitled (#400)*, 2000, colour photograph, 116.2 x 88.9 x 2.5 cm
Courtesy of the Artist and Metro Pictures

Cahun, Claude (1894–1954), *What Do You Want from Me?*, 1928, black and white photograph

Warhol, Andy (1928–87), *Self-Portrait*, 1963–4, silkscreen ink on synthetic polymer paint on canvas, 4 panels, each 50.8 x 40.6 cm
The Collection of Mr and Mrs S. Brooks Barron / akg-images © The Andy Warhol Foundation for the Visual Arts / Artists Rights Society (ARS), New York / DACS, London 2009

Warhol, *Self-Portrait with Skull*, 1977, Polaroid ™ Polacolor Type 108, 10.8 x 8.6 cm
Collection of the Andy Warhol Museum, Pittsburgh. © The Andy Warhol Foundation for the Visual Arts / Artists Rights Society (ARS), New York / DACS, London 2009

Freud, *Painter Working, Reflection*, 1993, oil on canvas, 101.3 x 81.7 cm
Copyright © Lucian Freud. Photo: John Riddy

Chapter 16 Farewells

Carracci, Annibale (1560–1609), *Self Portrait on an Easel in a Workshop*, c. 1604, oil on wood, 42.5 x 30 cm
The State Hermitage Museum, St Petersburg

While every effort has been made to trace the owners of copyright material reproduced herein, the publishers would like to apologise for any omissions and would be pleased to incorporate missing acknowledgements in future editions.

Select Bibliography

On Bonnard

Bell, Julian, *Bonnard*, London: Phaidon, 1994.

Hyman, Timothy, *Bonnard*, London: Thames and Hudson, 1998.

Terrasse, Antoine, *Pierre Bonnard*, New York: Harry Abrams, 1989.

Terrasse, Michel, *Bonnard at Le Cannet*, New York: Pantheon Books, 1988.

Whitfield, Sarah and Elderfield, John, *Bonnard*, London: Tate Gallery Publishing, 1998.

On Botticelli

Brion, Marcel, *Botticelli*, G. Cres, 1932.

Ettlinger, Leopold D. and Helen S., *Botticelli*, London: Thames and Hudson, 1976.

Hatfield, Rab, *Botticelli's Uffizi Adoration: A Study in Pictorial Content*, Princeton, NJ: Princeton University Press, 1976.

Horne, Herbert Percy, *Botticelli, Painter of Florence*, Princeton, NJ: Princeton University Press, 1980.

Levey, Michael, *Botticelli*, London: National Gallery, 1974.

Lightbown, R. W., *Sandro Botticelli: Life and Work*, London: Thames and Hudson, 1989.

On Caravaggio

Berenson, Bernard, *Caravaggio: His Incongruity and his Fame*, London: Chapman and Hall, 1953.

Hibbard, Howard, *Caravaggio*, New York: Harper and Row, 1983.

Langdon, Helen, *Caravaggio: A Life*, London: Chatto and Windus, 1998.

Longhi, Roberto, *Caravaggio*, trans. B. D. Phillips, Leipzig: Edition Leipzig, 1968.

Mancini, Giulio, *et al.*, *Lives of Caravaggio*, London: Pallas Athene, 2005.

Wilson-Smith, Timothy, *Caravaggio*, London: Phaidon, 1998.

On Carracci

Bellori, G., *The Lives of Annibale and Agostino Carracci*, University Park, PA: Pennsylvania State University Press, 1968.

Benati, Daniele, *et al.*, *The Drawings of Annibale Carracci*, Washington, DC: National Gallery of Art, and London: Lund Humphries, 2000.

Chamberlaine, John, *Original Designs of the Most Celebrated Masters of the Bolognese, Roman, Florentine and Venetian Schools*, London: W. Bulmer, 1812.

Dempsey, Charles, *Annibale Carracci and the Beginnings of Baroque Style*, Glückstadt: Augustin, 1977.

Dempsey, Charles, *Annibale Carracci: The Farnese Gallery, Rome*, New York: George Braziller, 1995.

Malvasia, Carlo, *Malvasia's Life of the Carracci*, trans. Anne Summerscale, University Park, PA: Pennsylvania State University Press, 2000.

Martin, John R., *The Farnese Gallery*, Princeton, NJ: Princeton University Press, 1965.

Posner, Donald, *Annibale Carracci: A Study in the Reform of Italian Painting around 1590*, London: Phaidon, 1971.

Robertson, Clare and Whistler, Catherine, *Drawings by the Carracci from British Collections*, Oxford: Ashmolean Museum, and London: Hazlitt, Gooden and Fox, 1996.

On Courbet

Clark, T. J., *Image of the People: Gustave Courbet and the 1848 Revolution*, London: Thames and Hudson, 1973.

Faunce, Sarah and Nochlin, Linda, *Courbet Reconsidered*, New Haven, CT and London: Yale University Press, 1988.

Fried, Michael, *Courbet's Realism*, Chicago: Chicago University Press, 1990.

Herding, Klaus, *Courbet: To Venture Independence*, trans. William Gabriel, New Haven, CT and London: Yale University Press, 1991.

Lemoyne de Forges, Marie Thérèse, *Autoportraits de*

Courbet, Paris: Editions des Musées Nationaux, 1973.

Lindsay, Jack, *Gustave Courbet: His Life and Art*, Bath: Adams, Dart, 1973.

Mack, Gerstle, *Gustave Courbet*, New York: Knopf, 1951.

Nicolson, Benedict, *Courbet: The Studio of the Painter*, London: Allen Lane, 1973.

Nochlin, Linda, *Art Bulletin* 1967

Nochlin, Linda, *Gustave Courbet: A Study of Style and Society*, New York: Garland, 1976.

Richardson, John, *Corot and Courbet*, London: David Carritt, 1979.

Rubin, James, *Realism and Social Vision in Courbet and Proudhon*, Princeton, NJ: Princeton University Press, 1980.

Rubin, James, *Courbet*, London: Phaidon, 1997.

Zutter, Jörg, *et al.*, *Courbet: artiste et promoteur de son oeuvre*, Paris: Flammarion, 1998.

On David

Bordes, Philippe, *Jacques-Louis David: Empire to Exile*, New Haven, CT and London: Yale University Press, 2005.

Brookner, Anita, *David: A Personal Interpretation*, London: Oxford University Press, 1974.

Brookner, Anita, *Jacques-Louis David*, London: Chatto and Windus, 1980.

Johnson, Dorothy, *Jacques-Louis David: Art in Metamorphosis*, Princeton, NJ: Princeton University Press, 1993.

Maurois, André, *J.-L. David*, Paris: Editions du Dimanche, 1948.

On De Chirico

Crosland, Margaret, *The Enigma of Giorgio de Chirico*, London: Peter Owen, 1999.

De Chirico, Giorgio, *The Memoirs of Giorgio de Chirico*, trans. Margaret Crosland, New York:

Da Capo Press, 1994.

Foucault, Michel, *This is not a Pipe*, trans. James Harkness, Berkeley, CA: University of California Press, 1983.

On Degas

Armstrong, Carol, 'Reflections on the Mirror', *Representations* no. 22, 1988.

Brown, Marilyn R., *Degas and the Business of Art: A Cotton Office in New Orleans*, University Park, PA: Pennsylvania State University Press, 1994.

Degas, Edgar, *Dix-Neuf portraits de Degas par lui-même*, Marcel Guerin, 1931.

Degas, Edgar, *Degas by Himself: Drawings, Prints, Paintings, Writings*, ed. Richard Kendall, London: Macmillan Orbis, 1987.

Dunlop, Ian, *Degas*, London: Thames and Hudson, 1979.

Gordon, Robert and Forge, Andrew, *Degas*, London Thames and Hudson, 1988.

Kendall, Richard, *Degas: Beyond Impressionism*, London: National Gallery Publications, 1996.

McMullen, Roy, *Degas: His Life, Times, and Work*, Boston: Houghton Mifflin, 1984.

Moore, George, *Degas, the Painter of Modern Life, Impressions and Opinions*, New York, 1891.

Reff, Theodore, *Degas: The Artist's Mind*, Cambridge, MA: Belknap Press, 1977.

Sutherland Boggs, Jean, *Degas*, Chicago: Art Institute of Chicago, 1996.

Sutton, Denys, *Edgar Degas: Life and Work*, New York: Rizzoli, 1986.

Vollard, Ambroise, *Degas*, Les Editions G. Cres et Cie, 1924.

On Delacroix

Davies, Elspeth, *Portrait of Delacroix*, Edinburgh: Pentland Press, 1994.

Delacroix, Eugène, *Journals*, Covici-Friede, 1937

Deslandres, Yvonne, *Delacroix: A Pictorial Biography*, London: Thames and Hudson, 1963.

Johnson, Lee, *Delacroix*, London: Weidenfeld and Nicolson, 1963.

Johnson, Lee, *The Paintings of Eugène Delacroix*, Oxford: Clarendon Press, 1989.

Murgia, Adelaide, *The Life and Times of Delacroix*, trans. Peter Muccini, Feltham, Middlesex: Hamlyn, 1968.

Segal, Beth Wright, ed., *The Cambridge Companion to Delacroix*, Cambridge: Cambridge University Press, 2001.

On Dürer

Bailey, Martin, *Dürer*, London: Phaidon, 1995.

Bartrum, Giulia, *Albrecht Dürer and his Legacy: The Graphic Work of a Renaissance Artist*, London: British Museum Press, 2002.

Brion, Marcel, *Albrecht Dürer: His Life and Work*, trans. James Cleugh, London: Thames and Hudson, 1960.

Conway, William Martin, *Literary Remains of Albrecht Dürer*, Cambridge: Cambridge University Press, 1889.

Eichberger, Dagmar and Zika, Charles, eds., *Dürer and his Culture*, Cambridge: Cambridge University Press, 1998.

Grote, Ludwig, *Dürer: Biographical and Critical Study*, Lausanne: Skira, 1965.

Hutchinson, Jane C., *Albrecht Dürer: A Biography*, Princeton, NJ: Princeton University Press, 1990.

Koerner, Joseph Leo, *The Moment of Self-Portraiture in German Renaissance Art*, Chicago and London: University of Chicago Press, 1993.

Levey, Michael, *et al.*, *Essays on Dürer*, Manchester: Manchester University Press, 1973

Panofsky, Erwin, *The Life and Art of Albrecht Dürer*, Princeton, NJ: Princeton University Press, 1955.

Smith, Alistair, *The Complete Paintings of Dürer*, London: Penguin, 1987.

Strieder, Peter, *The Hidden Dürer*, trans. Vivienne Menkes, Oxford: Phaidon, 1978.

Waetzoldt, Wilhelm, *Dürer and his Times*, trans. R. H. Boothroyd, London: Phaidon, 1950.

On Gentileschi

Bal, Mieke, *The Artemisia Files: Artemisia Gentileschi for Feminists and Other Thinking People*, Chicago: University of Chicago Press, 2005.

Garrard, Mary, *Artemisia Gentileschi: The Image of the Female Hero in Italian Baroque Art*, Princeton, NJ: Princeton University Press, 1989.

Greer, Germaine, *The Obstacle Race: The Fortunes of Women Painters and their Work*, New York and London: Tauris, 2001.

On Goya

Baticle, Jeannine, *Goya: Painter of Terror and Splendour*, London: Thames and Hudson, 1994.

Ciofalo, John, *The Self-Portraits of Francisco Goya*, New York: Cambridge University Press, 2000.

Gállego, Julián, *Autorretratos de Goya*, Zaragoza: Caja de Ahorros de Zaragoza, Aragón y Rioja, 1978.

Gassier, Pierre and Wilson, Juliet, *Goya: His Life and Work*, London: Thames and Hudson, 1971.

Glendinning, Nigel, *Goya and his Critics*, New Haven, CT and London: Yale University Press, 1977.

Holland, Vyvyan, *Goya: A Pictorial Biography*, London: Thames and Hudson, 1961.

Hughes, Robert, *Goya*, London: Harvill, 2003.

Licht, Fred, *Goya: The Origins of the Modern Temper in Art*, London: John Murray, 1980.

Licht, Fred, *et al.*, *Goya in Perspective*, Englewood Cliffs, NJ: Prentice Hall, 1973.

Muller, Priscilla, *Goya's 'Black' Paintings: Truth and Reason in Light and Liberty*, New York: Hispanic Society of America, 1984.

Sánchez Pérez, Alfonso and Sayre, Eleanor, *Goya and the Spirit of Enlightenment*, Boston: Museum of Fine Arts, 1989.

Sayre, Eleanor, *Late Caprichos of Goya: Fragments from a Series*, New York: Walker, 1971.

Stoichit, Victor and Coderch, Anna Maria, *Goya: The Last Carnival*, London: Reaktion, 1999.

Symmons, Sarah, *Goya*, London: Phaidon, 1998.

Tomlinson, Janis, *Graphic Evolution: The Print Series of Francisco Goya*, New York: Columbia University Press, 1989.

Tomlinson, Janis, *Goya in the Twilight of Enlightenment*, New Haven, CT and London: Yale University Press, 1992.

Waldmann, Susan, *Goya and the Duchess of Alba*, Munich and London: Prestel, 1998.

Wilson-Bareau, Juliet, *Goya: Drawings from his Private Albums*, London: Hayward Gallery with Lund Humphries, 2001.

Young, Eric, *Francisco Goya*, London: Thames and Hudson, 1978.

On Guston

Ashton, Dore, *A Critical Study of Philip Guston*, Berkeley, CA: University of California Press, 1990.

Auping, Michael, *et al.*, *Philip Guston: Retrospective*, Fort Worth: Modern Art Museum, and London: Thames and Hudson, 2003.

Corbett, William, *Philip Guston's Late Work: A Memoir*, Cambridge, MA: Zoland Books, 1994.

Mayer, Musa, *Night Studio: A Memoir of Philip Guston by his Daughter*, New York: Alfred A. Knopf, 1988.

Serota, Nicholas, ed., *Philip Guston: Paintings 1969–1980*, London: Whitechapel Art Gallery, 1982.

Storr, Robert, *Philip Guston*, New York: Abbeville Press, 1986.

On Klee

Kudielka, Robert and Riley, Bridget, *Paul Klee: The Nature of Creation*, London: Hayward Gallery with Lund Humphries, 2002.

Werckmeister, Otto T. *Making of Paul Klee's Career, 1914–1920*, Chicago: University of Chicago Press, 1989.

On La Tour

Bury, Adrian, *Maurice-Quentin de la Tour: The Greatest Pastel Portraitist*, London: Skilton, 1971.

De Goncourt, Edmond and Jules, *French XVIIIth Century Painters*, London: Phaidon, 1948.

La Tour, Maurice-Quentin de, *La Tour*, Bates and Guild, 1907.

Wilenski, R. H., *French Painting*, C. T. Branford, 1949.

On Manet

Adler, Kathleen, *Manet*, Oxford: Phaidon, 1986.

Brombert, Beth Archer, *Edouard Manet: Rebel in a Frock Coat*, Boston and London: Little, Brown, 1996.

Fried, Michael, *Manet's Modernism, or, The Face of Painting in the 1860s*, Chicago and London: University of Chicago Press, 1996.

On Mengs

Mengs, Anton Raphael, *Sketches on the Art of Painting*, trans. John Talbot Dillon, London: R. Baldwin, 1782.

Röttgen, Steffi, *Anton Raphael Mengs 1729–1779 and his British Patrons*, trans. Eileen Martin, London: Zwemmer, 1993.

On Michelangelo

Barolsky, Paul, *Michelangelo's Nose: A Myth and its Maker*, University Park, PA: Pennsylvania State University, 1997.

Bull, George, *Michelangelo: A Biography*, London: Viking 1995.

Condivi, Ascanio, *The Life of Michelangelo Buonarroti*, trans. H. P. Horne, Boston: D. B. Updike, 1904.

Hall, James, *Michelangelo and the Reinvention of the Human Body*, London: Chatto and Windus, 2005.

Holmes, George, *Art and Politics in Renaissance Italy*, Oxford: Oxford University Press, 1993.

Hughes, Anthony, *Michelangelo*, London: Phaidon, 1997.

Murray, Linda, *Michelangelo: His Life, Work and Times*, London: Thames and Hudson, 1984.

Nagel, Alexander, *Michelangelo and the Reform of Art*, Cambridge: Cambridge University Press, 2000.

Paolucci, Antonio, *Michelangelo: The Pietàs*, Milan: Skira, 1997.

Wind, Edgar, ed., *The Religious Symbolism of Michelangelo: The Sistine Ceiling*, Oxford: Oxford University Press, 2000.

On Munch

Berman, Patricia, *Art Bulletin*, 75, no. 4, December 1993.

Müller-Westermann, Iris, *Munch by Himself*, London: Royal Academy, 2005.

Prideaux, Sue, *Edvard Munch: Behind the Scream*, New Haven, CT and London: Yale University Press, 2005.

On Parmigianino

Ashbery, John, *Self-Portrait in a Convex Mirror: Poems*, Harmondsworth: Penguin, 1976.

Freedberg, S., *Parmigianino: His Works in Painting*, Cambridge, MA: Harvard University Press, 1950.

On Poussin

Blunt, Anthony, *Nicolas Poussin*, London: Pallas Athene, 1995.

Kitson, Michael. *Nicolas Poussin*, London: National Gallery, 1995.

Kitson, Michael, *Nicolas Poussin and Claude Lorrain, Studies on Claude and Poussin*, London: Pindar, 2000.

Poussin, Nicolas, *Lettres*, Paris: Cité des Livres, 1929.

On Raeburn

Andrew, William Raeburn St Clair, *Life of Sir Henry Raeburn*, London: W. H. Allen, 1886.

Greig, James, *Sir Henry Raeburn*, London: The Connoisseur, 1911.

Thomson, Duncan, *Sir Henry Raeburn 1756–1823*, Edinburgh: National Galleries of Scotland, 1994.

On Rembrandt

Alpers, Svetlana, *Rembrandt's Enterprise: The Studio and the Market*, London: Thames and Hudson, 1988.

Bonafoux, Pascal, *Rembrandt: A Self-Portrait*, Geneva: Skira, 1985.

Bredius, A. *Rembrandt: The Complete Edition of the Paintings*, London: Phaidon, 1971.

Brown, C., Kelch, J., and van Thiel, P., *Rembrandt: The Master and His Workshop*, New Haven, CT and London: Yale University Press, 1991.

Brown, J., *Kings and Connoisseurs: Collecting Art in Seventeenth-Century Europe*, New Haven, CT and London: Yale University Press, 1995.

Chapman, H. Perry, *Rembrandt's Self-Portraits: A Study in Seventeenth-Century Identity*, Princeton, NJ: Princeton University Press, 1990.

Gasser, M., *Das Selbstbildnis*, Zurich: n.p., 1961.

Mander, Carel van, *Het Schilder-Boek*, Haarlem: n.p., 1604.

Schama, Simon, *Rembrandt's Eyes*, London: Allen Lane, 1999.

Schwartz, Gary, *Rembrandt: His Life, His Paintings*, London: Penguin, 1991.

Slive, S., *Rembrandt and His Critics 1630–1730*, The Hague: Martinus Nijhoff, 1953.

Small, A., *Essays in Self-Portraiture: A Comparison of Technique in the Self-Portraits of Montaigne and Rembrandt*, New York: P. Lang, 1996.

Van de Wetering, E., *Rembrandt: The Painter at Work*, Amsterdam: Amsterdam University Press, 1997.

White, Christopher, *Rembrandt*, London: Thames and Hudson, 1984.

White, Christopher and Buvelot, Quentin, *Rembrandt by Himself*, London: National Gallery, 1999.

Wright, Christopher, *Rembrandt: Self-Portraits*, London: Gordon Fraser, 1982.

On Reynolds

Mannings, David, *Sir Joshua Reynolds*, New Haven, CT and London: Yale University Press, 2000.

McIntyre, Ian, *Joshua Reynolds: The Life and Times of the First President of the Royal Academy*, London: Allen Lane, 2003.

Northcote, James, *The Life of Sir Joshua Reynolds*, London: Henry Colburn, 1819.

Wendorf, Richard, *Sir Joshua Reynolds: The Painter in Society*, Cambridge, MA: Harvard, 1996.

On Rosa

Kitson, Michael, *Salvator Rosa*, London: Arts Council, 1973.

Lady Morgan, *The Life and Times of Salvator Rosa*, London: Henry Colburn, 1824.

Scott, Jonathan, *Salvator Rosa: His Life and Times*, New Haven, CT and London: Yale University Press, 1995.

On Seurat

Herbert, Robert, *Georges Seurat 1859–1891*, New York: Metropolitan Museum of Art, 1991.

Rewald, John, *Seurat: A Biography*, New York: H. N. Abrams, 1990.

On Van Eyck

Albus, Anita, *The Art of Arts: Rediscovering Painting*, trans. Michael Robertson, New York: Alfred A. Knopf, 2000.

Friedlander, Max, *Early Netherlandish Painting*, vol. I, *The Van Eycks – Petrus Christus*, Leiden: A. W. Sijthoff, 1967.

Hall, Edwin, *The Arnolfini Betrothal: Medieval Marriage and the Enigma of Van Eyck's Double Portrait*, Berkeley, CA and London: University of California Press, 1994.

Harbison, Craig, *Jan Van Eyck: The Play of Realism*, London: Reaktion, 1991.

Panofsky, Erwin, *Early Netherlandish Painting, its Origins and Character*, Cambridge, MA: Harvard University Press, 1953.

Seidel, Linda, *Jan Van Eyck's Arnolfini Portrait: Stories of an Icon*, Cambridge: Cambridge University Press, 1993.

On Van Gogh

Dorn, Roland, *et. al.*, *Van Gogh Face to Face: The Portraits*, London: Thames and Hudson, 2000.

Erpel, Fritz, *Van Gogh Self-Portraits*, trans. Doris Edwards, Oxford: Bruno Cassirer, 1964.

Hulsker, Jan, *The New Complete Van Gogh*, Amsterdam: J. M. Meulenhoff, 1996.

Schapiro, Meyer, *Van Gogh*, New York: H. N. Abrams, 1952.

Silverman, Debora, *Van Gogh and Gauguin: The Search for Sacred Art*, New York: Farrar, Straus and Giroux, 2000.

Uhde, Wilhelm, *Van Gogh*, London: Phaidon, 1972.

Van Gogh, Vincent, *The Letters of Vincent Van Gogh*, London: Constable, 2003.

On Velázquez

Acker, Thomas, *The Baroque Vortex: Velázquez, Calderón and Gracián under Philip IV*, New York: P. Lang, 1996.

Brown, J., *Images and Ideas in Seventeenth-Century Spanish Painting*, Princeton, NJ: Princeton University Press, 1978.

Brown, J., *Velázquez: Painter and Courtier*, New Haven, CT and London: Yale University Press, 1986.

Brown, J. and Elliott, J. H., *A Palace for a King: The Buen Retiro and the Court of Philip IV*, New Haven, CT and London: Yale University Press, 1980.

Brown, J. and Garrido, Carmen, *Velázquez: The Technique of Genius*, New Haven, CT and London: Yale University Press, 1998.

Carr, Dawson, *et al.*, *Velázquez*, London: National Gallery, 2006.

Harris, Enriqueta, *Velázquez*, Oxford: Phaidon, 1982.

Hind, C. Lewis, *Days with Velázquez*, London: Adam and Charles Black, 1906.

Justi, C., *Diego Velázquez and his Times*, trans. A. H. Keane, London: Grevel, 1889.

Kahr, Madlyn Millner, *Velázquez: The Art of Painting*, New York and London: Harper and Row, 1976.

McKim-Smith, G., *et al.*, *Examining Velázquez*, New Haven, CT and London: Yale University Press, 1988.

Orso, Steven, *Philip IV and the Decoration of the Alcázar of Madrid*, Princeton, NJ: Princeton University Press, 1986.

Ortega y Gasset, José, *Velázquez, Goya and the Dehumanization of Art*, London: Studio Vista, 1972.

Palomino, Antonio, *Lives of the Eminent Spanish Painters and Sculptors*, trans. Nina Mallory, Cambridge: Cambridge University Press, 1987.

Picasso, Pablo, *Les Ménines et la vie*, trans. Alfred Rosset, Paris: Editions Cercle d'Art, 1958.

Rousseau, Theodore, *Juan de Pareja*, New York: Metropolitan Museum of Art, 1975.

Ortiz, Antonio Domínguez, *et al.*, *Velázquez*, New York: Metropolitan Museum of Art, 1989.

Stowe, Edwin, *Velázquez*, London: Sampson Low, Marston, Searle and Rivington, 1881.

On Vigée-Le Brun

Sheriff, Mary, *The Exceptional Woman: Elisabeth Vigée-Lebrun and the Cultural Politics of Art*, Chicago and London: University of Chicago Press, 1996.

Vigée-Lebrun, Louise-Elisabeth, *Memoirs of Madame Vigée-Lebrun*, trans. Lionel Strachey, New York: George Braziller, 1989.

Select
General
Reading

Alpers, Svetlana, *The Vexations of Art: Velázquez and Others*, New Haven, CT and London: Yale University Press, 2005.

Arasse, Daniel, *Vermeer: Faith in Painting*, trans. Terry Grabar, Princeton, NJ: Princeton University Press, 1994.

Armstrong, John, *The Intimate Philosophy of Art*, London: Allen Lane, 2000.

Artists' Self-Portraits from the Uffizi, Milan: Skira, 2007.

Ashton, Dore, *About Rothko*, New York: Oxford University Press, 1983.

Bailey, Martin, *Vermeer*, Phaidon, 1995.

Barrell, John, *The Political Theory of Painting from Reynolds to Hazlitt: The Body of the Public*, New Haven, CT and London: Yale University Press, 1986.

Bätschmann, Oskar, *The Artist in the Modern World: The Conflict between Market and Self-Expression*, New Haven, CT and London: Yale University Press.

Baudelaire, Charles, *The Painter of Modern Life and Other Essays*, trans. and ed. Jonathan Mayne, London: Phaidon, 1995.

Bell, Julian, *Five Hundred Self-Portraits*, London and New York: Phaidon, 2004.

Berlin, Isaiah, *The Roots of Romanticism*, London: Chatto and Windus, 1999.

Bond, Anthony and Woodall, Joanna, *Self-Portrait: Renaissance to Contemporary*, London: National Portrait Gallery, 2005.

Borzello, Frances, *Seeing Ourselves: Women's Self-Portraits*, London: Thames and Hudson, 1998.

Breslin, James, *Mark Rothko: A Biography*, Chicago and London: University of Chicago Press, 1993.

Brewer, John, *The Pleasures of the Imagination: English Culture in the Eighteenth Century*, London: HarperCollins, 1997.

Brilliant, Richard, *Portraiture*, London: Reaktion Books, 1991.

British Self-Portraits: From Sickert to the Present Day, London: Arts Council, 1962.

Brooke, Xanthe, *Murillo in Focus*, Liverpool: National Museums and Galleries of Merseyside, 1990.

Brookner, Anita, *Soundings*, London: Harvill, 1997.

Brookner, Anita, *Romanticism and Its Discontents*, London: Viking, 2000.

Brown, Katherine, *The Painter's Reflection: Self-Portraiture in Renaissance Venice 1458–1625*, Florence: L. S. Olschki Editore, 2000.

Bruce, Vicki and Young, Andy, *In the Eye of the Beholder: The Science of Face Perception*, Oxford: Oxford University Press, 1998.

Bryson, Norman, *Vision and Painting: The Logic of Gaze*, New Haven, CT and London: Yale University Press, 1983.

Bryson, Norman, *Tradition and Desire: From David to Delacroix*, Cambridge: Cambridge University Press, 1984.

Campbell, Lorne, *Renaissance Portraits: European Portrait-Painting in the 14th, 15th, and 16th Centuries*, New Haven, CT and London: Yale University Press, 1990.

Clark, T. J., *The Painting of Modern Life: Paris in the Art of Manet and his Followers*, New York: Alfred A. Knopf, 1985.

Clark, T. J., *Farewell to an Idea: Episodes from a History of Modernism*, New Haven, CT and London: Yale University Press, 1999.

Comini, Alessandro, *Schiele in Prison*, London: Thames and Hudson, 1974.

Conrad, Peter, *Modern Times, Modern Places*, London: Thames and Hudson, 1998.

Danto, Arthur, *Encounters and Reflections: Art in the Historical Present*, Berkeley, CA and London: University of California Press, 1997.

Danto, Arthur, *The Madonna of the Future*, New York: Farrar, Straus and Giroux, 2001.

Derrida, Jacques, *Memoirs of the Blind: The Self-Portrait and Other Ruins*, trans. P.-A. Brault and M.

Naas, Chicago: University of Chicago Press, 1993.

Elger, Dietmar, *Andy Warhol: Self-Portraits*, Ostfildern-Ruit: Hatje Cantz, 2004.

Elkins, James, *Why are our Pictures Puzzles: On the Modern Origins of Pictorial Complexity*, New York and London: Routledge, 1999.

Feaver, William, *Lucian Freud*, London: Tate Publishing, 2002.

Finn, David and Licht, Fred, *Canova*, New York: Abbeville Press, 1983.

Foucault, Michel, *The Order of Things: An Archaeology of the Human Sciences*, London: Routledge, 2001.

Freedberg, David, *The Power of Images: Studies in the History and Theory of Response*, Chicago: University of Chicago Press, 1989.

Freedberg, S. J., *Circa 1600: A Revolution of Style in Italian Painting*, Cambridge, MA: Harvard University Press, 1983.

Fried, Michael, *Realism, Writing, Disfiguration: On Thomas Eakins and Stephen Crane*, Chicago: University of Chicago Press, 1987.

Fried, Michael, *Art and Objecthood*, Chicago: University of Chicago Press, 1998.

Gayford, Martin and Wright, Karen, eds., *The Penguin Book of Art Writing*, London: Viking, 1998.

Gedo, Mary Mathews, *Picasso: Art as Autobiography*, Chicago and London: University of Chicago Press, 1980.

Goffman, Erving, *The Presentation of Self in Everyday Life*, Garden City, NY: Doubleday, 1959.

Goldschneider, Ludwig, *Fünfhundert Selbstportrats von der Antike bis zur Gegenwart*, Vienna: Phaidon-Verlag, 1936.

Goldstein, Carl, *Visual Fact over Verbal Fiction: A Study of the Carracci and the Criticism, Theory and Practice of Art in Renaissance and Baroque Italy*, Cambridge: Cambridge University Press, 1988.

Gombrich, Ernst, *The Image and the Eye: Further Studies in the Psychology of Pictorial Representation*, Oxford: Phaidon, 1982.

Gombrich, Ernst, *The Uses of Images: Studies in the Social Function of Art and Visual Communication*, London: Phaidon, 2000.

Goncourt, Edmond and Jules de, *Pages from the Goncourt Journals*, trans. Robert Baldick, New York: New York Review of Books Classics, 2007.

Greenblatt, Stephen, *Renaissance Self-Fashioning: From More to Shakespeare*, Chicago and London: University of Chicago Press, 1980.

Grosser, Maurice, *The Painter's Eye*, New York and Toronto: Rinehart, 1951.

Hall, James, *The World as Sculpture: The Changing Status of Sculpture from the Renaissance to the Present Day*, London: Chatto and Windus, 1999.

Hammer, Martin, *The Naked Portrait, 1900–2007*, Edinburgh: National Galleries of Scotland, 2007.

Hanson, Anne Coffin, *Manet and the Modern Tradition*, New Haven, CT and London: Yale University Press, 1979.

Harbison, Robert, *Reflections on Baroque*, London: Reaktion, 2000.

Harris, Ann and Nochlin, Linda, *Women Artists 1550–1950*, Los Angeles: Los Angeles County Museum of Art, 1976.

Haskell, Francis, *Past and Present in Art and Taste*, New Haven, CT and London: Yale University Press, 1987.

Haskell, Francis, *The Ephemeral Museum: Old Master Paintings and the Rise of the Art Exhibition*, New Haven, CT and London: Yale University Press, 2000.

Herrera, Hayden, *Frida Kahlo: The Paintings*, London: Bloomsbury, 1991.

Hertel, Christiane, *Vermeer: Reception and Interpretation*, Cambridge: Cambridge University Press, 1996.

Hess, Thomas, and Ashbery, John, eds., *The Grand Eccentrics*, New York: Collier Books, 1971.

Hickey, Dave, *Air Guitar: Essays on Art and*

Democracy, Los Angeles: Art Issues Press, 1997.

Holmes, George, *Art and Politics in Renaissance Italy*, Oxford: Oxford University Press, 1993.

Hughes, Robert, *Nothing if Not Critical*, London: Collins Harvill, 1990.

Johns, Christopher, *Antonio Canova and the Politics of Patronage in Revolutionary and Napoleonic Europe*, Berkeley, CA and London: University of California Press, 1998.

Jones, Roger and Penny, Nicholas, *Raphael*, New Haven, CT and London: Yale University Press, 1983.

Kahlo, Frida, *Images of Frida Kahlo*, London: Redstone, 1989.

Kelly, Sean and Lucie-Smith, Edward, eds., *The Self-Portrait: A Modern View*, London: Sarema, 1987.

Kinneir, Joan, ed., *The Artist By Himself: Self-Portrait Drawings from Youth to Old Age*, London: Elek, 1980.

Knafo, Danielle, *Egon Schiele: A Self in Creation*, Rutherford, NJ: Fairleigh Dickinson University Press, 1993.

Kris, Ernst and Kurz, Otto, *Legend, Myth and Magic in the Image of the Artist: A Historical Experiment*, New Haven, CT and London: Yale University Press, 1979

Lacan, Jacques, *Ecrits: A Selection*, New York: Norton, 1977.

Levey, Michael, *Rococo to Revolution: Major Trends in Eighteenth-Century Painting*, London: Thames and Hudson, 1966.

Levey, Michael, *Sir Thomas Lawrence*, New Haven, CT and London: Yale University Press, 2005.

Levey, Michael, ed., *The Soul of the Eye: An Anthology of Painters and Painting*, London: Collins, 1990.

Licht, Fred, *Sculpture, Nineteenth and Twentieth Centuries*, London: Michael Joseph, 1967.

Lindsay, Jack, *Death of the Hero: French Painting from David to Delacroix*, Studio, 1960.

Lomax, Yves, *Writing the Image: An Adventure with Art and Theory*, London: I. B. Tauris, 2000.

Morley, Simon, *Writing on the Wall: Word and Image in Modern Art*, London: Thames and Hudson, 2003.

Nagel, Thomas, *The View from Nowhere*, New York: Oxford University Press, 1986.

Nagel, Thomas, *Concealment and Exposure*, Oxford and New York: Oxford University Press, 2002.

Phillips, Tom, *The Artist as a Portrait*, Great Haseley, Oxfordshire: Roy Davids, 2000.

Piper, David, *The English Face*, London: National Portrait Gallery, 1992.

Pope-Hennessy, John, *The Portrait in the Renaissance*, Princeton, NJ: Princeton University Press, 1966.

Protter, Eric, ed., *Painters on Painting*, Mineola, NY: Dover, and London: Constable, 1997.

Rideal, Liz, *Mirror, Mirror: Self-Portraits by Women Artists*, London: National Portrait Gallery, 2001.

Riley, Bridget, *The Eye's Mind*, London: Thames and Hudson, 1999.

Robert Arneson: Self-Portraits, Philadelphia: Moore College of Art, 1979.

Rosen, Charles and Zerner, *Henri, Romanticism and Realism: The Mythology of Nineteenth Century Art*, London: Faber and Faber, 1984.

Rubin, William, ed., *De Chirico: Essays*, New York: Museum of Modern Art, 1982.

Schapiro, Meyer, *Modern Art, Nineteenth and Twentieth Centuries*, New York: George Braziller, 1978.

Schapiro, Meyer, *Words, Script, and Pictures: Semiotics of Visual Language*, New York: George Braziller, 1996.

Schoenbaum, S., *Shakespeare's Lives*, Oxford: Clarendon Press, 1991.

Sherman, Cindy, *A Play of Selves*, Hatje Cantz, 2007.

Sleptzoff, L. M., *Men or Supermen?: The Italian Portrait in the Fifteenth Century*, Jerusalem: Magnes Press, 1978.

Soby, James Thrall, *Giorgio de Chirico*, New York: Museum of Modern Art, 1955.

Springer, Peter, *Hand and Head: Ernst Ludwig Kirchner's Self-Portrait as Soldier*, Berkeley, CA and London: University of California Press, 2002.

Storr, Robert, *Chuck Close*, New York: Museum of Modern Art, and London: Thames and Hudson, 1998.

Sturgis, Alexander, *et al.*, *Rebels and Martyrs: The Image of the Artist in the Nineteenth Century*, London: National Gallery, 2006.

Sylvester, David, *The Brutality of Fact: Interviews with Francis Bacon*, London: Thames and Hudson, 1987.

Sylvester, David, *Magritte: The Silence of the World*, New York: H. N. Abrams, 1992.

Taylor, Charles, *Sources of the Self: The Making of Modern Identity*, Cambridge, MA: Harvard University Press, 1989.

Tufts, Eleanor, *Luis Meléndez: Eighteenth-Century Master of the Spanish Still Life*, Columbia: University of Missouri Press, 1985.

Uglow, Jennifer, *Hogarth: A Life and a World*, London: Faber and Faber, 1997.

Updike, John, *Self-Consciousness*, London: Penguin, 1990.

Varnedoe, Kirk and Gopnik, Adam, *High and Low: Modern Art, Popular Culture*, New York: Museum of Modern Art, 1990.

Walsh, John, *Portrait of the Artist*, New York: Metropolitan Museum of Art, 1972.

Wheelock, Arthur, *Vermeer and the Art of Painting*, New Haven, CT and London: Yale University Press, 1995.

Wollheim Richard, *The Thread of Life*, Cambridge, MA: Harvard University Press, 1984.

Woods-Marsden, Joanna, *Renaissance Self-Portraiture: The Visual Construction of Identity and the Social Status of the Artist*, New Haven, CT and London: Yale University Press, 1998.

Index

This text is set in Centaur, a typeface based on
several Renaissance models and first developed as
titling capitals by Bruce Rogers for the Metropolitan
Museum of Art in New York in 1914.